Coffee Hour in Flensburg

Coffee Hour in Flensburg

Stories of War and Peace, of Adventure and Love

Erika Dethlefs Passantino

Janda Books, Canton, GA

Cover design by Fiona Passantino

ISBN 13: 9781732996427
ISBN-10: 1732996423

Printed in the United States of America

Table of Contents

Preface

Great Creator, hear me, for this, my grandchild.
Teach me to sing the clay,
And once more I ask for your guidance
That all my mothers and fathers be remembered.

Each design has meaning in this beautiful life.
We must remember and thank them, all of them;
The sun, the plants,
The grandmothers and the grandfathers.
All of them, and you, are part of this and in this way,
we must remember.

(Poem piped into the galleries of the National Museum of American
Indian Art, New York, probably Navajo)

Acknowledgments

There they sit at coffee hour, in the parlor of my soul. They have remained at my side over years and continents, regaling me with stories. They are the forbears and the two people who occupied every thought and surprise of this journey–my parents. Thanks, and love, go out to them!

Along the way, there were friends and teachers who encouraged me. Thanks, a symphony of it, is due Jedwin Smith and the "School of Hard Knocks," the writer's group in Decatur, Georgia. Under Jedwin's gentle guidance, this talented group raised questions about flow, language, sequence and clarity.

There were kind readers who searched for non-sequiturs, duplications or plain nonsense: My friend, Martha Glenn, pushed me on when I was about to give up. Encouragement came from Bob Passantino, who gave advice on the process of publishing. Thanks also to the Soleil Writers Group, my new home, and to a kind reader, Don Converse. Our friend, Wilma Libar, applied her multi-lingual talents to the search for errors in fact and history. The editor, Mari Ann Stefanelli, gave sage advice, and Jane Shaw and Suzanne Mansell urged me to continue.

This book would not exist had it not been for Josh Langston. He did the heavy lifting, bringing this book to life through his publishing house, Janda Books. Leading me every step of the way from editing to design and production, Josh gave image to mere words–deep thanks.

Finally, a book is only as attractive as its cover, the lure we writers throw out to the world, inviting the browser to take a quick look. Who better than my beloved daughter, Fiona, to have designed the cover. Her talent is huge. How does a mother deserve that?

And Richard, my husband and best friend who, through his own suffering and steely endurance, became the model of a strong human being. He had patience with a wife chained to the keyboard; Richard, I love you.

We Three, the farewell photo, 1946

A Letter to my Children

When you were young, our family would sit around the table in our house on Waneta Road—your dad, Richard, myself, and you, our son and daughter. Born in Washington, D.C., you both grew to sense the significance of place, the daily presence of political life.

Sometimes talk would turn to my own childhood. You said you wished to have known these two spirited and unpredictable people who were your grandparents on your mother's side—shadowy figures, their existence conveyed through a faded photograph or a reference here and there. Now, as a last link to them, I feel compelled to leave you a record. The intensity of memory makes the past dominate the day, weighing heavily.

And so, with a view that spans three generations, I am deeply grateful for the life given to me. I see and admire you as loving spouses and parents, and I understand more deeply the truth in the Navajo text: "All of them, and you, are part of this, and in this way, we must remember."

This book, started as a letter, grew in volume and importance to my very life. It is a memoir, a history lesson, and a love story that revealed itself out of correspondence and records. I must tell you how my parents discovered love, made it live to the very end.

Finally, I was forced to come to terms with what it meant to be German in their generation, suffering through two world wars, what it means in mine. What are the lessons to be learned for the future?

This book is dedicated to:

My husband, Richard,

our son, Stefan, and his wife, Kathleen,

our daughter, Fiona, and her husband, Barry,

and our grandchildren, Cole, Cameron, Sophia, Tilo and Sabine.

In deep love,

Erika Dethlefs Passantino

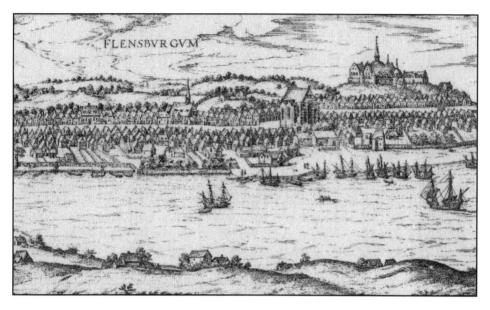

"Flensburg, Seen from the East," section of a copperplate, ca. 1588, by Frans Hogenberg in vol. IV of 'Theatrum Urbium' *by Georg Braun.*

Chapter 1

The Ancestors

Stories

Imagine coffee hour in 1950s Flensburg, the Nordic city hugging the border between Germany and Denmark. My father, a man with a soul as large as all creation, lay in that big American bed, his long, arthritic limbs frozen into contorted shapes, their swollen joints causing never-ending pain. Pillows, bedrolls and all manner of support did little to shift weight from one body part to the other. Silently, never complaining, he would look out of the window, his gaze very far away. His eyes lit up when I entered the room and sat at his bedside to tell him about school. I was a teenager. I called him Vati.

My mother, whom I called Mutti, was short, stout, and lively; her Beethoven shock of white hair, with one dark streak running from the center of her forehead, was held in check by large combs. Having ended her nap, she was now dressed in her afternoon outfit as she set a tray on the table at the foot of Vati's bed–fresh coffee, a bit of cake, nice china. It was coffee hour, the central-European counterpart to British tea time, a quiet point in the day that invited reflection. Mutti's typewriter was temporarily pushed to the side. Later, she would return to it carrying out business matters and typing letters to her sisters and friends. Mutti was now the leader of the family; she and I were Vati's sole care givers. Only a local doctor made occasional house calls.

My parents' bedroom had once been the apartment's grand parlor with large windows and a lovely corner bay that offered views from our hilltop all over Flensburg Fjord and as far as Denmark just to the north of us. At our feet, the old town embraced the harbor; the copper spire of Marienkirche (medieval St. Mary's Church) rose from the city's tile roofs to the height of our windows. On Sunday mornings, church bells and brass music flowed from this tower into our rooms, celebrating the Lord's day with those stark melodies of Lutheran Pietism, the chords of which went straight to the soul and reminded one of moral imperatives.

Early in the last century, our row of grand apartment houses had been built on the edge of a high plateau once occupied by Duburg Castle. Originally owned by Queen Margaret I (1353-1412), wise ruler of Denmark, Norway and Sweden, this fortification had guarded the harbor, but fell into decay, used only by traveling royalty, public authorities, and perhaps a robber baron here and there.

Now a park dropped into town. If there was a lookout point from which Vati could survey the world, this was it.

Flensburg harbor and our house on the hill, today

Usually a ferocious wind hurled the trees about, making them gyrate like crazed rock musicians. Even double windows, the kind that open out and a second set that opens in, could barely prevent the cold, howling wind from seeping in–it was our perpetual background music. My memory, however, chooses an afternoon of bright sunlight bathing the room, so it must have existed. I had spent the last hour or so trying to concentrate on my homework, but instead had stared at the scene outside our bay windows.

4

"It's coffee time," Mutti called out to me, "come sit with us, I have a bit of cake as well. You can go back to your work later." The aroma of coffee and warm cake scented the room. This was our time for reminiscing. We three would talk. Partly for my benefit, partly to banish pain and depression, my parents passed along stories and experiences. My, could they tell stories! Not the made-up kind, but those personal and rich in life. They had the texture of our humanity and ranged from the momentous to the minute: Vati's memories as a young man in the trenches of World War I, or how he got to own this imposing apartment building where we now lived.

In the telling and remembering, Vati could momentarily escape the ever-present pain, return to a time when he was strong, creative and powerful. His ice-blue eyes would once again show that glint, express that rich soul, convey the joy of achievement, even if just for a few moments.

Mutti in turn described the setting sun's light on the pine forests around Berlin, their red-golden bark shining against deep green foliage and yellow sand, surrounding watery marshes. She avoided talking about the bombed-out city, an event we both had experienced together. The Berlin of her youth may have disappeared; the place of memory, however, was alive and colorful.

Other times she described—eyes shooting flames at the memory—how she, a classically trained pianist, stormed out of an audition in 1920s New York:

"After waiting for hours, I was called to the interview, asked to play a nice piece. Which I did. Then, can you imagine? This guy, this impresario, asked me to raise my skirt so he could enjoy my shapely legs!" In the telling she once more relished the moment when she urged the gentleman to go to hell. No history class in school, no book, could match these lessons.

These were the two sides joined to form our family—one male, one female; one rural, one urban; contrasts almost to the extreme:

The father, Carston, a farm boy from the Scandinavian North of Germany, home to a thousand years of wind, rain, canals, and potato fields. Steadfastness and love that never ended, even in the worst of times. The mother, Margarethe, a girl from Berlin, the piano protégée, descended from nineteenth-century bourgeois tradition. She harbored creativity, fast words, a ready laugh, sometimes naughty in thoughts, a bit naughty in life.

~*~

Some time ago the *New York Times* published an article on both the value and hazard of oral history as a valid account of events. It reported how Italian scholars together with historians at the University of Indiana are reevaluating a discipline that has had scant respect, for how trustworthy are

"…memories not just of what you did, but also of what you wanted to do and think you did?" New scholarship treasures this ambivalence as just another stone in the structure that creates historic reality; for does reality exist only in the archives, in the biographies of important men, or does it reside in the texture of the broad culture, in the simple lives of simple people?

This thought is made all the more complicated in my own telling, for I am a trained art historian and as such am compelled to ask questions at every turn about feeling, illusion, symbol, objective reality, about the bending of fact or the existence of truth.

All of these tales became my parents' immortality as well as a lesson so vivid that I credit them with my love of history. And if stories are history, let me begin with one of the earliest, told many times as far back as I can remember. It lies like a rock foundation under Vati's tales that enlivened coffee hours in Flensburg.

Vati's Haferhocken Geschichte, [The Story of the Oat Tents]

It was harvest time on Grandfather's farm, way up north, in the region we call Jütland. The year was 1895, and all family members were needed in the fields. My dad, a blue-eyed, freckled boy of five, too young for harvesting, was ordered to drive the cows through the village and out to pasture. He was to watch them all day and bring them home at night. His mother fretted at the thought of sending out such a young child but obeyed her fearsome husband; she packed a favorite lunch and sent him off.

The boy followed his herd down the village road. How tall those cows were, how slowly they lumbered, how proud he was when the neighbors called out to him! With triumph he discovered that he was tall enough to open the heavy gate to the pasture. There Carsten sat in the sun, on a bale of straw, the cows calmly grazing, and the hours dragging hazily.

Suddenly, a thunderstorm rose from the North Sea, huge clouds rushing over the endlessly flat land, followed by thunder and beating rain. Terrified, Vati crawled into one of the Haferhocken, little tents of bundled oats set up to dry. There, sleep overcame his fear.

By six o'clock, when cows know it is time to be milked, there was no little boy to drive them. They must have banged their horns on the gate until it gave way, marched through the village, turned the corner into the large farmyard. No cowherd.

Grandmother became frantic, the field hands were called to the search, and the villagers joined in. At last, there in the field, in the little tent, two feet were sticking out into the evening sun: the sleeping boy. The march back to the farm surrounded by family and workers must have been triumphant, but Vati was too modest ever to bring up that part. The important end of the story was: All was good and safe.

~*~

And so, it is that, whatever image of my father aris
bridges and subways, the soldier in war, the tall, elegant trav
little boy in the field will always define him. This story brought
the man to a scale a child could embrace.

Today I ask myself: "What made my parents such tellers   ...o
were they?"

Margarethe Jenny Friederike Müller (1895-1966), born in Berlin, and
Carsten Jonas Dethlefs (1890-1959) born in Nordhackstedt, in the far north of
Germany, were of the generation born at the close of the 19th century. They
survived World War I and immigrated to the United States separately. There
they fell in love and married in 1927.

Life in America would become both exciting and profitable for them.
However, after some years they returned to Germany, where I was born and
where the family became caught up in the horrors of World War II. These years
were followed by extensive travel in search of a new beginning, and lastly, a
final return to Flensburg. Neither parent lived past their 70th year. These late
years are the setting of coffee hour.

Their rich spirits allowed my parents to be guided by ideas,
inquisitiveness, quest for change. They even achieved a measure of success,
although not commensurate with their talents. Most of all, both mother and
father differed from their families and compatriots through their stubborn
disregard for bourgeois notions of what life should be. By refusing to fit the
mold, they also gave up its protective shield. Over the years, wars, illness, and
impulsive decisions ground their promise to shreds. Yet, they may have
gradually braced themselves so that, when they had run out of options, been
battered too many times, it would come as no surprise that they had grown
hardy. Today I understand their strength; today I wish I had some of it.

Certainly, a child's early memories and stories dished out at coffee hour,
are illuminating. They may be cozy, enlightening or even instructive. But how
can this view paint people and places in tones other than crayon reds, blues
and greens–no subtlety in their shades? As an only child, born late in my parents'
lives, I was too young for true understanding. And no matter how much these
stories are contemplated, they remain such: the view from three to four feet of
a child's height.

So, the writer turns elsewhere for help. In my case it was the discovery
among the left-overs of my mother's life, of a black portfolio with green
envelopes bound together. I had seen it a hundred times, had watched Mutti
search for papers or photographs inside it, never bothered to look at it until I,
myself, stood at the doorstep of final thoughts. I have since made it my business

to open this portfolio whenever, in the course of writing, I confronted questions or doubts. Many were the answers found there, and the reader will find references to this gold mine strewn throughout my writings.

And then I realized that even this is not enough. To make sense, to give clarity, or in many cases, horrifying reality to a child's magic vision, I had to confront history–the cold, clear, documented kind; had to turn to records and archives now open to us via the internet. And out of these strands, memory, family lore and fact, I braided my story.

Still, what remains is the vision of one set of eyes, one heart, one mind.

Berlin, Prinzenstrasse 19, late 19th century

The Müller Family

Mutti's childhood played out in the urban density of Kreuzberg, then the heart of Jewish Berlin. Commerce and small industrial sites were squeezed into dense apartment settlements. The area was gradually declining and becoming the Lower East Side of this immigrant city. Margarethe's stories were complex, never repeated but expanded, embellished, given a Berlin edge. At times, wicked humor heightened the action and brought forth a naughty smile. Her recollections spread before us the flavor of imperial power and its slide into world wars.

The cast of characters that enlivened Mutti's tales was a genteel, formerly wealthy family, a house full of women. They occupied the *"belle étage,"* the more fashionable second floor, of Grandmother's apartment building that had shops and workshops on street level. Impoverished, tubercular families and minor factories were crammed into the even darker inner court and back building. This back building will play an important part in the later story.

Mutti loved Berlin deeply, knowing that it had been a state of mind as much as a place, and that both were now gone. Like an invocation, she recited the names–Prinzenstrasse, Moritzplatz, Alexanderplatz, Schloss, Leipziger Strasse, entire neighborhoods that were flattened by carpet bombing, street battles and finally Russian occupation and the Berlin Wall that cut the city in half making prisoners of them all.

Helene Herrmann as a young girl

To this day, I could repeat for you the sounds, smells, hustle of the town in its golden age. If only my mother could have lived to see the rebirth of this remarkable city: *Mitte*, with its great museums, Kreuzberg–now a haven for artists and progressives, cheap housing, endless parties. Today, life in Berlin is celebrated like nowhere else, and with good reason: death had come knocking so many times. The current mayor refers to his town as "poor but sexy."

Mutti's stories about her mother, Helene Juliane Antonie Herrmann (1855-1925), presented a Victorian lady who found herself raising four daughters on her own and supporting two maiden sisters, blind Tante Ida and emotional Tante Amalie. The family clung to the status of the *haute bourgeoisie*, no longer having the funds but pretending nevertheless. In Grandmother's house, you did not call your mama "Mutti" or some other plebeian abbreviation; no, you said *"Maman,"* the French way. After all, the Prussian king, Frederick the Great, spoke French to one and all; English to his cousins, German only to his horse.

The apartment house on *Prinzenstrasse* 19 had been part of Grandmother's huge dowry. It was said that, newly in love, Grandmother had declared she would kill herself if forbidden to marry this man. This decision, however, meant having to live in Kreuzberg, abandoned by family and friends. This fact alone raises many questions.

Sadly, the grandparents' marriage ended in divorce when Mutti was all but five years old. Grandfather, Maximilian Müller (1852-?), was a compulsive gambler. After years of paying his debts, when all but the house in Berlin had been gambled away, Grandmother threw him out and got a divorce, a thing of great shame piled on top of the financial punishment. Henceforth the man was dead for the family, his whereabouts unknown, his name never to be mentioned in their house, nor a generation later, in ours.

However, adult whispers and knowing glances would refer to him as being talented, charming and "from the East," sometimes a euphemism for being Jewish in spite of the name Müller which may have been assumed to give cover as was the case with so many German Jews. That may have been the reason for living in Kreuzberg.

Helene Herrmann Müller with her daughters, Lotte, Adele, Käthe, Margarethe, ca. 1910

Mutti told how the daughters, Adele, Käthe, Lotte, and Margarethe, were often left at home to fend for themselves. One time, they decided to create a swimming pool in the living room, opening all faucets and flooding the apartment. Another, they played circus acrobats, suspended upside-down by their knees on the outside of the windows, their sailor suit dresses drooping over their heads (blue with white trim on weekdays, white with blue trim on Sunday; same dress for all, summer and winter). Tante Amalie, walking home from a shopping trip, turned the corner, and saw the girls hanging there. She promptly fainted in the street–in those days, ladies were expected to faint rather than do something. The porcelain lamp and two candlesticks in our living room, painted with genteel Victorian scenes are her work, they have traveled with us through wars and moves too numerous to count; they are tangible evidence of her existence, a token of the world that ended when World War I detonated a way of life.

Mutti told how blind Tante Ida was given piano lessons at home to pass the time. Mutti, age five, watched the teacher and, to the amazement of the adults, later played the entire lesson from memory. From then on, her life was shaped by the demands of the talent: Eight hours of practice each day, training at a renowned conservatory, sometimes in the company of a young genius from South America, Claudio Arrau, or a member of the Mendelsohn family. I was told that when she was twelve, the newspaper published an article on the youngest music teacher at the conservatory.

Mutti explained the harsh discipline music demands of her students—the sheer physical power required every day; she compared it to the strength needed to chop wood; she was proud of that. Yet, in her youth nothing was allowed that could have damaged her hands; only swimming was permitted as sport. It is hard to imagine that she had even a semblance of natural youth within the confines of that family, that city, that talent.

Music flowed through Mutti like an electric current that connected hands and keys at the

Margarethe seated by the piano, Berlin, ca. 1915

moment of touching; all else appeared to be unconscious. This gift soon made her the focus of family attention and devotion. Later, as a student, she tried to supplement the cost of her training by playing the piano in movie houses where silent films were given musical interpretation. In fact, music *was* the narrative, not the accompaniment to the action.

Even as a small child, I knew how she could improvise on the piano, gliding from melody to melody, from dramatic moment to crescendo with transitions of total ease, and I grasped, not without a dull pain, that Mutti was alive in a different way the moment she sat at the piano—more alive than at any other time. My inadequacy in the face of such a bond burned deeply.

But could I, at the time of Mutti's telling, there in that Flensburg apartment, understand what it had meant for a young woman to entertain an entire movie house full of spectators—perhaps rowdy, drunk, sentimental, critical, engrossed or bored—to take them on an emotional ride with an hour or two of uninterrupted sound? How could I fathom the feat of a player who had to stare up at the screen, and on a moment's call, translate a flickering image into a wall of sound, evoking a storm at sea, a police chase, or the river of tears shed by the heroine's dark-rimmed, staring eyes? The sheer guts of it? And she did this while World War I was raging outside.

Mutti was twenty-three years old at the time, and starvation as well as lack of medicines had given her tuberculosis. During the long hours of studying for her music exams, she was so hungry that she chewed on a candle, the only light left by which to work. And yet, she passed the exam. Her task? To be able to play any Beethoven sonata on demand.

Mutti told about the day in 1918 when the German army started the revolution at the close of World War I. The emperor had long ago fled to his relatives in Holland, safely watching the end from a manor house near the German border.

On her way home, Mutti had to pass the palace square. Turning the corner, she saw angry and desperately hungry soldiers and workers, the Socialist revolutionaries, throw furniture and velvet curtains into the streets where people were fighting over the scraps. Flames were shooting from the roof, guns were fired. Terrified, Mutti ran home, only to see Tante Amalie leaning out of the living room window, her blouse open, pointing to her chest and shouting: "Here, you criminals, shoot a fine bourgeois heart!"

This war, this revolution, brought the end of a dream, the end of an era, the beginning of Germany's slide into disaster: Hunger, inflation, more despair and finally World War II.

So, I ask myself, how must my mother have felt, telling such stories to a daughter who could only stare back in disbelief, not yet gifted with understanding?

To help cure Mutti's tuberculosis, her oldest sister, Adele, established in New York, sent mother and daughter to Italy for a year, a shining, glorious memory of happy times. Grandmother insisted that, in addition to hikes and wine in charming gardens, an hour a day be spent reading from Goethe's *Italian Travels,* [*Kennst Du das Land wo die Zitronen blühen?* Do you know of the land where the lemons bloom?]

In that beautiful land, at that lovely time, it must have felt like a rebirth. Mutti built up a store of images–happy fellowship around a fine table, her love for Italian men–tales that have gone through our family for generations now. Oh, that boyfriend Beppo–he alone was fodder for story after story: Beppo taking her sleigh riding in the Dolomites; Beppo's sister, cloistered as a nun against her wishes, throwing herself off the monastery's cliff, the family

burdened by the sin; Beppo, the beautiful Italian, turning to the modern world, to the joy of living, to an early love. "But," she would say at coffee hour in Flensburg, "...you don't marry them!" Right, Mom, little did you know.

By 1925, now 30 years old, Mutti emigrated to America. She would join her sister, Adele, and try to establish herself as an artist in a country that was just discovering the modern ways of art and living.

Helene and Margarethe in Italy with Local Friends, ca 1920

The Dethlefs Family

Vati's background could not have been more of a contrast. In that tattered document folder, I find a sepia photograph–Vati's confirmation. His parents, his numerous siblings and relatives are standing in the courtyard of a farm in far northern Germany near the Danish border. The old thatched roof hovers over them like a huge hat.

Vati, fourth from left in the photo on the following page, is small at fourteen for a man who would grow to six feet five inches. He is wearing a tight black suit and bowler hat to signify the important day that had made him an adult; his face shows a shy smile. From now on, he was allowed to sit on the bench, not stand, at the dinner table; no longer was he required to line up at the end of the meal to shake his father's hand and say *"Tak for Måltide"* ("thanks for the meal" in Danish).

In this family photo, my grandfather, Claus Dethlefs (1856-1936) stands next to grandmother, Christine Nommensen (1862-1956), who was pregnant as usual. Grandfather appears indistinguishable from the other farmers in the photo. As a young man, he had ridden north from Sandschleuse to purchase land for this farm, eventually marrying a Danish girl. Over the years he rose to some prominence but was feared for his haughty ways and violent temper (he is supposed to have thrown a farm worker out of the stable window, window frame and all). Even in old age his fierce blue eyes gleam from the photograph

Carsten Jonas Dethlefs confirmation, ca. 1904

taken of the white-haired couple on their wedding anniversary: Grandmother bland but formal, grandfather imperious.

This Dethlefs family draws its lineage back to Christian Albrecht, Duke of Holstein-Gottorp. Christian Albrecht had inherited the duchy from his father, who had recently died in battle against the Danish king. He was a highly educated young man, who, in 1665, at the age of twenty-four founded the University of Kiel that carries his name to this day. Educated or not, in the days of Absolutism, a duke had the right to take every young girl in his realm as a mistress, or worse perhaps, to rape her—*droit du seigneur* was the French way of gilding the concept. Resulting children were given some sort of livelihood and a coat-of-arms. The young girl who gave birth to our ancestor is said to have been Sophie Dethlefs.

In our case, the gift was Sandschleuse, a lock on a narrow waterway called the *Alte Sorge* [Old Worry]. Our ancestor was given the right to charge a toll from any boat passing through. The "blessed" family was supposed to be proud and grateful. Well, ours was.

This marshy ridge, all swamps, canals and drooping willow trees, comes close to connecting the bays of the North Sea with rivers and fjords of the Baltic. The Viking capital, Haithabu, lay a few miles to the east and is still visible today. Most likely, Viking seafarers chose this site because they could easily carry their boats over the narrow strip of land, ever ready to sail to Russia, down the Volga, or to the west, across the North Sea to plunder England and Scotland. Sandschleuse may well have been one of those ancient connectors.

The Dethlefs family was Frisian and Viking to the core, and adventure was written in their genes. Vati would grow into a very tall man, narrow frame, all bones and strength. The eyes in his long head were so narrowly placed that he had to wear children's glasses, and there was that huge bent nose. And, oh yes, stubbornness, the Vikings' passport.

Sophie named her son Claus, who in turn named his eldest Christian Albrecht in honor of this distinguished heritage. For generations, the oldest son of the oldest son has been either a Christian Albrecht or a Claus. To this day there are such gentlemen, descended from Vati's oldest brother, Christian Albrecht. My Berlin mother, ever irreverent, used to ridicule this family pride, saying that in other places and times, this would be a bastard lineage, which of course did not endear her to her husband's clan.

The Grandparents, possibly on their 25th Wedding Anniversary, 1908

As it may be, the family had an intense sense of self. They multiplied furiously and participated in the huge population surge that in turn filled the ships with immigrants to America. Since the oldest son invariably inherited the farm, and Grandfather had no intention of spending money on his children's education, all the others had to fend for themselves.

After having acted as county councilman, Grandfather retired to a nearby small town. It was also said in the family, that he hired himself a chemistry teacher, fulfilling his own life-long wish. Others say "No, this teacher was a spiritualist or an alchemist."

Recently, I even learned that one day, Grandfather decided that was not enough. He packed a bag and traveled to the town where his oldest daughter was married to an engineer. Arriving at their front door, he declared: "My life in the village bores me; my wife bores me. I will now live in the city and start a new life." His daughter's answer was: "You fathered eleven children with this woman, you belong at her side. Go home." She handed him his suitcase and sent him on his way.

There are no stories about whether Grandmother appreciated his return. For close to twenty-five years, she had given birth to child after child, managed a household of some twenty-five members, including farm workers who needed to be fed three times a day, and had seen to the moral and religious education of her brood.

Vati told a story about the Saturday night bath: Grandmother gathered all the kids in the wash-kitchen for their baths and commanded:

"Who did not go to church last week?" Five kids hesitated to answer.

"Well, you will go this Sunday. Stand over here so I can crack an egg on each of your heads, massage them into your scalp, wash you down so you can be clean for church!"

To the others she called out: "You get to sleep in, but tonight you will polish all the family shoes!" Did I mention there were well over a dozen family members? Vati recalled that, actually, there was fun in that task, the kids got to chat and sing, perhaps some old tunes in the finest "Plattdütsch" dialect:

Ick wull, wi weern noch kleen, Jehann,

Dor weer de Welt so groot...

[Jehann, I wish we were still small,

that's when the world was so wide...]

Or better:

Dar Du mien Levsten buest,

Dat Du wohl weest,

Kümm bi de Nacht, kümm bi de Nacht, ik bin alleen....

Moder slaapt, Vader slaapt, ik slaap aleen.....

[That you are my beloved, you know so well.

Come in the night, come in the night, I am alone...

Mother sleeps, Father sleeps, I sleep alone....]

Yes, Grandmother knew how to manage a family.

Soon after Vati's confirmation, he was sent off and indentured to a carpenter in Flensburg. This form of near-slavery required the apprentice to live with the master's family. As was so often the case, they treated him badly. Vati worked all day on construction sites, and upon returning to the master's home, was expected to clean the house, do the dishes, and sleep in the attic.

Every day he pushed his work cart up Toosbüystrasse, a very steep street leading from the harbor to the upper city. Stopping to catch his breath,

Flensburg, view of the Burgfried and Toosbüystrasse, ca. 1915

he glanced at the fancy row of apartment buildings that had recently been built on the old castle's grounds, the Burgfried, imposing structures in stucco or red brick, elegant facades with bays and balconies held up by caryatids and statues of Hercules.

Homesick, tired, but driven by stubborn pride, Vati pushed his cart up the hill, and to the rhythm of his steps recited to himself, "Someday, I will be rich, I will live up there, in one of these houses. I will show them who I am!"

It would take him almost thirty years to make this dream come true, but he eventually bought the corner property that rose over all of Flensburg and was visible way into Denmark. To do this, he had to work his way through an architecture and engineering school, immigrate to the United States, and return a rich man.

The graduation photo on the following page of freshly minted engineers shows Vati standing in the back row, a young man not yet fully grown and the least comfortable in this boastful group. The other young men already display a sense of superiority. My father looks shy and tentative, out of place; was he a scholarship student? I was never told.

But first, Vati had to serve in the army. There is a photo showing a line of young men in what looks like parade uniform, lined up before a store in some small town near Berlin. The image hardly suggests the power and bellicosity behind this Prussian military.

There is a fine and somewhat later photo of a tall man in the uniform

Vati's graduation from technical college, Rendsburg, ca. 1910

of the Imperial Guard: long coat, white gloves, pith helmet, and gold-trimmed uniform. (Photo on page 21.) The Guard marched through the streets of Berlin, decorating and adding importance to the Emperor's every move. World War I ended this pomp in the German trenches of both France and Russia.

An architect and engineer by training, Vati was soon conscripted into war action as soon as World War I began. He was sent on the most dangerous missions, those of rebuilding bridges destroyed by the retreating opposition. I have postcard-size photos of groups of soldiers sitting in shabby East European cafés, trying to look worldly and optimistic. How many survived?

These photos were taken and then distributed to the soldiers in the form of postcards which could be

In Berlin, Carsten and fellow recruits of the Imperial Army

sent home as a greeting. Notes to the family were written on the reverse. The dates range from 1914 to 1917.

Today, the cities and dates there noted tell another story of war: lives of individuals and their role in the big picture. There is a card that shows Vati sitting with a group of men at a party with musical instruments, relaxed poses and smiles. Most of them appear to be Romanians in uniform. Vati is always easy to spot: he is the tall one, in the center, whose eyes are so blue they appear white in the sepia prints.

The reverse gives the date July 6, 1917. Vati's greeting reads as follows: "I safely returned and am sending you a photo of

Postcard from the front, 1914. The text on the reverse states that this train served as barracks for the soldiers before they were sent into battle

our station, taken on my first day after return from leave. I am well, but drowning in work; of course, everything stopped while I was gone. I returned last Sunday from a trip of almost four days. The fact that I returned late was not discussed....Warm greetings, Carsten"

A quick dip into internet listings of date and place, reports that this city, the proud center of Romania's leadership in the oil industry, was the first site of drilling for oil and gas, the world's first pipeline. In the face of German advances in the course of World War I, the site at Moreni had been completely destroyed by the retreating forces. When taken by the Germans in 1917, it was rebuilt to light a local town by natural gas, the first in the world. The oil holdings were turned over to a German company and, in the end, all was lost in 1918, on the last day of war, when Romania re-entered the war on the side of the Allies and was thus a winner.

In the face of such new knowledge, I stare at the photo that shows Vati seated in a prominent fashion, suggesting that he was the leader of this group. It raises the question of what might

Postcard from the front, Moreni, Romania. Carsten is seated, second row, center

Carsten Jonas Dethlefs, member, Imperial Guard, ca. 1913

have been his role in the big picture. Could he have been one of the engineers who built that oil refinery? He never mentioned it.

Finally, Vati was moved to the trenches between France and Germany, to this day the worst condition of war in all memory. There is also one last photo note, dated December 1918, shortly after war's end. Shown are two men, one is seated, while the other stands, both in sadly battered uniforms—the image of defeated soldiers. The note states that Vati was in Germany now, but unable to return home for Christmas. The photo itself may date from late in the war when he was sent to the trenches between France and Germany. He never spoke about those experiences, except for saying that it was slaughter and psychological horror of the worst kind—and for what gain?

Here I must add another detail of loss and suffering in World War I that I encountered only recently. My cousin, Sophie, sent me copies of old letters that had been in her mother's collection. There, old and many times folded, is a letter, in English, from a British ambulance driver who, stationed along the Belgian front in 1918, discovered a dying German soldier, very young, by the side of the road. He stopped his ambulance and soon discovered that help, any help, would be too late. He lifted the young man into his ambulance and delivered him to a burial place for soldiers. Then, having found identification and a home address, he wrote to the dead man's mother in Germany, telling her that he had not died alone and was given proper burial. The letter ends with a warm expression of

Postcard from the front; defeated soldiers, December 8, 1918

condolence. How many miles from Vati's station in the trenches did this happen? When did he learn?

For me, Belgium, poor, much-loved Belgium, and its blood-soaked soil will never be the same.

Recently a friend who knows and lived through wars, asked me: "What was it like to fight this horrible war, what did your father say?" But immediately we both realized that the horrors of the trenches would never be conveyed to a child, in fact veterans and families of soldiers will tell you that the true, soul-stunting facts are never discussed with those who did not share the experience. I have observed relatives and friends who, after a beer or two, and in the company of other veterans, will exchange things seen and felt, pain that avoids description but rises from a word, a gesture, like a code known only to those who saw—and what they saw had become enshrined in deep corners of the mind. Those who returned would never be the same.

Therefore, my description, in fact most of my text, has a cloistered, almost hermetic quality: I can tell what I heard, I can tell what I saw and experienced; I cannot quote conversations or descriptions of how it must have felt.

Years later, Vati would teach me the military songs of World War I: *Ich hab mich ergeben, mit Herz und mit Hand, Dir Land voll Lieb und Leben, mein deutsches Vaterland..."* [I have dedicated myself, with heart and hand to you, my country, the land filled with love and life, my German fatherland] or *"Ich hatt' einen Kameraden, einen bessren findst Du nicht..."* [I had a comrade, you could not have found one better...] Both songs, he pointed out, were later usurped by the Hitler regime. In actuality they dated from the 1848 student uprising, the first liberal efforts in Germany—a melancholy era of history and a chance for democracy missed.

Here I must inject the present and try to explain part of what it means for my generation to be German—collective guilt by ethnic belonging, a constant questioning and search for the meaning behind hellish events; a search for the place or time where these events' roots may lie buried in history and culture; it is a cosmic guilt, ever present, awakened at unanticipated moments, raising more questions, never answering a one.

So, it was that the song about the *Kamerad* lingered in my mind. I could not remember the other verses and looked them up in my book of German songs. Then it hit me: Here are two comrades-in-arms, marching in formation so close that one soldier feels himself part of the other, same pace, same stride. A bullet flies... *"Was it meant for you or for me? You are torn from me as though a piece of me. You reach for my hand in farewell. Kamerad, I cannot give it to you, for I am reloading*

21

my gun. May you live in everlasting life, my good comrade, my good comrade." Strange, this is a song we sang many times in school and on hikes, never stopping to think what the words meant. *"For I am reloading my gun..."* Today I look at the terror of the idea.

Vati, when telling about World War I, would hint that, in his view, these sacrifices and patriotism weren't worth a damn. He relayed stories about brutality in the German military, of mental cruelty so terrible that one time, in desperation, he swung his fist at his sergeant in front of the entire company. Unable to bear the abuse, but knowing that he might be shot for it, he feigned an epileptic attack, threw himself on the ground, and pretended to foam at the mouth.

When, after all this, the young veteran returned from the trenches, Vati was told by potential employers that his degree was not an academic but a technical one, hence not entitling him to advanced positions.

Now, this man had a mission born in those hard times, and at one point he realized it could only be carried out via America; *there* they would be happy to have him.

Chapter 2

The Immigrants

Adventure

For a few years, Vati's life in America was good. He furiously attacked his engineering assignments, and whatever money he could save, he invested in the New York Stock Exchange. He took deep pleasure in watching his fortune grow—a symbol of pride and validation. The ability to work in the English language seems to have come to him quickly.

On high seas; photo by my father, mid-1920s

There are few references to life outside of work: Together with a cousin from the Island of Föhr, he built a sailboat to enjoy the Long Island Sound. A photo shows friends and relatives sitting aboard in bathing costumes of the time, a pretty young lady quite close to handsome young Carsten.

Early on, Vati spent time helping develop Palm Beach, Florida. At coffee hour in Flensburg, he regaled us with descriptions of

Sunday outing on the sailboat

the island in its early years, foundations disappearing in the sand overnight, storms washing away a year's worth of work. According to him, there were unsound engineering practices in the face of such conditions, and he added:

"Well, can you imagine, they offered to pay me in real estate on the island instead of money! I looked at the sand, looked at them and told them, no thanks, give me some lots on the mainland." Need I tell you how fine it might have been to be neighbors with Mar-a-Lago?

The hotel on Sunrise Boulevard, a few blocks from the beach, and built under his supervision, is still standing today and was recently added to the Register of Historic Places. Glistening white, the building's Moorish loggias, lush courtyards and suspended bridges tell of a time when Palm Beach was a piece of heaven. Today, aged occupants amble along the hotel's grounds. Both building and inhabitants have lost defining features: the plaster curls to numerous coats of paint, the residents to too many face lifts. Yet both tell of the solace that rises out of long-gone habits of living: morning constitutionals at the beach, fully clothed; leisurely lunch dates, white gloves; card games by the pool. One can sense the charm of tea dances under the bougainvilleas, the band's melodies dripping like syrup from the violins.

Lately, both building and residents convey the irrefutable fact that this heaven may be an early taste of the

The Palm Beach Hotel under construction, 1924

24

real one not too far away.

Records do not indicate what role Vati played in these projects, but he told me he soon became discouraged. He returned to New York City and eventually became a partner in the concrete construction firm, P. N. Petersen Company. A few photos allow the

Section of Pulaski Skyway, Newark, NJ, 1928

imagination to build a sense of his life: a dock under construction in the East River and a section of Pulaski Skyway. Later he also had a contract to build part of the Fort Tryon subway line, but I could not find any records.

Margarethe Müller becomes Margaret Muller

Meanwhile, in early June of 1925, Mutti arrived in New York City on the "Arabic." There, she joined her sister, Adele, who at age sixteen, had run away from home, making her way to America before World War I and eventually marrying a writer.

There is a photo of Mutti standing in Riverside Park, her obvious beauty obscured by a huge hat. She appears shy and tentative, but as we know, once seated at the piano she came to sparkling life.

Mutti's collection of old records includes a letter received from her mother. It is dated June 18, 1925. In four pages of old German script with a fine, steady hand, Grandmother Helene Müller expresses her relief to read of her daughter's safe arrival. She consoles Mutti after learning of intense sea sickness; she marvels at a description of the modern comforts to be enjoyed in sister Adele's New York apartment. The words are strangely motherly and becalming, considering that Mutti was 30 years old at the time; they suggest special concern for a

Margarethe Müller in Riverside Park, 1925

fragile psyche:

My dear Gretel: We received your mail after a long, worried wait. Not until June 8 did we have reassurance that the Arabic had landed.... Your description of illness and suffering worried me deeply....Your courage toward life will be steeled and in hindsight all terrible things will no longer loom so large....The worst thing is standing all alone, being abandoned by all loved ones and family. My dear Gretel, this is what I had to endure many times... so very alone, and for me it was an unhappy marriage!... But all this is over now.

Grandmother's letter in German script, June 18, 1925

Yet, Grandmother still worries about Adele's reaction to troubles of the past, suggesting that the long-ago divorce from her father had been the cause for Adele's departure from Germany. She ends with a report on the family dog running around the Berlin apartment searching for Gretel; Mutti's friends visiting to cheer up both Grandmother and dog.

The letter adds a shred to the notion that Maximilian Müller was indeed Jewish as earlier descriptions suggested: "*...abandoned by all loved ones and family...*" Was that why they lived in Jewish Kreuzberg? Together with the earlier reports that he or his family "came from the East," these references resemble the furtive shame that hits you when someone says, "Your slip is showing." Much can be inferred from that remark; even more about hate, or bare tolerance, of Jews, whether open or disguised.

Family records show that Helene Herrmann Müller died June 30, 1925, days after this letter was written; in fact, with mail delivery at the time taking about three weeks, this greeting would have arrived in Mutti's hands after her own mother's death.

Years later, when Mutti would talk about this event in her life, she felt reassured by her sisters' letters suggesting that Grandmother had died peacefully in her sleep, cared for by the remaining unmarried daughter. Today, the letter bears qualities of a broken heart, a final greeting.

The letter's last page with salutation is missing from the carefully preserved missive and its envelope. Was it destroyed? Why? A reminder of the guilt carried by those who leave? Questions, always questions.

Adele and Stephen

As to Mutti's sister, Adele: She would become important to my life and much loved, as Tante Adele. Feisty and ever driven with the need to change the world, she joined a crowd of left-wing New York intellectuals. I was told years ago that she worked as a translator with the American offices of the League of Nations; other sources hint at more radical activities.

What Adele lacked in beauty, she made up with a sharp mind, stoic determination and a smile that gave a hint of her deep generosity. At some time, she had fallen in love with—and married—a man named Stephen Naft (1878 – 1956), a brilliant, charming, politically engaged writer. My parents' photo album holds two photos showing the couple, the only images of Stephen Naft known to exist, according to his biographer.

Young Adele, New York, 1910 or later

Is that the man in those photos of mom and aunt, in fancy 1920s dress, the man with the Don Juan moustache and wavy dark hair pomaded just so? Is that Stephen Naft? And why is he looking away from his wife and turning to my so-much-prettier mother?

I did not know I had an Uncle Stephen. No one ever spoke about him. Only once in a while, during our coffee hours in Flensburg, did I notice furtive glances between my parents, followed by: "Oh, well, Stephen Naft..." then silence and a new subject. But the name hovered in my brain and just sat there.

Naft was born Siegfried Nacht in Vienna, son of a prominent Jewish physician. He published under the names of Arnold

Stephen Naft with Adele and Margarethe, ca. 1928

Roller and Stephen Naft, among others, and was affiliated with free thinkers and followers of the anarchist/syndicalist movement on either shore of the Atlantic. He corresponded with Rudolf Rocker, Upton Sinclair and Bertrand Russell among many other political activists. Research revealed many internet listings, even a monograph, entitled in translation: *The Wild Sheep: Max and Siegfried Nacht. Two Radical, Jewish Presences,* written in 2008 by a Swiss social scientist, Werner Portmann. There, amid discussion of the era's political ferment and the activities of two Jewish intellectuals from the *shtetl,* appeared the name Ada (Adele) Naft-Müller, married to Stephen. Her husband, in turn, praised her charms in a letter:

> *"Ma compagne, who speaks English, German, French and Spanish and takes dictation as fast as one can speak, and in addition writes in perfect English..."* Never did a woman have more cause to feel flattered or take more pride in her attractions and endowments as a wife.

Did the four of them really spend a vacation weekend in Atlantic City, New Jersey? The photo was most likely taken by Vati. Who was this person? Back to Mr. Portmann's book and the anarchist brothers: There once was a wealthy doctor, Fabius Nacht, who lived in the *shtetl* of Buczacz in Galizia (now Ukraine but originally part of the huge Austro-Hungarian empire). He was the first

formally trained physician in town, opened the first hospital for the Jewish population and saw to it that his two sons, Maximilian and Siegfried, attended the University of Vienna. However, in addition to this fine education, the brothers also absorbed the injustices of *shtetl* life and the political ferment of the early 20th century. This imperative demanded service to humanity as a whole, just as their father had served his people.

Stephen Naft with Adele and Margarethe, Atlantic City, NJ, ca. 1928

The brothers became anarchists, journalists and publishers, stirring up revolution wherever they went; they were jailed, numerous times and in various countries, as political agitators. They crisscrossed Europe, sometimes on foot: Paris, London, Switzerland, North Africa. Siegfried spent a year in a Spanish prison because he was caught with a pistol in Gibraltar, just when the King of Spain was visiting.

Siegfried/Steven finally landed in New York around 1912, where he worked within the syndicalist/anarchist movement of mostly wealthy intellectuals. His publications, some translated into multiple languages, painted the picture of a social utopia that would bring justice to the workers, safety to the man in the factory, and a salary that would allow him to feed his family. He worked on a global scale, wrote for revolutionary publications and was connected to many of the leading thinkers of the movement.

In New York, the creators, and perhaps future leaders, of this glorious world lived for their high-minded intellectual pursuits, their parties, and their weekends in Woodstock.

Meanwhile, the couple fought against racism, insisted on the equality of women and men, and envisioned a world free from religion, that is, the right of individuals to live as their hearts demanded. They formed a support group for Max Nettlau (1865-1944), the highly respected German anarchist and historian, the "Herodotus of Anarchy," having written a ten-volume history of the idea. Later, Adele and Stephen helped remove him from Nazi Germany to Amsterdam, where his enormous archive became the bedrock of the Institute for Social History, founded 1935. Nettlau lived there to his end, never having been discovered by the occupying German forces.

On a recent visit to Holland, I dug for additional information in this beautiful, well-financed institution. There I found more notes, even a long letter Adele wrote to Nettlau in 1924, regarding the current discussion about the developments in Russia and the Syndicalist's disapproval: "If you really think that we are great admirers of Russia, you are wrong." However, she also expresses her support for the rights of workers worldwide and her admiration for the banking strike in Europe. This letter, too, is in the collection of the Institute, together with Christmas greetings.

Mr. Portmann's book and letters give a hint of uncle Stephen's later activities, including a note on his divorce from Adele. His efforts did not move the world's powers to heed the anarchists' calls for justice. All around, not much good came of it.

During World War II, desperate for money, Stephen Naft served on the FBI's international branch as a political informer, making use of his ability to speak both Russian and German fluently. He taught at the New School for Social Research and New York University. Uncle Stephen, the savior of the working man, died penniless in the 1950s, twice divorced and blind, his dream of a just world and a return to Europe forever unrealized.

~*~

In 1925, this circle of radical intellectuals had taken Mutti in, and rich were the stories spread before Vati and me at coffee hour in Flensburg. She recalled being the group's official entertainer, playing at fancy political dinner parties on Park Avenue and Long Island. Mostly, she said: "There were meetings in Village apartments, boys from the Ivy League, artists, intellectuals of all varieties, gorgeous women…smoke and discussions so thick nothing good could come from that. They were just playing around."

Also, Mutti thought, the revolutionaries were too messy, "nobody did the dishes or cleaned out the ashtrays. So, I did it." Eyes ablaze, she regaled us with her conclusion that the movement was for men only, all the women were expected to do was sleep with the anarchists and by all means keep their mouth shut. Certainly not Mutti's kind of folks. Her statements conveyed the idea that politics and intellectual debate were not part of her sphere of interests, that she was non-political. However, many activists in these groups came from wealthy New York families and did prove useful; they opened doors and brought her gigs where she was able to repeat the improvised piano patter so well developed in Berlin movie houses. And, of course, she *was* pretty.

This circle also introduced her to the city's artistic avant-garde of the 1920s. Soon she sang in Arturo Toscanini's choir and at Temple Emanu-el on Fifth Avenue, met–and adored–the great singer Paul Robeson, and his friend Harry T. Burleigh (1866-1949) the famous singer, collector and recorder of spirituals who also sang at the temple. Mutti would say that H. T. Burleigh (as he was commonly addressed) came to the Naft's apartment to make music. To do so, he had to climb the fire escape because, as a black man, he was not allowed to enter by the building's front door. Burleigh's biography mentions the spiritual "Deep River," one of his earliest arrangements fashioned for classically trained musicians.

To my delight, I recently gained new insight into H.T. Burleigh's life and work, one that makes the idea of my mother's friendship with the musician all the more precious. NPR radio broadcast a piece that presented Burleigh, then a very young singer, as having been the artist who sang spirituals for Antonin Dvorak while the composer was in the USA. In fact, one opening chord of his New World Symphony echoes "Deep River," surely an expression of admiration for both the music and its singer.

Many years later, in Nazi Germany, Mutti would crank up the Victrola, insert the silver needle into the sound arm, and call forth the magnificent voice–the sheer power–of Paul Robeson, singing "Deep River." And yet, one senses that in spite of Robeson's original and expressive power, the arrangement had been somewhat muted. Did it reflect early efforts of the arranger, of black artists in general, to take on the tone of the larger culture, just to be allowed to participate? Perhaps their own true words or sounds, those that came from the soul, were left for safer corners of their lives, not the public arena.

I still own this record; it has accompanied the family in all its travels, and it was played in war-time Graz, Austria, and later Flensburg, at coffee hour.

The Couple–Drop Dead Love

The story of how my parents met, fell in love, and married in 1927, was one of my favorites at coffee time. In its absolute, struck-by-lightning suddenness, it always gave me the feeling of having been ordained by a higher power and thus unshakable. Later reports from family suggested the opposite: that their marriage was stormy, that they spent many months, even years apart, that they had other lovers. But not that I would have noticed–never did I hear so much as a raised voice.

Mutti and Vati's meeting was happenstance. Still single in their thirties, both were returning from Germany and happened to be on the same ship, the *Hamburg*. Vati had abruptly ended his home visit in a rage, furious at the fact that his mother had organized an engagement party with a local farmer's daughter without telling him. Mutti had visited family, and since her profession required eight hours of practice each day, she had permission to play in the ship's music room.

Vati took his daily constitutional, making the rounds on deck, each time glancing through the salon windows at the lovely lady with dark hair pounding away at the piano keys. Once he had the courage to approach her, they fell in love with a huge thud, became engaged during the Captain's Dinner the night before landing, and got married in New York on the following weekend, ages 32 and 37.

There are photos of the couple aboard ship. Vati, very tall, lanky, tweedy, his red hair blowing in the wind, has his arm around my rather short mother who is wearing a billowing dress. A stylish hat curves down over her face. They are the golden, international couple of the twenties, living The Life. The famous Murphys, or stories by F. Scott Fitzgerald, come to mind.

The couple on board ship, fall 1927

The hectic pace of life in New York

Seated on deck chairs, 1927

City must have hit them the moment they landed. What one might have called a wedding was a trip to City Hall, lunch with the witnesses, Stephen Naft and a person called Ella. Strangely, there is no record that Vati's sister, Christine, her husband or the cousin with whom he owned the sailboat were in attendance. In the evening, the assembled signed a postcard to Mutti's sister, Käthe, that seems to have served as the official wedding announcement: *"I am Mrs. Dethlefs now."* Vati added a greeting, written twice across the postcard's face, a view of New York skyscrapers. The witnesses signed on the back.

Margaret Muller retained her name professionally and continued to perform. From then on, my parents shared the fate of many expatriates–the loss of rootedness. They lived in two worlds (or many worlds in their case) which is both an enriching gift and an eternal drive for the Other, the place and ways left behind. If means permit, the need is satisfied with repeated travel, and my parents each crossed the ocean numerous times in search of the right place, the soul's origins. There may lie the reason many immigrants return to the place of their childhood.

If you travel, as we did a few years ago, into deepest Sicily, in search of traces of the Passantino family, you will suddenly come upon a large Statue of Liberty, plaster, painted green as fresh grass, guarding a front yard that exudes Queens. The proud owner, sitting on his stoop, cell phone in hand, will explain: "Toity years of Bensonhoist, now we are all back here."

This inner current is paired with the realization that "belonging" will never again happen, that knowledge of different ways to live and think have forever made the expatriate the person who looks in from the outside–both

Postcard announcing the marriage, Oct. 1927

"at home" and in the new land. Strangers ask: "Where are you from?" Immediately, a barrier is raised; you are not part of the fabric; you must be judged, examined against the general template of your ethnicity.

For yourself, the "old country" is physically comforting in theory only. On visits you share the songs, you understand the unspoken, the gesture, the motivations, good and bad. Soon, however, you become impatient with real or perceived shortcomings of people and place left behind. Your information, even your language, have grown stale with years. The locals, on the other hand, have moved on. So, you return to the "new country," its drive, its growth, its wealth of differences born out of the gift brought by many cultures. At times you may even long for more of the unknown, for adventure.

In the "new country," you sense sharply the need to build your own traditions, you choose, discard, select, instruct, and cling to that which cannot be let go. And yet, your patterns feel artificial, being the result of choice and, therefore, not unconscious. You cannot select or discard traditions that grew into the soul, that are the base chord of existence. Lucky the expatriate by choice, not the victim of exile or persecution.

On upper Broadway, I used to look into the faces of old German Jews, souls doubly tortured by unspeakable crimes inflicted upon them by the very culture they nurtured and that nurtured them, and to which they had made so many gifts. These aged folks become fewer with each passing year; they seem to walk as in a bubble, lost and drawn into themselves. They appear to be in a dialogue with that inner world that has no partner other than the past. Worst of all, these very victims are at times berated for being so "darned Germanic."

The Art Singers of New York

Sometime around 1926, Margaret Muller, her name now anglicized, had become affiliated with the Institute of Musical Art of the Juilliard Foundation of New York City (forerunner of the Juilliard School of Music), then the hot-bed of progressive music and internationalism. She took their entrance exam and passed—no surprise, considering she had a degree from her Berlin conservatory in piano, organ and voice.

Eventually, three talented female musicians established *The Art Singers of New York:* Mutti, a German mezzo and pianist; Allie Rönkä, a Finnish soprano from Minnesota; and young Millie Kreuder, a contralto from New York and a native American. The years of their greatest success appear to have been from 1927 to 1929. There also was a tour of college music schools in Minnesota. These, and other, events are documented in a binder with publicity photographs and reviews of concerts in New York, New Jersey, and Virginia. They give a sense of the times. The music is commented upon, but so are the dresses and the graceful intonations. Photos show the three women ready for performance, their smiles, their undulated, bobbed hair and beaded gowns telling of the revolutionary glamor that had grown from new wealth and the freedom of the 1920s.

The Art Singers of New York, 1928

"...The audience was widely enthusiastic not only because it liked their charming personalities, but because it is very seldom we hear such wonderful singing...Their accompanist, Miss Margaret Muller, also from New York, was indeed excellent. She is a first-rate pianist, but at no time did she forget that she was there to support the singers and not to display her own unusual abilities."

East Orange, undated announcement of an October 28 concert at the Columbian Woman's Club:

"...The musical program to be given by the Art Singers...promises a delightful half hour or so for the guests." Featured numbers included a

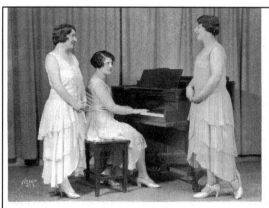

The Art Singers, shown above are a very delightful ensemble who will be presented in concert at the Washington Auditorium, Tuesday, September 3, by the Music & Drama Club. From left to right they are, Allie Ronka, soprano; Margaret Mueller, mezzo and accompanist and Mildred Kreuder, contralto.

Miss Ronka is an Ely girl of whom the people of the city are exceedingly proud. She is a graduate of the Da. kish State Teacher's College and taught in the schools of the county for three years. For the past several years Miss Ronka has held full scholarship at the Institute of Musical Art in New York City under the vocal guidance of Mrs. Wood Stewart. She has done concert and radio work in New York City and is the first soprano of the Symphonic Singers under the concert management of Arthur Judson.

Margaret Mueller is a graduate of the Berlin Conservatory of Music. She is an excellent concert pianist and has studied for several years in Italy and France.

Mildred Kreuder, contralto of the Art Singers is from New Jersey. She has had all her musical training at the Institute of Musical Art in New York city as a scholarship student under Mrs. Wood Stewart.

The Art Singers of New York, concert article, 1928

piece by all three singers: "Go Down Moses."

"*Vocal Trio in Triumph Here*" (unidentified clipping with a note: "Virginia:")

> "*An enthusiastic audience of music lovers heard a well rendered and pleasing concert...The advance notices were entirely too conservative....The trios, of which there were four, were a very pleasing addition...Miss Margaret Muller, mezzo and accompanist, augmented the harmony, beauty, strength and technique of the misses Ronka* [sic] *and Kreuder, not only by her accompaniment, but by carrying her vocal part in a pleasing manner.*
>
> *All of the young women are studying in the Institute of Musical Art of the Juliard Foundation of New York City under Mrs. Wood Stewart...*" [Juilliard misspelled].

The most significant concert, both in locale and program, was the appearance on March 17, 1929, at Steinway Concert Hall, New York, presented by the League of Composers: "New Works by Young Americans and Young Europeans."

An array of international works included two pieces sung by Mildred Kreuder, with "Margaret Muller at the piano." The significance of this series can be understood when reading an announcement of the next program: The first full stage performance in America of Stravinsky's "Les Noces" conducted by Leopold Stokowski.

According to Mutti, the Art Singers were the first white musicians to sing spirituals in public, using Burleigh's arrangements.

To my astonishment and joy I found a pack of small, silver records packed away in that black portfolio. They must have been "demo" recordings of the Art Singers of New York used for publicity. They are to be played with wooden needles, and I have heard them only once or twice in the past; wooden needles have all but disappeared by now. "Deep River" is among the titles. Far-away sounds seemed to emanate from under water, yet, these are surely the voices of Millie, Allie and Margaret on those silver recordings, very graceful–truly Victorian, I would say today.

Among the lovely publicity photos is a portrait of Mutti. Her even features and elegant hair underscore her self-possessed good looks; her eyes also convey the maturity of a modern woman. Gone is the shy Victorian girl in Riverside Park only three years earlier. Often as a child I would study these photos as though hoping to find my mother in this person who looked like, yet did not quite seem to be, my mother. Perhaps it was that other side of her,

Margaret Muller, publicity photograph, 1928 (photo Apeda)

the one that remained inaccessible—deeply precious, but buried in sadness.

And there is another story that clings to my memory: As young female musicians trying to build a career in 1920s New York City, the Art Singers knew that pregnancy was not an option. This dilemma caused them to walk up fire escapes themselves to visit a nurse, Margaret Sanger, who clandestinely gave information on birth control. Many years later, when I had grown to be a teen, Mutti would give advice as an aside, trying, I think, to give me food for thought about moral issues and freedom of choice for women.

Of course, Mutti marched with the Suffragettes in New York; of course, she believed in what she called "trial marriage," summing up her story with an admonition: "Of course, you don't marry a man without having lived with him for a while."

Yet I, the product of 1950s Schleswig-Holstein, the willing disciple of the Nordic farmer family, half-listened and thought my mother was crazy. I felt sorry for myself to be thus burdened.

Were you alive today, Mutti, I would ask your forgiveness.

And so, as I contemplate these remarkable happenings, and my mother's role in them, I try to understand what it must have meant for her to explain their significance to her child, how to share her pride at having been part of this world. All I could give her in return were unwilling attention and total lack of comprehension. Where did she turn to find recognition, some kind of

Margaret in front of the Packard

36

validation? How could she keep on living?

Yet, pictures and stories convey the notion that the couple's life was good for a few years. Mutti proudly stands in front of a fancy Packard; Vati, on a Sunday walk, clad as a true gentleman. One senses a man who feels he has arrived. Never mind the tense face that speaks of the hardships drawn ever more sharply into his features.

Leaving America: Why?

All my adult life I have pondered my parents' moves, changes of locale, travels. I have not arrived at a single root cause but instead at several probable motivations. By the late twenties, photographs prove that Vati's health had seriously deteriorated. His face is gaunt; he looks exhausted. In his early work of

Carsten out for a Sunday stroll

building bridges and docks, he had made countless descents in unpressurized caissons to inspect ongoing work. No one yet knew what had caused John Roebling, the builder of the Brooklyn Bridge, to become a paraplegic, forced to watch the completion of his work from a wheelchair. To a degree, this would become Vati's fate as well. I ask myself whether he was aware of that fact.

Today we understand that bubbles develop in the spinal cord from pressure changes. Engineers, especially, were at greater risk than the workers who made the trip once a day.

I remember Eberhard, my neurologist cousin in Germany, telling me many years later, that caisson disease, "the bends," together with rheumatoid arthritis, were the causes of Vati's increasing inability to move his limbs. There was talk as well that an American doctor had told him to stop all work. He was not about to, and by the late 1920s he had achieved great financial success, especially in the stock market.

On Mutti's part, stories mentioned her suffering greatly from the summer heat in New York, making life unbearable for her. She would spend nights lying naked on the kitchen floor, hoping for cooling effects, or sitting on the roof all night.

She had lost a baby, a boy, through miscarriage.

Also, there was Mutti's asthma. Increasingly, the attacks became so violent she had to give up her music; singing had become impossible, and there was no strength left for the piano.

No strength to perform.

Had the Art Singers of New York disbanded, gone their separate ways? It was never mentioned during coffee hour in Flensburg.

Photos of Mutti suggest sadness, perhaps depression. We all know, or believe, that asthma is an illness the roots of which reside in the body as much as they do in the soul. But living without music? That loss, and the end of promise, shadowed all her subsequent life, regardless of place. In later years she would still play, at times for hours, anything. She had perfect pitch, could entertain a crowd well into the morning just as well as she could play the organ on Easter Sunday.

The final section in the same photo album which contained the rare photos of Uncle Stephen Naft, shows lovely photos of camping trips to Vermont and Minnesota: Vati with some other guys, proudly showing the fish caught on the lake, Mutti gamely posing in hiking gear.

I did not learn about the troubles, the struggle. Instead, I was regaled with the hilarious account of Mutti held captive in the outhouse by a large bear until someone rescued her at sunrise.

However, there also is a photo of my mother sitting on a large rock by the lake, looking pensive, as though wishing herself away. Does this image offer a glance into the condition of her mind and soul at the time; was it her illness? The loss of a baby? General depression? Perhaps both, husband and wife, were vacationing in hopes of finding a healthier climate or to chase away the demons.

In my effort to understand, I turn once more to my parents' photo album. Suddenly, there, stuck behind other pasted-in images, is a photo, cut in half, showing my parents seated near a door with their backs to the camera. Mutti is slumped in her chair—is she crying, suffering an asthma attack? Vati is seated nearby. His expression cannot be seen, his pose is

Margaret on a rock by the lake

Fishermen in Minnesota

watchful but not leaning toward his wife as though to comfort her. I have looked through this album a hundred times; never before did I even notice this fragment showing my parents in a difficult moment.

Who took this photo? Why was it cut in half? Why was it inserted behind other photos and not pasted into the album? Was it meant to make clear the impossibility of continuing life as it was, in New York?

So, for the hundredth time, I turn to that black portfolio with photos and letters, this document map that accompanied us on all our moves. And for the first time in my almost eighty years of life, I remove the rubber band from a stack of letters I had always put aside, lacking the curiosity to open them. The envelopes show dates from August through September 1932. It is a one-sided correspondence revealing only Vati's letters addressed to, and saved by, his wife.

Mutti's responses were not saved, while she kept his, for years and years, through moves, war and bombs. These letters are long, yellowing around the edges, and written in Vati's fluid, strangely delicate script that belies the writer's large hand.

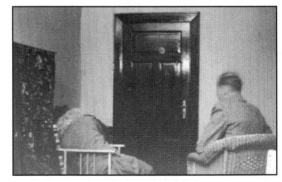

The couple, turning from the camera, New York, 1932?

Again, was this packet saved by happenstance? Were these letters a plea to some god, that he might add them to the scales of justice? Was it yet one more furtive message left to the future in hopes of finding understanding or forgiveness, sent into the unknown, the way a stranded sailor lets loose a note in his last whisky bottle. This bundle, so carefully collected, may have been a message to me, proof of

39

the couple's love. Finally, I tremble at the thought that it was Mutti's silent assumption of guilt for all that was to be endured as a consequence. Viewed by their child, close to a century later, it demands to be studied.

Vati's letters from New York to Mutti in Germany present the sequence of events before the fateful move that would lead to an ever more tragic spiral of fate.

No record remains of the couple's trip to Germany, its duration or places visited, but correspondence shows that Vati returned to New York alone, his wife having refused to join him.

References suggest that Mutti spent time in Berlin, perhaps looking after the property, now no longer occupied by family. She also traveled to see her sister Käthe and husband, Karl, in Lamsdorf, Silesia, a small town in south-eastern Germany, now Poland. From the hindsight of history, it is astonishing that neither the correspondence nor later references suggest that the political developments in Germany were of great concern to my mother.

I look at the dates of these decisions and the urgent question arises: These two people, my parents, were German to the core. Were they returning to the "Fatherland"? One cannot talk about Germany and the early 1930s without the issue of Nazism rising. The post-World War I German Depression piled misery upon misery on a people barely recovering from the ravages of the war. Half of the factories had ceased production; more than a third of the population was unemployed; the elected government was powerless. Finally, the vote of 1932 had given Hitler the largest numbers, if not the majority, in Parliament, a position from which he gradually instituted his control, raining upon a devastated population threats, brawls, legal actions and murder, all culminating in the infamous "Kristallnacht" of 1938.

My parents, Nazis? Does the idea, the image, fit? I have always considered myself exempt from that pain, but do I know, really know? Did I, too, become burdened by the collective guilt that shaped our generation of Germans?

Carsten on his return trip from Germany, 1932

40

So, I search for the truth in this packet of old letters. They are loving notes, pleading, giving the image of a man who loved and longed for his wife. Several times, Vati raises the issue of danger, once asking whether it would not be better to wait. Since the answers are absent, the final action has to speak for itself: It appears that whatever darkness rose on the horizon, it could not compare with Mutti's inability to remain in America.

Margaret visiting her sister, Käthe, in Lamsdorf, Germany, 1932?

The first letter, dated August 11, 1932, on board ship, reports on the crossing and conveys greetings from crew and officers. "Why," they asked, "did your wife not come back with you?" As always, the letter is addressed to "Muttchen" (little mother) and signed by "Dein Alter" (your old man).

August 11, 1932, return trip on board the *Deutschland*:

"We again have the same table and deck stewards. All of them send you greetings. By now you must be in Lamsdorf....Here you are sorely missed. Everything is just half as good when my old lady is not around.... I give you hearty greetings and a kiss, Your Old Man."

August 23, 1932, on P.N. Petersen Company, Inc., Letterhead Long Island City, NY

The letter opens with: *"It has now been three days since I gave you a sign of life aside from that one postcard..."* There follows a report on one couple returning to the States because of the political situation.

"[T]he situation here seems to be a bit more positive. Petersen [his partner] *had stayed in town to greet me.* Vati closes with concern for Mutti's health:

"...I think that once your health improves your spirits will pick up as well. These last days lay on my soul like a heavy nightmare, but I think we will find a solution....Greetings from all my heart; kisses, your Old Man."

In following letters, he pleads with Mutti to reconsider, to return for at least a few years until things calm down in Europe, assuring her that much new work is coming through for his partner who wants him to return to work. He asks for patience.

New York, Aug. 26,

> *"Here things seem to improve, although slowly. You could certainly have your permit extended if you so wish. Stay well, do not worry, instead, think of your old man who longs for you."*

New York, Sept. 1,

Vati reports on a subway station that is near completion, another that is to be started in two weeks; payment is also forthcoming soon. The stock market is very good. He gets the feeling the political conditions in Germany are worrisome–a crazy time, he calls it, but returns to his business dealings:

> *"Petersen said that I could return to the company, but we did not discuss details... he thought I should think it over....I have so much time to think...we both did things the wrong way, and if we wanted, we could make our lives much much better and more beautiful. The good will is there after all on both sides, but surely you must realize that I mean well and love you. Now, take a kiss from me... your Old Man."*

New York, Sept. 8,

> *"It is terrible that I cannot give you a birthday kiss and hope that this is the last birthday we have to celebrate separately....Yesterday evening, I began making drawings for our home, and I enclose the first sketches. You must now let me know which ones you like best and give me some suggestions for changes. Now, my precious, best wishes...a fat birthday kiss, your Old Man."*

New York, Sept. 15,

> *"...You want to have assurance and can no longer endure being dragged along. My dear heart, when I wrote you on Aug. 8, I had been here for just a few days and had nothing positive to tell you... I will wait until beginning or mid-October and will then leave, no matter whether settled or not....You see, my dear, how hard it is."*

The letter of Sept. 20 gives a list of ships and their departure dates for Germany, which suggests he was planning to travel to Germany and accompany her back to the States. Finally, he proposes to give her a pleasant surprise by coming directly to Berlin as soon as possible.

New York, Sept. 24,

In this last letter, Vati asks for understanding but leaves the final decision to her.

> *"I do not lay any unspoken blame on you if you decide to remain in Germany... I also would never expect you to return here if you will have to suffer from the climate as you did before....Take a kiss from your Old Man.*

It becomes clear that the political situation was considered, but of little concern to Mutti; in the end, it was her decision that mattered. This return to Germany in late 1932 became fate for my parents, and I can only guess at regrets, pain and perhaps accusations that grew from that decision. Over all the years of our life in Germany, it was never discussed in my presence.

Chapter 3

The Price of Love

The Price

Early on I told of two kinds of stories that nourish memory. There are the lovely, fuzzy or breathtakingly adventurous ones dished up with the crumb cake on a sunny afternoon. Then there are those that lurk in a glance, or in a word furtively uttered mid-sentence, hinting at a story not meant to be passed down the generations.

For the child grown to adulthood, and looking back on stories or quick remarks, these fragments grow into questions. What were the motives, the gains, the losses, the life-shaping consequences?

My parents' return to Germany in the early thirties must rank among the most fateful of their lives, its consequences of monumental import and suffering. It must have weighed heavily on their marriage over all the years remaining them. Now that I know, or better, can guess at the reason, I can also try to grasp the circumstances.

Were health and homesickness really the reason for my mother's demands to return to Germany? Was that all? How to ignore the fact that returning to Germany in the early 1930s was a statement that today weighs like lead in the hand. Germans from the east of Europe were called to the "Fatherland," young Americans of German descent were invited for lengthy stays, given education laced with indoctrination, all very delicately applied in the beginning, growing darker and more dangerous by the month. The thunder

45

of propaganda, the terror of persecution, the bombastic speeches, rallies, parades, all conveyed the rise of a power with terrifying goals.

Today, I may mention in conversation the fact of my parents' return to Germany, and I can see doubts rising:

They returned to Germany in 1932?

From the letters presented in the previous chapter, it becomes clear: the decision rested with my mother, that my father gave up everything–his wealth, his business, his friendships in New York–to build a life in Germany where his wife could be healthy and happy.

Perhaps they both weighed the personal against public events and conditions, and the former weighed heavier. Since there remain no answers to my father's letters, I cannot say whether his concerns were ignored or even acknowledged. The political dangers appear to have been set aside. It was not sympathy with the new regime, at least that is what I hope.

And yet, happiness seemed to have returned to them. Had they both longed to be "home" as they often mentioned? Did they hope that Germany would rise from the ashes? When I look at a photo of my parents at that time, they seem to radiate energy; they have a kind of glamor, like visitors who have just briefly touched down–Father and Mother have presence, be it in Germany or

Margarethe and Carsten Dethlefs visiting the family in Nordhackstedt, Germany

anywhere else. Talent, travel and their ability to adjust to multiple circumstances gave them a carriage different from that of others. However, photos do not convey the price paid.

There were now enough resources to fight Vati's possible disability and illness as the doctors' prognoses had suggested. Arriving in Germany with hard currency, my parents had the opportunity to buy up half the country. Which they did.

Shortly after their return, Vati remembered, and acted upon, a childhood dream now made possible by German economic troubles as well as inflation. As luck would have it, my parents were visiting Vati's brother in Flensburg, and during a stroll through town, Vati discovered that the finest apartment building on the promontory overlooking the old city of Flensburg,

House in Flensburg

the very street he admired so longingly when, as a carpenter's apprentice, he pushed that heavy cart of tools and wood up the hill, well, that building was for sale! His papers include a large, folded photo of the corner building, turret and all. This building, its very prominence in the city, would help him assert his power. Perhaps it even allowed him to spit in the eye of those who would not struggle but accepted their role in life without trying to escape. This need for victory would not have been part of his soul, but it must have felt good at the time. Many years later, and in much more devastating circumstances, it would be this building alone that rescued this family

Langenhagen

There is a photo, taken in the garden of Vati's boyhood farm, on the occasion of the 1933 Golden Wedding Anniversary of Vati's parents, an event that involved, I would guess, at least a week of country parties.

One can imagine that the receptions were a regional event, and the photo of the golden couple shows their formality. By then, Grandfather had long ago given up farming; he continued to be politically involved. Making sure the area was connected to the outside world by train from Flensburg, a line that led all the way to Sylt, today bringing many of the rich and famous of new Germany to the island's spas and fancy restaurants.

The group photo was most likely taken by Vati, since he is not in the picture while Mutti is standing in the back row.

Golden wedding anniversary, the Dethlefs family, 1933

There are some of Vati's siblings, except for those living in the States. To Mutti's right, stands her niece, Dina, who would have such an important role in our future life.

I used to adore my father unquestioningly, still do. This tall, solid man in whose eyes I could do, or be, no better than I did or was. Whatever problems arose in the family, I always loaded onto Mutti, the temperamental and unpredictable one, who was different and had a love greater than the one for me.

Only lately have I revisited my mother woman-to-woman, from the point in life whence one looks at its totality and judges one's own efforts in the face of circumstances. Putting aside the devastating decision to return to

The golden wedding anniversary, Christine and Claus Dethlefs, Erika's grandparents, 1933

Germany at the door of disaster, I look at a woman so cheated by fate, so valiant in her insistence on spiritual survival, that only admiration can be her testimonial.

What was it like to be an artist from the golden age of Berlin, to marry a man who loved her and her talent but could not help her achieve a successful career in America; how did she cope with the loss of her gift to asthma?

Also, it is hard to understand some of my father's decisions. At heart the farm boy, how could he, on the light side of this, insist that the few American vacations they took together were in a cabin in Vermont or on an island in the Minnesota lakes, reached only by canoe, where one lived in tents and fished all day?

What do I know about my parents? What, for that matter does one know about anybody? Does one connect at the one point of thousands, in that place where one's own experience touches that of others? And where does filial love enter into this picture–does it enhance or distort? How can I trust the stories, especially since I was so young when my parents died, that we never had a chance to know each other adult-to-adult. Over the years, my appreciation of both has changed–even in my memory–as I try to understand the motives that may have guided their actions.

One thing I know, the older I get the more I admire them, love them, each in his or her own way. Their spirit is with me, always, and alive.

The following chapters will retrace the steps beginning with their return to Germany and the search for permanence, location by location, trying to unfold the way fate and decisions together form biography.

Vati made huge investments, among them the purchase of a brick and cement factory in a small village near Eutin in Schleswig-Holstein. Scenic and romantic as the area may be, and as lavish their house in comparison to the surroundings, it was not city life. Mutti tried to survive.

The brick and cement factory,
Langenhagen, Schleswig-Holstein

Already in the early 1930s clouds were gathering over Germany. Reports spread of growing attacks on Jews, Socialists, in fact on most intellectuals. This news must have wafted even to the bucolic North. I suppose that, like most Germans, my parents ducked, turned inward, away from the present day, hoping for the best.

In this setting, there were frequent house guests, lots of money, a housekeeper, even a talking parrot. But there also was a husband who loved riding his tractor and working in the clay pits, supervising the manufacture of building materials. In the course of time, he forgot his promise that a house would be built in Hamburg in order to provide an urban environment within driving distance. How could he impose upon this woman the life of a German wife, in the far rural North of Germany, no less?

Of course, Mutti fit into this rural setting like a clown at a funeral. Pictures show her smiling tentatively, getting fat, taking on minor office chores for the factory. There was the grand piano by the window, but played for whom? Is it enriching enough to play for a husband whose love is unquestioned and to whom one owes a debt of such proportions, a man who gave up the core of his energies and hopes to follow Mutti back to Germany and who was now her only audience?

It was in Langenhagen that Mutti started her habit of going to spas at least once a year, a pattern I always resented and belittled, believing this to be just one more example of her spoiled diva airs, as were massages, hats with veils and jewelry. At spas, Mutti would meet people, have a few charming weeks, perhaps a mild flirtation, and return refreshed to her sober life and stoic husband.

But I am moving ahead, and there is much to be told about my father, who also deserves a new, closer look. How might he have been as a husband? Was he willing to adjust to the needs of this unusual woman he had married? Was he driven by circumstance to make the decisions he made, or did he eventually fall into the role of the German *paterfamilias* who expects his decisions to be law? Never in all my memory do I find an instance where a single harsh word was exchanged between my parents, but then, in piecing things together, just how much time did they spend in normal marriage and family life? Not too much until much later, I must now admit.

The house in Langenhagen

When considering the events that followed the move to Germany, doubts about happiness arise in large numbers. A remark Mutti made late in life now gives me food for thought. She told me that, had it not been for the war, the bombs, and the Russian occupation, the years in Graz, in the middle of World War II, were her happiest. That would exclude the years in America as well as those between 1932 and 1943 before we moved to Graz.

Later, once I reached some understanding of family life, I observed my parents having good moments together. Later, when illness, poverty and years of separation had made a mockery of their dreams, they became a bastion of strength in the face of fate and outside forces.

A Child

After ten years of marriage, a major event was about to change their lives: Mutti expected a child at age forty-two. By accounts from both, this was a happy event and all was done to make the situation comfortable.

Yet, during the months of pregnancy, Vati decided to take a trip to Africa—a long-held dream following an invitation from a German plantation owner in Angola who had become a friend. It was the first and only luxury he permitted himself: seven months of travel by ship, of staying on the coffee plantation and there, fatefully for the future, falling in love with Africa. But, does a husband leave a pregnant wife, one forty-two years of age? Did he leave because Mutti was becoming unbearable in her spoiled, pregnant ways? Was he terrified of the certain prospect of his debilitating illness, at that time still held at bay? The French have a saying: *Tout comprendre c'est tout pardonner* [to understand everything is to forgive all]. Do I forgive him because of who he was, or was he entitled to this adventure?

Vati with newborn daughter

Later on, there were times—years perhaps, I don't remember—when my parents lived separately, the situation always explained as circumstance. What circumstance? I know Vati, too, went off to spas (this was after all the preferred health cure for wealthy Europeans). Was it because his hands were beginning to get stiff, his feet swelling? Still, there were little asides, such as his telling the story of how he met and became friends with Melitta, the wife of the man who invented the coffee filter. These stories, Mutti's too, were always told with smiling tolerance on both sides, not implying or suggesting anything improper.

The setting of my birth was a hospital in Kiel, the large university town near their home in Langenhagen. Her husband had returned just in time to fondly pat Mutti's belly and ask: "How are the two of you?" This she told me with great warmth, suggesting that Mutti never resented the trip, and that both were happy to see each other.

My birth, in May of 1937, was difficult, as could be expected, and it left Mutti quite ill. Asthma continued to sap her energies, she walked on two canes and was sent to a spa for three months immediately after my birth. In addition to a nurse, my cousin, Dina Dethlefs, was brought in to live with us. She became both my substitute mother, older sister, and eventually a much-loved member and protector of the family.

Later, I seem to have fallen ill. One night the nurse knocked on my parents' bedroom door, handed them a limp baby and declared that she could no longer assume responsibility. She was dismissed on the spot, and Dina took charge. People other than my mother cared for me day by day. Today we know how important is a newborn's bonding with mother—was that chance taken from both of us? Is that where we lost the opportunity to connect deeply?

Photos show a strapping baby on a white bearskin, or sitting in a high chair, spoon in hand, and looking quite well fed indeed. They show a single child doted upon by an army of adults, the center of all attention. Stories lead me to believe that the dirty part of childcare was left to others. Years later, Mutti herself told me she became seriously interested in me only once I talked and could listen to her stories.

Mutti, having produced an heir, now had greater status. Photos show her with a happy smile. In her words, she had fooled Adolf Hitler, she had deprived him of an inheritance, the Great

The family in Langenhagen

Dictator having announced that all childless couples automatically made him their heir. I have not found documentary proof of this assertion. Yet, it was the reason my parents had briefly entertained the idea of adopting Dina.

Baptisms, too, were frowned upon, prompting my parents to stage a private ceremony in our house, officiated by the village pastor. I doubt seriously that mom and dad had ever set foot in his church; it was a gesture of defiance, and to this day, I treasure the pewter bowl used as my baptismal font.

Vati's life took on new meaning, causing him to close the factory an

hour earlier, just so he could give me my bath. My earliest memory centers on my father and has to be from age two to two-and-a-half. It was a sunny day, we were still living at the factory, and I was walking across the yard, Vati holding me steady. I can still feel how I had to stretch high to reach his enormous hand. We climbed a ramp into the brick-drying shed, a long structure, open at the sides, with rows and rows of shelves upon which bricks and roof tiles dried before firing; cobwebs were drooping from the shelves.

In this huge open space, the rafters were exposed, creating spaces where swallows had made nests, many

Mother and daughter

nests. Parents were swooshing in and out

with worms in their beaks, the baby birds making a racket. All you could see in the nests were wide-open beaks, pink in the center. Their nests were sheltered from the rain by an exposed roof made of the same clay tiles that were drying in the racks.

I remember Vati lifting me onto his shoulder and blowing air through his tight lips, making a squeaking noise that imitated the baby birds. The effort made his eyebrows bob up and down; fascinated by the sound, I turned from the birds to his face: Vati's blue eyes, the color of liquid icebergs, were smiling; his impressively long, curved nose descended between them in a very narrow ridge. The only other time I have seen a face like that would be many years later, in a museum in Schleswig, where it appeared on the mummified body of a Viking who had died in the peat swamps. Well, on that sunny day in Langenhagen, with the swallows, we both were happy. Since the factory was sold on September 1, 1939, the day the war began, this very early memory set the stage for a tight bond between father and daughter, no matter where fate would place us.

Lamsdorf/Łambinowice

Thereafter things get hazy. Mutti and I were now living in Lamsdorf, Silesia, between the towns of Oppeln and Neisse, today a part of Poland. We were at the home of Mutti's sister, Tante Käthe, and her husband, Onkel Karl, a pharmacist.

I do not remember when we left Langenhagen, nor do I recall the trip in our old Packard. I do not know when Vati moved away, nor do I recall having been told a reason for his absence. All I have to guide me is a drawing showing the car trip. It is part of a book documenting the family's many moves. It is simply entitled *Erika*, a lovely book, like notes of a journey, commissioned from a watercolor artist.

Another written record is called *Unser Kind* [Our Child], a small notebook containing Mutti's handwritten notes on her daughter's development. They tell of my early experiences and offer tiny glimpses of family life that require in-fill by an adult mind and amplification with historic fact. As always, however, every piece of information raises the question "Why?"

Yes, they sold the factory on the day Hitler declared war. Yes, Mutti and I had spent the previous Christmas with my aunt and uncle, where Vati had lent a hefty sum for the building of a pharmacy. Now we lived with them; even Dina had come along, staying for a while until I was adjusted to the change.

Many years later I learned that while we were there, Vati lay in a hospital

1939

MIT VATI, MUTTI UND GEPÄCK
GEHTS NUN VON LANGENHAGEN WEG.

On our way to Silesia, formerly East Germany; drawing from the "Erika" book

in Kiel with appendicitis. Alone?

The rather grand house in Lamsdorf combined my uncle's pharmacy with living quarters above; my earliest memory is a lovely garden, white with blooming snowdrops. An upper terrace off the dining room was shaded by an acacia tree spreading above us like a scented roof. There was a *Herrenzimmer*, the gentlemen's room, to which my uncle retreated in the evening to smoke his cigar after having put on his velvet corbeled smoking jacket and velvet slippers–both fascinated me. This was the one room in the house where entrance was forbidden.

I remember a morning: standing in astonishment in the family bathroom. I watched handsome Onkel Karl shave and trim his black moustache. Tante Käthe, as was her wifely duty, had spread her husband's clothing out on the bed for the day, right down to his kerchief and a newly starched, white pharmacist's coat. I loved it. If I had been especially good, I was allowed to accompany him to the pharmacy downstairs and "help," selling tiny white mints to the customers, the only non-medicine sold there, all else was chemical smells and lovely white jars lining dark shelves.

Of the six pregnancies this couple experienced, only one resulted in a live birth, their son, Eberhard, who grew to become a highly respected brain surgeon and researcher on Dopamine. I do not remember ever seeing Eberhard in Lamsdorf. He had been conscripted into Hitler's army as a field doctor, later made prisoner of war by the Russians, not to return to Germany until sometime in the later forties. Over the years he, and his family, became loving supporters of our lives.

Other photos show me at age

Erika in the yard with new toys

three or four: on my tricycle in the garden, with my beloved dolls in 1942, the last photo taken in Lamsdorf, shortly before the flight. It gives no hint at war or danger, only the magic childhood of a golden child.

There were trips to spas during Vati's rare visits. Bad Landeck and Lindewiese come to mind. There were summer evenings on the terrace, and if I remember correctly, we never lacked food—who knows what medications

Erika on the terrace with dolls, 1942

Onkel Karl bartered for it? There is vague, delirious memory of serious illnesses, pneumonia and hepatitis. Do I recall, or was I told later, that in my fever I demanded to see my father, insisting that I would not get better until I had him with me?

According to Mutti, Vati was then working and living in Innsbruck, Austria. What was he doing there? Stories have it that Vati was reached by wire, that he caught the next train and arrived in the morning. For days he sat by my bed, never leaving. I remember feeling his large hand on my forehead and knowing that all would be fine now. Again, the little

handwritten book fills in the blank:

"In July 1940 Erika greets her most beloved dad with great joy. Once, when I was fussing over a blemish on his face, Erika interjects: 'This is my Vati, nobody is allowed to mess with him.'"

A later note states:

"She grows, becomes very independent and gets acquainted with the switch."

Interestingly, my response is also recorded:

"You old goat; if you make me angry, I will simply travel to Vati!"

The "Our Child" book; notes in Mutti's handwriting

Agnes

In Lamsdorf I spent most of my time in the company of Agnes, the Polish cook. A member of the family, she seemed to love and be loved, even after war and flight separated us, but of course, she knew her place. Mutti, for her part, would rise late, dress beautifully, her dresses always having a deep front opening into which she buttoned lovely embroidered or lacy triangles and a diamond pin. She would put on her hat with veil and go out with Tante Käthe. At times she played the piano–or had terrifying asthma attacks. I see her sitting in the kitchen, her head and arms on the table, gasping for air and unable to move from exhaustion.

Vati was not there.

Agnes's kitchen was my headquarters; I had a place on the wood-box next to the huge stove; there I learned (was I only four or five years old?) how to pluck and dress a chicken, to make noodles– practical things, useful and undemanding that I found to be extremely fine; they filled me with pride. I learned how to iron clothes from watching Agnes iron my wide silk hair ribbons. These ribbons were important, because in Mutti's view, girls from good houses did not have bangs. Their hair had to be short and tied on one side with large ribbons, always freshly ironed. Girls from good houses also did not wear earrings, nor did they wear anything but smocked dresses of fine cotton. I, of course, longed for all the things girls from

Erika and Agnes on a walk outside the Berlin Zoo, January, 1943

not-so-good houses had. I dreamed of having long dark hair, dark eyes, a delicate body covered by multi-colored, diaphanous gowns, bangs, even earrings–none of which were to be; it took me years to come to terms with that.

Best of all Agnes experiences were her songs–music called *Küchenlieder* or *Gassenhauer*, kitchen songs, street music of the people, sentimental or ghastly–the very opposite of Mutti's "high music." Today I would say that many songs reached back into ancient history, even the Crusades, such as the one that talked about the Black Whale Pub in Ashkelon: *"Im Schwarzen Walfisch zu Askalon vertrank ein Mann den Tag, bis daß er steif wie ein Besenstiel am Marmortische lag-ah-ahg..."* [where a man drank away the day until, stiff like a broomstick, he lay on the marble tahahahable...] or others that dealt with ancient battles, or maidens who lost their loves to war. From this rich trove of folk culture sprang the songs that Berthold Brecht and Kurt Weill made famous in the "Threepenny Opera." These songs, Agnes sang loud, with feeling, sounds trailing like syrup down the scales. When the washer girl was at the house, the two sang together, and I chimed in.

Pure Heaven.

After having cooked and served the mid-day meal, Agnes took me for a walk (the family, not having done much in the morning, were sleeping the nap to which their bourgeois station entitled them). She got dressed, turned to me and asked, "Where do we go now? Whom do we see?"

I answered, "To the barracks, to visit Schorsch."

Her boyfriend, Georg, was stationed there. After a short walk, waiting for him to appear, we leaned against the street lantern, singing *"Vor der Kaserne, vor dem grossen Tor, stand eine Laterne und steht sie noch davor..."* [In front of the barracks, at the large gate, there stood a lantern; does it still stand?] the "Lili Marleen" song we thought was very appropriate.

Did we know—would we have caught the irony had we known—that somewhere in the world, thousands of miles away, Marlene Dietrich was singing this same song in German, hoping to draw German soldiers from fighting? Surely the adults in the house knew about the growing threat, but Agnes and I simply lived for the fun of it. Eventually, Schorsch came out briefly, the two would whisper, arrange a date for the evening; a blown kiss, and we headed home.

I loved Agnes.

She was the source of my first religious education as well. A devout Polish Catholic, she instructed me on proper ritual: If you met a nun in the street, you greeted her with a curtsy, made the sign of the Cross, and uttered a quick *"Gegrüßt sei Maria"* [Greeted be Mary]. At church, you used holy water and curtsied toward the altar. Later on, when we lived in Austria—every bit as devoutly Catholic—I would get annoyed with Mutti for not knowing how to behave. That is when she told me that we were Protestants, different.

Once back from my walk with Agnes, it was time for coffee and for my special time with mother. She would read to me or tell stories. Everything she did was fascinating and terrifying at the same time. One never knew whether her mood would swing, her asthma return. All was tentative and yet exceedingly absorbing.

Language, to my mother, was like music. With ease she could sail from English to French, to German, to Yiddish (for her, family was always the *Mishpocheh*, a foolish person always *meshuggah*). And when she was angry, she yelled "*Shaddap,*" which I thought was expressive and concise, until arriving in New York many years later and being told by Vati's relatives never to use such language.

"But Mutti said it all the time!" I had answered.

Raised eyebrows, knowing nods adult-to-adult. I soon understood that these people had never liked my mother one little bit and pitied their poor brother.

The Piano and I

Sound defined my mother, carried her magic at the piano and her ability to shine at parties. Still, music and pain were close neighbors in her soul ever since the days in New York when she discovered that asthma no longer allowed her to exercise her profession. Love and loss painted the color of her day depending upon her thoughts and memories; lack of air made her lungs constrict to the point of fainting.

As to her child, I proved not to have been blessed with the talent–not at all. This realization must have come early to both of us. I simply knew the piano would never make beautiful music for me. I came to fear and hate its very existence, the way it confirmed what I knew all too well: this black hulk, with its elephantine legs, wide mouth and gleaming teeth was not on my side. Even when the keyboard was closed, that mouth showed a narrow sliver of white. It said, "Wait! We will be open, and then you will see you can't handle us!"

To compensate for my failure at the piano, I was trained to sing, beginning somewhere around age four. Every day we practiced charming melodies. I stood next to the monster, one hand on its cover, as singers do, trying to keep the rhythm, keep the flow of voice, adjust to the timing set by those teeth.

In the evening, when guests appeared to make and hear music, I was told to perform for the assembled, who clapped and laughed. I was passed from lap to lap, and someone invariably asked what I wanted to be when I grew up.

My answer, which I knew was expected of me, was always "opera singer!" Everyone laughed and cheered.

"Opera singer, of course!"

Who were these people? Well, an answer came to me recently. I was looking at the *Unser Kind* book. There, in Mutti's brief entry for Lamsdorf in 1941 it says: *"Einquartierung ist ihr Entzücken"* [home occupants are her delight] referring to officers placed in private homes before being sent to fight and die in battles on the eastern front. I had always read right over these words; now they burn. These were the young men who brought me dolls from Paris, who stroked my hair. Sometimes their eyes were very sad.

The story in the book further suggests the precocious child I had become: Mutti notes it as the accomplishment of a 4-year-old:

"She declares that she will marry seven men, so that each day she can go to a café with a different one. She embarrasses her mother by declaring that her mother, too, has two husbands, the other one, Onkel Fritz, living in Hamburg! She states that one of the soldiers is so pretty, as pretty as her daddy, and therefore she would marry him; and anyway, her daddy already has a lot of money in the bank for her."

Surely, if ever there was a child trained not to be a child, I was it.

In spite of that, the family decided it was time for me to go to kindergarten (nursery school in Germany). I was livid. There, in the playroom, were several children whom I refused to acknowledge, sniveling, pushing, yelling–and only two adults.

Where was my personal adult? Still today I can feel the outrage.

According to reports, I screamed for two solid days, until I was sent home and did not have to return. Is this the first instance of my desire to be alone, to be happy in solitude? Never then, nor in later life, did I know loneliness or boredom; being alone has always been like swimming in a low chord, a resting point for the soul, a sufficiency that would come to good use in many a setting. It is also the beginning of my life-long habit of talking to myself–aloud.

After the kindergarten debacle, a babysitter, Maria, was hired for me. I disliked her, she was too young, only about 14, and I am ashamed to say, I bossed her around and tortured her. There is a photo of us: Maria had taken me for a walk in the neighborhood. She is standing by, quite helplessly, while I put money into the collection box of a Hitler Youth. It was *Winterhilfe*, the winter collection, that must have served the war effort. Judging from the photo, I took that very seriously, making my coin clank in the metal box. A child does not know, cannot imagine, the forces behind such an action. Eventually I would learn.

Later, too, memory would settle on moments and events which, in isolation seemed innocent and meaningless. When contemplated from the view of half a century, however, these fragments take on a sinister mean.

One such event was my temper tantrum, perhaps at age four, when Mutti and Tante Käthe were getting all dressed up because *"Herr Oberst"* [a colonel] was coming with his carriage to take them for a ride–a ride to where? All I remember is wanting to be taken along, kicking and screaming, to no avail. Mother and aunt, in their finest–hats with little veils, leather gloves, fur collars, fancy handbags on the arm–disappeared when the two-horse

Erika with Hitler Youths collecting money, 1942

carriage arrived. What had brought about this honor bestowed by a powerful member of the Hitler military? What were they doing?

How can I confront this fact? Does this fragment of experience add to the question lurking behind the fact that it was my mother who insisted on living in Germany, no matter the political consequences? My mother who came out of Jewish Berlin, whose ancestry might well have been questioned?

Questions–never any answers.

Gradually, and noticeable even to a child, there were moments when Onkel Karl studied the atlas, and the adults listened to speeches I now realize were those of Adolf Hitler. Onkel followed the news, reporting on movement of "the front" and tracing places on the map. He looked grave and quickly turned away, so I could not see his face.

It seems Vati visited occasionally. For whatever reasons, my parents decided a cure was called for. This one put both of them on a vegetarian, "body cleansing" diet. Somewhere in the Eastern mountains, in the winter, all three of us stayed in a fancy resort hotel. I watched my parents getting massages, being wrapped in mud and thick towels, going to the dining room only to find carrots and raw cabbage on the plate. However, there was snow, and I had my first try at skiing.

There is a photo of a little girl looking worried; but was it fear of being on skis or did it reflect a harrowing experience–a quick image that would ring in the future?

Vati and I were walking in the snow. Suddenly he turned away from me and vomited. Fascinated, and terrified, I saw fresh red blood sinking into deep white snow, an image that is burned into my soul. I asked him what was wrong, and he said it was an ulcer, that his stomach was bleeding, but that he would soon be better. On our way back to the hotel, Vati took my hand, and I noticed that his huge fingers were stiff and swollen, no longer bending around my hand as I had remembered.

Why had Vati gone to Innsbruck? Why had we not left the country when it was still possible? Some years later, I asked him this question, and he told me that by then, his American passport had been taken away, and Mutti, never having taken out her American citizenship, could no longer leave Germany. Piece by piece the regime confiscated my father's properties. Two apartment houses in Kiel that overlooked the harbor were disowned and razed because U-Boots were launched there. There was a movie house in Berlin. Bank accounts were frozen, insurance policies as well. Was there simply no money to leave? Did Vati know that his illness would make it impossible for him to work and support his family back in America? When he sold the brickyard, would the revenue not have been enough to get us out? Was it too late? I will never know but will also never cease to ask.

Erika on skis at a resort in the Sudeten Mountains

Danger at the Door

Once, late during our stay in Lamsdorf, an experience broke the illusion of a golden childhood; it is an image I have learned to interpret and will never forget. Mutti and I were standing at our bedroom window. It had snowed furiously during the night, and I was placing a sugar lump on the window ledge in the sure conviction that the owl, not the stork, would bring me a brother. Mutti held me up so I could reach and search for the owl.

As I struggled to place the sugar, I looked up, across the road, over the fields. There, in great distance, I saw humped figures moving very slowly in deep snow, more like lumps than humans. Slowly they were digging or moving things, too far to discern. I remember asking what these people were doing.

Mutti explained that these were prisoners of war, being forced to clear snow from the train tracks. The sight terrified me, as though an unnamed terror was slowly closing in on us, perhaps this was the "front" the adults were always talking about. This front was obviously dangerous and coming closer and closer judging from the family's faces and murmured comments.

Only recently have I made a chilling discovery that will forever throw dark terror over this scene, and in fact over every memory of that time and place. Google Earth led me to Łambinowice, in Poland, "*Lamsdorf*," in German, where a photo shows an expanse of meadow with a large memorial cross at its center. Farther along, there is a museum as well as numerous grave and memorial sites dedicated to the dead of that horrific place. The accompanying text tells of this site as a prison colony for many years, first in the 1860s, during the Franco-Prussian War, holding more than 3,000 prisoners, followed by even larger prison sites during World War I, with more than 7,000 dead. During World War II, it became the infamous "Stalag VIII-B" camp, later increased by "Stalag VIII-F," the former housing prisoners from every region of the world, the latter reserved for Russian and Polish POWs. Together, this compound wrought deaths in the hundreds of thousands. After war's end, this camp housed displaced Germans with more death—in short, Lamsdorf is a monument to human cruelty, a sadder place the mind cannot conceive.

Searching "*Lamsdorf*" further, I discover entire web sites established by former prisoners—Americans, French, British—that show photos of soldiers in the camp, letters and descriptions. These texts explain that "*Stalag*" was an abbreviation for the word "*Stammlager*" which denoted this was a holding center for up to 100,000 prisoners who were not all housed right there but assigned to numerous forced labor camps, their names and tasks documented.

Conditions were desperate, and one website quotes a former inmate:

"Prisoners worked 12-hour days... Occasionally the prisoners were put to work on snow clearance on major roads...work clothes were limited."

Is this what I saw that morning at the window, putting out a sugar lump for the owl? When the adults around me saw these scenes, what did they think, do, say? So, I ask myself: Were the barracks where we sang "Lili Marleen" actually "Stalag VIII-B"? Was Schorsch a prison guard? Did Agnes know? Were the huddled lumps of humanity I had seen in the snow the prisoners of the camp? The visiting German officers who played the violin so beautifully, who brought me French dolls and candies, were they involved? Why did my uncle's family settle in Lamsdorf? How is it possible to build a child's world of illusion in the midst of such reality? Today I carry guilt by the mere fact of having been there. Questions, always questions.

Brandenburg–Berlin

It must have been early 1943 when we left Lamsdorf. I assume that the "front" had indeed moved closer and closer. Grave conversations, desperate decisions must have taken place. How do you walk out of a business, leave a way of life, a home? Strangely, I do remember that the old Packard, the one proudly displayed in photos of early New York days, the one that was shipped all the way to Germany in that fateful move in 1932, this Packard was left for the Russians. I saw it in the garage, sitting on blocks, the tires long ago confiscated. Why is that the one thing I remember of fleeing from the approaching Russians?

For the rest, memory fails; details are lost. There remains, however, a weightless fragment, like a leaf blown by the wind: Mutti and I are together in some dark room; it might have been the attic. She is sorting through things, packing a few bags. Perhaps I was bored, a pest. In an effort to keep her four-year-old child occupied, she handed me a magnificent pink beaded gown and a scissor:

"Here is something nice for you to do while I pack. Make yourself a princess gown." I remember the touch of that fine silk, the hundreds of shiny beads and pearls jumping around on the floor as I cut through the fabric. I was delighted. However, I do not remember ever playing with the princess gown.

In my current, sleepless search for understanding, I comb through these early images, add them to others. Finally, from the totality of my own life, I find the symbolic content of this scene and gain a softer image. It is archeology: excavating layer after layer of human experience, each informing the next.

I now see Mutti's effort with clarity. Handing me a scissor to cut up her beaded gown was a deeply symbolic act, discarding a part of her life. This was the beaded gown worn during performances in New York, at the height of her career as a pianist, a gown she had kept like a talisman and hauled from residence to residence–that gown was now the last fragment of a world forever gone. Its destruction at the hands of a child was the only possible gesture of closure.

The four-year-old child in that scene was, of course, unaware the family had been packing up, preparing to flee westward from eastern Germany in the face of Russian advances. Whatever future, if any, there might have been, would certainly not include beaded gowns, and Mutti certainly was not going to leave the gown for the Russians.

I do recall that we suddenly lived in the city of Brandenburg near Berlin. There was a new pharmacy. I do not recall the trip, but we were now in an apartment, still with Tante Käthe and Onkel Karl.

Where was Vati?

Agnes had accompanied the family in the move to Brandenburg. I know because there is that photo of the two of us on the sidewalk visiting the famous Berlin Zoo.

Other outings with Mutti were memorable, especially the ones to nearby Potsdam, ancient seat of the Hohenzollern emperors, where Mutti and I visited her cousin, Martin Winzerling, a lawyer. There he lived with his elegant, slender wife, Tante Ella, who was Swedish. Two daughters from her previous marriage had returned to Sweden, and judging from photos displayed in silver frames, they were extremely beautiful in that Ingrid Bergman way.

Their fancy villa was furnished with white Scandinavian furniture; they served dinners on numerous plates with tiny portions, carried in and out by a maid in black dress and white apron. The sparsity of meals made Mutti eat before each visit.

Short, rotund, and balding, Onkel Martin was clearly a favorite of Mutti's. His vest pocket was adorned with a golden chain from which hung a *pince-nez* that was endlessly fascinating to me. When worn, it was clamped over the ridge of his nose without temple wires–a most compelling object. I have no proof, but I believe Onkel Martin would later play a major role in our lives.

Adult conversation at the dinner table was animated and friendly. Onkel Martin loved to tell jokes; he was his own most appreciative audience, and his face would turn red, his eyes tear with amusement. In general, I did not understand a word. Yet, sound of voice and body language told even a young child that this person was important, a family member to be treated with respect.

After our visits, Mutti and I walked along the lovely promenades of Potsdam, with high wrought-iron fences, yellow-orange chestnut leaves on the sidewalk. Walking through them, and making them whirl around us, they swooshed under our feet, and we sang.

This we did to the sounds of *"Üb' immer Treu und Redlichkeit bis an Dein stilles Grab, und weiche keinen Finger breit von Gottes Wegen ab"* [practice faithfulness and probity up to your cool grave, and never move, even a finger's width, from God's paths...Music: Mozart's "Papageno"]. This tune chimed from the bells of the ancient garrison church, the *Garnisonkirche,* that had once crowned, baptized and buried kings since before Frederick the Great. Lately it had bestowed symbols of power and legitimacy upon President Paul von Hindenburg and Adolf Hitler.

We must not have stayed in Brandenburg very long, but enough for another image to be etched into memory: Mutti and I are standing in line at the butcher's for our 1/4 pound of meat redeemed through ration stamps. Next to me stood a little girl, barely older than myself. Pinned to her winter coat was a yellow star. I asked Mutti what that meant, she motioned me to be quiet, and later she told me this girl was Jewish and had to wear the star as identification. We left quickly. I do not believe I was given an explanation beyond that simple fact, for I cannot remember fear or foreboding, just astonishment. No matter, this scene remained, while logistics of our move to Austria have vanished.

I don't know what longings or rationalizations drove my parents to think of building another home together, nor do I know what negotiations took place at that point. Clearly, Mutti and I could not have stayed with the relatives, themselves now refugees in a rather small apartment. Clearly, there was a child that deeply longed for her father and kept making demands to see him. Also, all financial sustenance came from Vati's side.

Could it have been love? That drop-dead love of the twenties, from the time on the boat for America? The love that drove a man to abandon his lucrative business and follow his wife to a now dangerous continent? Now that escape from Germany had long ago become impossible, was their decision to find a home together born out of the realization that the family might be safer together. I lie in bed at night and wonder.

It must have been early 1943 when preparations were made for this new beginning. I was told Vati had moved to Graz in southern Austria and was renovating an old ballroom in a beer garden into an apartment for the three of us. He had called for us to come. How did he get the job with the government to review building projects in the countryside? His American passport had already been confiscated, so he was now technically stateless except for the fact that with his Viking looks he could have been a poster boy for Aryanism? Who was his protector; could it have been Onkel Martin of Potsdam? Had this uncle found a safe place for us far from the center of power, Germany?

I do not remember preparations for travel. Before leaving, however, Mutti wanted to visit her childhood home in Berlin where the old apartment had been kept for storing grandmother's and the sisters' belongings.

I remember entering this dark building on Prinzenstrasse 19, climbing stairs to an even darker corridor which led into an apartment full of trunks and boxes, heavy velvet curtains tightly drawn. Mutti went through some of the trunks, looked things over, put a few pieces into bags. Getting bored, I started my own search and came upon a set of dolls, from large to small, with black hair, wrapped in colorful blankets, moccasins on their feet. I was enthralled and asked to take the whole set. Mutti said no, these were Native American dolls that belonged to Tante Adele, now in America, who had brought them back from one of her trips to the West. No, we could not take them all, only one. I made a happy choice, and we returned to Brandenburg in the evening.

I cannot visualize whether snow or sun covered the events of those days, whether gardens were in bloom or trees bare. All memory will do is paint a picture of gray sky, gray masses of buildings, a world devoid of all color. Whether this was the outer, real aspect, or the way a child's brain stored what was seen but not understood, I do not know.

The following morning, we were to catch a train from Berlin to Graz. However, on that night came one of the huge bombing attacks on Berlin in 1943, aptly named "carpet bombing," that flattened much of the inner city. Tons of bombs were dropped, and thousands of people lost their lives, never mind their homes. War had entered the end phase, the part where terror is rained on the population in order to cause maximum damage but also demoralize the troops. Until then, stories of victory and glory had always been sent to the fighters on the fronts.

Somehow, we got from Brandenburg to the Berlin station; somehow, the train ran. Actually, the "coaches" crawled for hours through mountains of burning city ruins, smoke rising on either side of the rails. What had once been rows of apartment houses, were now mountains of rubble or gaping walls, wallpaper and some furniture still clinging to apartment floors not entirely fallen to the ground. It was as though a giant rake had come and removed roofs and surfaces down to jagged stalks that reached for the sky like a muffled cry. Once in a while a group of huddled figures rummaged through the still-smoldering debris. Perhaps they were in search of survivors or tried to salvage what little was left of their belongings. Others were busy clearing the tracks ahead of us.

We were alone in our compartment. Mutti stared out the window, tears rolling down her cheeks; did she know, or when did she learn, that this night a bomb had laid waste to her childhood home, demolishing all but the rear service building? Gone was the apartment, gone all the trunks and the Indian dolls. Much later we learned that this attack, too, had hit the aquarium of the Berlin Zoo with water and dying sea creatures gushing into the streets. Did it spill into that sidewalk where Agnes and I had our stroll?

While Mutti sat frozen, I stood by the window, just looking, perhaps numb, perhaps dispassionate, but not terrified. This is the world as it presents itself, a child has to take it as it is; judgment and understanding will come later.

Today it is hard to visualize, harder still to convey the scenes burned into our collective memory. That is why our generation must tell what we can, must remind all who are young that this cannot happen again, and if it should, as it surely might, we must fight those who want to go to war. It is these buried memories that caused a 70-year old woman to spend nights screaming uncontrollably when TV news brought image after image of the bombing of Baghdad. Screams lasted for hours, and efforts at consoling me had no effect; fear had returned. When I reported this to my doctor, he said nothing but added a term to his notes: "PTSD." Only recently, when electronic records were opened to patients, did I see this diagnosis.

Others who have experienced this shock will tell you it takes decades to confront these experiences and communicate them to others. Friends who are Vietnam veterans tell me it takes thirty years.

So, we must speak up, not obscure the past. The poet Albrecht Haushofer, speaking of the total sense of finality blanketing Germany at the end of the war, wrote:

In Schutt und Staub ist	*In rubble and dust*
Babylon versunken....	*Babylon has sunk...*
Das Efeu des Vergessens wird	*The ivy of forgetting will*
sich ranken	*Trail over and hide*
um ein Jahrtausend hoher	*A thousand years of*
Blütezeit,	*Flowering,*
um dreißig Jahre mörderischen Streit.	*Trail over 30 years of murderous strife.*
Wir sind the Letzten. Unsere	*We are the last ones. Our*
Gedanken	*Thoughts*
sind morgen tote Spreu, vom	*Will tomorrow be dead sheaf,*
Wind verjagt,	*Chased by the wind*
und ohne Wert, wo jung der	*And worthless where*
Morgen tagt.	*Young morning dawns.*

Berlin Again

Now that Berlin has risen, as though by miracle, from the devastation of being ruled by madmen, from being literally incarcerated by the Cold War, these images accompany the sight of the city: Berlin, the Phoenix.

Almost 70 years after the day when Mutti and I stared at that burning rubble, I visited her city. Rare is the house that shows ghosts of former neighbors, rare a crack in the pavement, all is new, built with almost manic effort to assert the present, to give hope and trust in the future.

You ride the S-Bahn; it still rattles a bit on those old tracks that lasted through the entire Eastern occupation. It stops at Prinzenstrasse, and you look out over modern housing. There are many trees and even more little Turkish kids playing under them.

The names of streets, once burned into my brain by Mutti's stories, flash by and now acquire the strange normalcy of daily life lived. Did her stories, often funny, mask her pain that a world had died?

I stare at the magnificence of the reborn city; not its beauty, it never was beautiful, but its energy, its sheer guts and the inhabitants' abiding sense of belonging together that was forged by hunger, fear and chaos. Is it this cohesion that brought forth a truly socialist society, that sense of having been through all this together and having prevailed?

I see fathers pushing strollers, moms guiding their tiny kids through traffic, on bikes no less, old people receiving home visits by an army of care-givers.

But most of all, come evening, a rare warm evening, and people by the hundreds fill up the public spaces, a glass of wine in one hand, a snack for the kids in the other. They sit on the grass, on the benches surrounding the playground, they quietly talk, kids run around, they look cheerful, healthy and well-to-do.

Oh, Mutti, if only you could have seen it. Surely you dreamt it.

Chapter 4

Graz and War

At Home in Graz

The train rolling through bombed-out Berlin that frightful day took us to Graz, Austria, and to happier times. This may sound strange; after all, this was early 1943. I was told that Vati would be there, and we would all be together; that he was fixing up a home for us. Why did we move to Graz? Was Austria a better place to wait out the war? Were we in danger and needed to hide?

Austria had been annexed, or liberated, depending upon your view of things, and so far, it had been spared serious impact of the war raging in the east, south, and west. Graz was to bring reunion for my parents after several years of separation. For me, it meant a first conscious

Early postcard of Kroisbach near Graz

sense of family: Mother and father were mine; they were present, the guides to everything safe: *eine feste Burg* [a mighty fortress], as Martin Luther wrote. Over time I would even gain a sense of who my parents were as individuals. It is hard to convey the riches they shared with me, the bastion they would become, during these dangerous times. Meager words will have to do.

Memories now have continuity; no longer does a word overheard, a sound remembered, float in vacant darkness. Had Mutti and I really lived with aunt and uncle since late 1939? Had my parents been separated for that long, and why? Was it really my insistence that had caused them to reunite when I declared I could not recover from grave illness unless my father was at my side?

Yes, I clearly see the room that day back in Lamsdorf. The doctor and relatives standing around–then Vati's large hand on my burning forehead and

his sure voice making a promise: "Ekalein, I am here, you will be better; we will all be together." I have to believe it.

Once in Graz, Vati had found an old pub with a beer-garden in the suburb of Kroisbach. On its second floor, the building contained a large open hall, once the pub's "ballroom." This, my father single-handedly converted into a fine apartment–high ceilings,

The old pub at Mariatroster Strasse 1, ca. 1995

large rooms with wood plank floors, proof that many generations had danced away the nights and worn away the wood.

This shabby structure, its strong bones prevailing over the ravages of time and neglect, sat at the corner of a major road leading out of town and a winding lane that climbed into the surrounding hills. Down the hill, it was just a short walk to the trolley line by the lake that took you into town or to Mariatrost, a beautiful Baroque pilgrimage church watching over the faithful from atop a mountain.

In those days, villas and small shops nestled themselves into nature, roofs rarely extending beyond tree height, houses and walls carrying that tired patina of southern Europe: ochre, sand, pink, a faded light blue, here and there trimmed in dirty white. These walls spoke of generations of living. Today the suburb sports fashionable condominiums, painted yesterday, the balconies dripping with geraniums, everything glistens, spelling wealth, not memories. However, the building where we once lived has remained run down. Our whole world had once looked worn like that, just being, making no demands.

Kroisbach with its lovely hills and protective charm is the core of my true childhood, one every kid should have—room to play, to roam, protected by a society that saw itself as guardian of every child, at least for a while.

I remember spring; Mutti and I spent time in a village near town until Vati finished the construction. Distant mountains and alpine meadows beckoned us for daily walks up to the edge of the woods where a bench offered a view of the land. There Mutti rewarded me with stories. There, she became fascinating, took possession of her child. We thrived; servants and relatives, even the piano, did not stand between us.

One day our furniture arrived. The grand piano was hoisted by ropes to the upper floor. Mutti and the grand piano were reunited. How did this fact affect my place in the constellation of Mother, Child, Piano? There is no doubt that, up to the time of bombs and danger, the order was Mother, Piano, Child. I simply knew there was a force greater than anything I could have affected.

Yet, I believe that, here too, Graz offered some healing; our relationship gradually changed. One of my favorite spots in the house would be sitting under the piano as Mutti played. The hammers were pounding inches away, causing the entire wooden body to vibrate. At times, it shook violently when a Beethoven sonata needed emphasis: Ba, Ba, Ba BOOM!

When Mutti played—never did she use sheet music, the sounds resided in her brain, her soul—Vati silently entered the room, took me on his lap, and we listened together. He worshiped her talent to the end of his days, appeared almost transported, so much so that I, too, felt joy. Peace enveloped all three of us, player and audience.

This scene would continue well into the grim last years of the second World War, always pitting pleasure of sound against my fear of the beast or the outside world. Much later would I learn that the force which had pounded torrents of sound from those white teeth would carry this woman from the heights of success, wealth, security and love, to a world of death, danger and poverty. And when most needed for sheer survival and for the strength to carry those who had once carried her, this force rose like a sword, a rock, a scaffold. It rose together with a gentle strength that would give love and help to husband and child. In the end, this force would become her core.

~*~

At Mariatroster Strasse, I had my own room, its window just above a little shed roof descending to the neighbor's yard.

On our first day, I looked out and saw a girl looking up. She appeared to be exactly my age, with beautiful brown eyes, her color cream and olive in the manner of southern Europe. Also, she was delicate–the way I had always dreamed of myself becoming once able to slip out of that tall, sturdy body of mine. I liked her immediately.

In that direct way of kids making contact, she asked: "What is your name?" Her question sang the lovely rounded vowels and soft consonants of Lower-Austria. I told her my name and asked for hers–it was Lisi Torsić–was she surprised by my more hardened speech?

Often, when I was sent to my room for some punishment or other, I crawled down the shed roof to play with Lisi. Later, back in my room and knowing that Vati would soon come home from the office, I pretended to have suffered great punishment, screaming through the door: "Vati, let me out, that woman has locked me up!" Vati opened the door, my parents grinned. I have the feeling Mutti knew all along I had escaped; after all, the kitchen window where she had fixed our meal, faced the same yard.

Lisi was my first great friendship, in fact my first lasting contact with a contemporary, and our devotion to each other colored all experiences. Soon her mother and grandmother, too, became family friends, and eventually we would become fellow refugees. Lisi's mother, Anni Torsić, was a very handsome woman of Austrian-Slovenian descent–blond hair, high cheekbones, a husky voice, fiery temperament. She was a person of great leftward leanings and firm convictions, a socialist approaching communism. She was single, having refused to marry Lisi's father after the two had a fight over politics. Principles did not allow her to sacrifice beliefs for the sake of marriage even if she was pregnant. Thankfully, in Austria the stigma of single motherhood was not as fierce as it would have been in Germany, so grandmother, mother and daughter lived quite happily, if modestly. Their warmth for each other was contagious.

The fact of an absent father in that family made Vati a most desirable person. Lisi insisted on joining every activity or conversation I may have had with him. Soon there was a fight when I insisted that sitting on my father's lap was *my* privilege. Vati, of course, brought peace by declaring that there were two knees, one for each child, one more way for our two families to bond.

Soon there were great evening get-togethers with laughter and other colorful visitors going in and out of our house. I remember musicians and an actor from the municipal theater. Simple dinners were served. Food began to get scarce, and Mutti was the belle of the dinner party for having managed to get the makings of potato dumplings and bean salad with onions.

Now both Lisi and I sat under the piano, listening, all the while hidden by the large silk piano cover that draped to the floor. Rarely did we comprehend the meaning of conversations, but we did get a sense of the adult world.

Our kitchen had a breakfast nook where we three ate our meals when alone. Only good vibes arise from that image. There was a black leather sofa, a table, and a large mahogany sideboard with marble top. The curved mirror above it now hangs in our bedroom, it was part of Grandmother's dowry, one of the very few pieces with a tangible link to her. It has accompanied me over all the years, and I enjoy dusting and touching it regularly.

In the large bedroom stood the American furniture brought from New York: nobody else in Graz had a gentleman's dresser with numerous drawers for shirts, a lady's dresser with seat and large mirror, and a double bed with narrow pillows. This bed became the site of Sunday morning stories. I crawled between my parents, and they took turns reciting to me the ways they loved me. It always started with a recital: "*Min Häsekin, min Mäusekin, min Butzebusekin, min Augenstern...*"[my bunny, my mouse, the star of my eyes...] Then I became excited, started jumping on the bed, adding my own chants: "My toy, my pillow, my breakfast...."

It was in Graz where the telling of stories became a ritual, simple and warm at first, later tinted by the reality of my parents' lives. There was of course the *Haferhocken* story, repeated a hundred times; Vati would also teach me bits of *Plattdütsch*, the dialect of our North German people that hovers somewhere between German, Dutch and English and is redolent of the sea. Endlessly he recited the ditty about the sleepyhead who did not want to get out of bed:

Jehann, staw op, de Vagel piepen,

Lat se piepen, lat se papen,

Ik bin moid un will noch slapen.

Jehann, sta op, de Grütt is goar

Wat? Is de grote Löppel ok schon doar?

[Jehann, get up, the birds are singing. Let them sing, let them peep, I'm tired and want to sleep. Get up, Jehann, the gruel is ready. What? Is the soup spoon ready too?]–I loved it.

On Saturdays we dragged a large tub into the kitchen for baths since the apartment did not have a bathroom. The toilets, shared with all living in the other parts of the building, were located in two little cubicles at the end of the long exterior walkway onto which all apartments opened; it was the *Gangerl*–passageway.

This walkway was the building's meeting place. Morning or night,

Our neighbors on the "Gangerl"

someone was sitting there, peeling potatoes, smoking a pipe, or just gabbing. Below, in the old courtyard that once held the patrons' coaches and horses, kids now ran around making a racket; no one cared.

The beer-garden itself was off to the side. Neglected picnic tables were rotting under majestic horse chestnuts. This was southern Austria, after all; people would smile, sit down, have a glass of wine, a slice of *Gselchtes* [ham], a piece of *Backhendel* [baked chicken] and talk some more. They would shrug, mumble some curse, smile, and return to matters at hand.

Summers we played in the sandbox under the chestnut trees. I had a special love for making huge mud holes with water in them and just covering myself with dirt. It was a great place to play and a great place to be a kid.

That spring, I suppose, was the time to go to school. Lisi and I entered first grade together. Still today, Schule Maria Grün is situated in the hills, next to a lovely Baroque pilgrimage church and elegant villas.

The small graveyard behind the church has the distinction of having been the temporary burial place of Napoleon's only official son, the King of Rome. His mother was Marie Louise, the Austrian princess whom Napoleon married upon becoming Emperor (*tu, felix Austria, nube!*–"you, happy Austria, marry!"). Unhappily, this child was either retarded–as rumors went, or was simply kept prisoner after his father's fall to prevent his rise to rule. Perhaps not even the Habsburgs wanted him in the end, otherwise they would have found a spot in Vienna where other royals were buried. Anyway, the young man died early of pneumonia or tuberculosis, and during the Hitler years his remains were transferred to Paris. Whatever the facts, a lovelier resting place no hapless ruler could have

Erika ready for school, 1943

74

asked for.

The school building next to the church still serves today. A large cube with big windows, its plain walls overgrown with vines. In my day, the rooms had wooden benches all in a row; in front of you sat the kid whose

Church and school Maria Grün

bench was attached to your desk. You made close acquaintance with the hair of the one in front of you, and at times you gave that braid a little pull, or being bored, carved your initials into the wood.

Our teacher was a kindly disciplinarian; we loved her very much. To this day I can remember being introduced to the alphabet and to writing through little drawings and wonderful stories. It was easy learning and much fun. Yet, I have no recollection whatsoever of classmates other than Lisi.

When listening, students sat upright with their arms folded behind their back. Any hands on the desk, if not writing, were returned to their place by the teacher banging on the desk with a long ruler–very near one's hands. That scared all of us, and yet we thought it proper, not cruel–why? Because, aside from the occasional ruler tap, the tone was warm, and we were challenged and given unstinting attention.

Very early and subtly, I believe, our energies were guided toward fitting into society's patterns, so that we would eventually be able to produce what society needed, derive satisfaction from what we could contribute. I have come to believe that these educational tools helped form a solid society where everybody had a role and a reason for existing–but might they also create conformist members who follow leaders without questioning?

Just how fundamental these attitudes can be if inculcated early in life occurred to me many years later, when I reached this country and first heard young people say "Hell, no!" which later became the even more amazing "Hell, no; we won't go!" The sky did not come down upon those chanting; the earth did not open up to swallow them; how could it be?

This education for self-determination that lies at the heart of American teaching, has to happen early. I came to understand this when my children, and we as parents, were educated in these principles at President Roosevelt's lovely National Child Research Center, a research site and nursery school.

But back to the days in Maria Grün. After school, the long way home was the fun part of the day. For the first few weeks mothers took turns meeting us, but soon we were trusted to make our own way, following the older children. Knapsacks bouncing on our backs, we dashed down the hill, past the church door where many a Friday or Saturday afternoon the priest would stand, calling the kids to confession. Instead, they just kept running and hollering: *Ich habe gelogen, ich habe gestohlen, ich habe der Katze den Schwanz lang gezogen* [I have lied, I have stolen, I have pulled the cat's tail]. I had no idea what these children were supposed to do inside the dark church. But anyway, nobody ever called for me, for some reason I was exempt. Why?

Gradually, however, strange events from the outside world entered our lives, quietly at first. Once, a group of gentlemen arrived in our classroom with folders and instruments. Our teacher was nervous and a bit subservient. The gentlemen started unfolding large forceps with which they measured the length and width of our heads, carefully recording the measurements in their files. With each measurement, they murmured "Slavic round-head," nodding sagaciously. Then they came to me. The man measured my head, looked at me, shook his head and measured again. Then he said, "Aryan long-head." All eyes turned to me, and the men asked me where I was from, who were my mother and father. Finally, they nodded to each other and said "Nordic." I was different, again. Was I different the way the little girl in Brandenburg, with the star on her coat had been different? Different good, or different bad? Nobody said anything.

Nevertheless, we were still sheltered from the frightful events of the world in a thousand different ways. There were brilliant winter days when we would sled home from school, two hills offering fast rides almost to our house. There were afternoons when we slithered down long, icy tracks in the middle of the road (by now there was almost no traffic left since private cars had been confiscated). Wildly and happily, we played until almost dark, quite far from home, near the baker and the milk store. Our mothers did not seem to worry, for we never had reprimands. The soles of our shoes were surely ruined, and two more sets of clothes were hung to dry by the oven in the living room.

On other days, I took my baby buggy filled with dolls to the top of the near hill, got in it with the dolls, and rode at a wild clip down to the main road, crossed it, ducked under a barrier and headed down a steep lawn, just as we did on our sleds.

Sunday afternoons were the best. After lunch, we were allowed to play in the woods beyond the café in the valley. In a large gang, we became princesses and robbers chasing each other all over the forest which, like most European woods, was actually cleared of underbrush and lay open and inviting. We hid under roots, under piles of leaves, climbed trees and ran like crazy along the paths.

Lisi soon became quite ladylike; I, however, enjoyed our wilder group, mostly boys–rough and physical. We had little brawls which taught me skills that would later come in very handy when, in foreign country after foreign country, I was forever the new kid on the block with a foreign accent, harassed and taunted. I fought back; I used my fists, and I often won.

It must be said again: It was there, in Graz, that I learned to be a child, that my parents learned to be a family, no matter the disasters outside our door.

Thinking about these years now, there was an event that shines in memory as extremely satisfying, even victorious–my opportunity to learn self-reliance.

To get to work in the morning, Vati would take the trolley into downtown, get off at *Hauptplatz*, the main square, and walk to his office in one of the Baroque buildings. Mutti and I often made that trip, picking him up at the office and going for a walk in the old town or taking the incline train to the top of *Schlossberg*, the huge granite block in the city's center that, according to legend, had fallen out of the devil's hands while he fled from God. It is a lovely park with beautiful views over the city.

The roofs of old-town Graz from the Teufelsberg, 1995

One morning Vati had left his glasses, even though Mutti usually dusted his coat, blew him a quick kiss, and did the checklist: "Handkerchief? Polished shoes? Glasses?" Well, that day, I insisted that I could bring them to the office *by myself*, repeating over and over "I can do it. I can do it!"

This event must have taken place early in our stay, for there seems to have not been danger of bombs or war, yet. I got to go off alone, taking the trolley, paying my fare, knowing to get off at the main square and march to the office building, glasses in hand. Lovely Baroque courtyards led to large stairs, and door handles so high, I had to stand on my toes to reach them. I remember hoping that an adult would be near to open the doors for me. Everything worked.

What a gift this had been from my mother–command over my environment. What pride did I feel once I got home! I had to have been six or seven years old. Oh, how I wish a bit of Graz for my grandchildren!

War Comes to Graz

Gradually and unavoidably, the large disaster threw shadows over the rhythm of our lives, even in Graz.

I cannot piece together the sequence of events that progressively made war a daily presence. How did we children notice that something was amiss–was it the first air raids? The shortages of food? Perhaps seeing our nervous parents, the ever-increasing presence of soldiers, tanks, and artillery lines passing our house, always heading east, out of town?

Mariatroster Strasse was a major road leading toward Yugoslavia and ultimately Greece. The soldiers marched in formation, singing *Die Fahne hoch, die Reihen fest geschlossen, SA marschiert....*[Raise the Flag: Horst Wessel Song].

As we did so often, we sat on the front stoop of our building, waved, and sang along. Soldiers waved back. No one mentioned where they were going, that they would not come back, or what the few who did would look like.

All this must have come about in the spring of 1944. By then our veranda and beer garden had been taken over by the government to make room for activities of the *Hitler Jugend*. Girls, age ten to fourteen, gathered for songs and crafts in the afternoons; boys' groups sang and marched. It all looked like great fun, and we marched right along, it was our garden after all.

But things soon changed. The girls started to collect clothes in the neighborhood, bandages were cut from bed sheets and rolled up. The boys suddenly seemed older. They still sang but mostly had to slither throughout the garden on their bellies, holding long sticks the size of guns. After some days, they would disappear and others, younger ones, arrived to do the same maneuvers.

Our play, too, changed in character. My dolls, worn from rough play (one had lost its legs, the other had a hole in its head) could not be replaced with new ones. Instead, I cherished them as *Kriegsverwundete,* war wounded, and carted them around in the buggy with bandages all over them. War had invaded the depth of life, its most innocent corners.

Often, sudden sirens ended all play, first as *Luftschutz* training (air raid training), soon as the real thing. More and more planes were flying overhead. The inn's former wine cellar, a deep stone vault, mossy and hung with bats, was converted into an air raid shelter. It still maintained that acrid smell of spilled unfermented wine. Benches were installed, and tunnels dug to the building next door, an escape for us and our neighbors, Lisi's family included. Our building's entrance had a shelter sign; anyone caught unawares by a raid could seek shelter in our wine cellar.

We still went to school every day. We had drills and learned to march in orderly fashion into its basement, which had bunk beds.

Food was becoming a problem, and my parents, now in their early fifties, suddenly became gardeners. In back of the old stable, little plots of land were made available for each family. Together with the neighbors we spent our evenings out there, my parents sitting side by side on a rickety bench, looking awkward and somewhat out of place. Vati dug into his farmer-boy past and soon enjoyed the task of growing vegetables, while Mutti sat by, quite helpless. She got tips from folks who knew that the tomato plants needed pinching, that the beans would take another two weeks before they could be harvested. Here and there, someone would grow a few flowers. I remember a pile of dirt covered with daylilies. We children did not understand–but I do now: they were an affirmation of life, a gesture of defiance against hunger and impending death.

Vati now took his bicycle and loaded it down with some of our belongings such as silver or pots and pans. He was going "to the country," I was told. He would return in the evening with carrots, potatoes, a bit of milk. This bartering–we called it *besorgen*–was strictly forbidden, and one could go to jail for it because food distribution was centered in the government's rationing system.

At other times we had visitors, farm women who came to town to do their own *besorgen*. They arrived, sat and talked for a while, looked around for what they needed; sometimes their eyes lit up at the sight of luxuries they had never dreamed of having. One woman gently ran her work-weary hands over a lovely set of damask napkins, saying, "Oh, my children will have lovely shirts."

Suddenly, the sewing machine was gone too, or a certain set of cups. Mutti insisted she did not need them. Then, in the evening, the woman's husband or some other messenger would show up with food.

Our Protector

Only recently did I start to pore over family photographs, trying to find clues in pictures, roaming through my memories for stories that might explain why we moved to Austria, how we survived as foreigners. Also, was the family history that my grandfather was of Jewish descent now dangerous? Might that have been the reason? Was it safer for Vati to be there as well? After all, at one time or another, the government had confiscated his passport and laid claim to his possessions. Did these officials know he was an American Freemason, member of an organization that claimed its roots in the building of the Temple of Jerusalem and thus considered Jewish?

I remember one day, when I could not have been older than seven, my parents had visitors and asked me to play in the adjoining bedroom, Mutti suggesting that I could dress-up with her jewelry and old evening gowns. In digging around in drawers, I came upon a most attractive white leather apron. Anxious to share the find, I put it on and danced into the living room to entertain the visitors. Suddenly, Vati rose, white as a sheet, and carried me out of the room in a great hurry. I will never forget the look on his face. Since he was a gentle man, utterly devoted to the late-in-life child, he had never even scolded me. To see this face, hear the harsh words, feel the jerky movements, frightened me; I stored the memory as one of the unexplainable, mysterious, actions grown-ups will take to punish you for something terrible you do not understand.

I don't know exactly what Vati did at his job, but it had something to do with rebuilding farm structures, a fact that put us in a good position for bartering. Under government auspices, he traveled around the countryside by train or on his huge bike, inspecting damaged buildings, and helping find funds to make repairs. Just how he got this job as a foreign citizen whose passport and properties had been confiscated, how he was not incarcerated once America entered the war, is another fact I cannot fathom. I have pondered this circumstance for a long time, never arriving at answers.

Now I suspect that we must have had a protector. Whether that is true I can only surmise since no one is alive to confirm it, and I was too young to ask. Today I believe it may have been Onkel Martin Winzerling, Mutti's cousin in Potsdam, whose fancy house we had visited a few times.

Over the years, I knew that Onkel Martin was a very important person. Today, with the help of the internet and records released from archives in the former East Berlin, I know that Onkel Martin was indeed a leading member of an accounting office called the *Rechnungshof des deutschen Reiches* [court of accounts of the German Reich]. Aside from his published dissertation on finance, still available today, records show that in 1931 he wrote a paper calling for stricter financial controls over state expenditures, called the "Winzerling Writ," which he was forced to retract later. However, his work must have been important enough, his actions useful enough, that by 1934 he was promoted to department head, in fact, he participated in the conjoining, of the Berlin and Munich branches of this office. By the time of our visits to Potsdam, in 1942, this office must have long been usurped by the Nazi machine and converted from an independent watchdog agency to an open money pit for the war machine with no questions asked or allowed.

From time to time Onkel Martin must have had business in Vienna or Graz, and his visits to our house were of the greatest importance to my parents. He brought me books or other goodies. I was allowed to join the adults for dinner but was sent to my room shortly thereafter. I loved this uncle and hated to go, so I hovered outside the living room door and overheard the conversations.

During later visits, Onkel Martin no longer told jokes; instead, he told Hitler stories, most of which I did not understand.

One, however, impressed me for I thought it was pretty funny: Hitler came to the *Rechnungshof* demanding money for the war effort. Onkel Martin described the scene:

"When told there was none, the Führer flew into an uncontrolled rage, threw himself on the ground and chewed on the carpet. Our group, all of us trained in obedience to authority, stood by helplessly, shifting from foot to foot, eyes pinned to the tip of our shoes, waiting for Hitler to finish. Eventually, the Führer rose, yelled, called us traitors to the cause and was led away by his entourage. All we could do was avoid each others eyes."

How was it possible, I now ask myself, that not one of these experts–or all of them–took action, seeing that the end was at hand?

Later on, Onkel Martin was overcome by horror of what had been his role in the regime. He sent his Swedish wife to Stockholm, refusing to join her there as a refugee. Instead, he stayed in Berlin and, after May 8, 1945, handed himself over to the Russian occupation forces. He was put on a train to Siberia. Many years later, someone returned from there and brought news that Onkel Martin had died on that train.

I wish I could say that Onkel Martin, his role, or his end, had ever been a subject of stories at coffee time in Flensburg. I did not learn about his fate until many years later. This subject, too, was one better forgotten than ever discussed. Sometime in the 1960s, after I left Germany, Tante Ella tried to get in touch with Mutti, but I never heard of a meeting between these two women.

Martin and Ella Winzerling visiting the family in Langenhagen. Seated: Onkel Martin and Mutti; standing, from left: Tante Käthe, Onkel Karl, Tante Ella, and Tante Adele

Some time ago, I had a portrait photo of this uncle; it has since disappeared. The single remaining image now in my possession is a group photo from early 1937, taken during a family gathering shortly before my birth. Although it reflects the days of Langenhagen, it is stunning for its assembly of characters: The well-to-do German Intelligentsia which made up the family, sitting together on a sunny afternoon. This photo, most likely taken by Vati, bears closer examination since it strikes me as symbolic of the powers then at work in the wider world.

Here sits Mutti, in an outdoor enclosure, her pregnancy discreetly hidden under a wide coat. Next to her is Onkel Martin, who by then must have been hustling money for Hitler's war. What did he know? I have searched his face many times, and it appears intelligent, kind, with a twinkle in the eyes. Was he the one who would later protect us? He certainly was powerful enough at the time, and his visits to our home in Graz must have had a reason. In this photo, his wife, Tante Ella, is dressed in white. She stands near Tante Käthe and Onkel Karl who would later shelter Mutti and me in their home in Lamsdorf.

On the far right is Mutti's eldest sister, my beloved Tante Adele, stopping by on her way from New York to London. At the time, she was an emissary of the anarchist revolutionaries that included her fire-brand husband, Stephen Naft. She had been sent to meet with donors and politically important people, including Bertrand Russell, to find help in the struggle for workers' rights. She had earlier tried, and succeeded, in enlisting help in support of Max Nettlau, the German anarchist historian. Today I know from publications and correspondence as well as a visit to Amsterdam, that her efforts helped remove Nettlau from Nazi Germany and transfer him and his enormous archive to Amsterdam, where it became the bedrock of the Institute for Social History.

Quite a party, all assembled to celebrate my mother who was about to give birth, way out there in the provinces of northern Germany. You wonder about the dinner conversations. Was it merely pleasant banter, back then, in 1937?

Living with War

War erases differences of status. Direct, physical danger reduces rich and poor, smart and dumb, to a common level where talent for survival is the supreme selector. It is the great testing ground for skills rarely needed in our everyday existence; it is, however, the ultimate test of character and goodness. We admire the heroes of war and secretly inquire within whether we would ever have the fortitude to match their acts of strength—be it as a prisoner, a hero who rescues fellow soldiers, or a plain citizen who hides others in danger. In theory, these acts of heroism appear to be natural, a matter of course. But until hunger, cold, danger, and the sheer animal will to survive have been experienced, it all remains theoretical. How would we act?

In the drive to wrest from ever-growing scarcity the few things that mean the difference between starvation and survival, a former pimp becomes a tycoon because he has a network, he is an expert in the things that matter most: supply and demand in the semi-legal realm. As the playwright and poet, Bertolt Brecht, so truthfully said: *"Erst kommt das Fressen und dann kommt die Moral"* (First grub, then morals).

The farmer, downtrodden and ridiculed for his lack of sophistication, suddenly is royalty, whose whim has to be satisfied, who has to be shown respect. Parents become feverish with the desire to protect and feed their children, and issues of right or wrong fade by comparison. In the face of concentration camps and examples of people shot on the spot for minor infractions, those who still manage to offer resistance, shall remain eternally our superhuman heroes, not just folks like the rest of us.

But back to Mariatroster Strasse and to our level of understanding. We children found much of this very exciting, and I am not alone in that assessment. Some time ago, I spoke with our friend, whose history—refugees on foot and horse-drawn cart, from Lithuania to Germany to Austria, to France, then to Colombia, and many years later to the United States—so parallels mine that we often revisited those years together. She, too, remembered much of the war as excitement, and said, "oh, we thought it was fun. How very much our parents protected and shielded us and later refused to talk about it!"

By then, air raids had become a fixture, their patterns dominating all our activities. Sirens howled, followed by planes that roared overhead, and we knew it was time to pack up and go to the shelter. The bombings came twice daily, one raid by day, around 2 pm, the other at about the same time at night.

Mutti had suitcases standing by the door. Long ago she had sewn some jewels and money into her considerably-sized corsets, just in case. She had also hoarded, of all things, French soaps, one cake of which she slipped into a pocket. She put on her fur cape, coat, hat and handbag, the way she had previously gone shopping or to a café; she wrapped me in a blanket and Vati carried me to the shelter. All the neighbors were there, tired, fearful, not too friendly. They sat around on the benches, listening for any banging or worse, all hoping for the siren to call out the end of the raid. To this day a siren gives me the creeps, as do thunder and loud popping noises.

It was during those days that Mutti's character, once expressed in music, now showed its full strength in the dark dampness of the shelters. I can only call it her greatness, and it came from the place in her soul where melodies lived.

There, in that cellar, illuminated by a single bare bulb, Lisi and I crowded around Mutti and soon asked:

"Please, tell us a story; about Mr. and Mrs. Bär, and how they went to parties where there was so much to eat, they couldn't finish…please…about Little Bär's new dress?" Soon other kids moved toward us and sat down in a circle around Mutti's feet. She spun a long and vivid yarn about a family of bears, magically transformed into human appearance through the powers of a lady called *Frau Nachbarin* [Mrs. Neighbor].

Mutti's vast reservoir of travel and experiences, of the good life in 1920s New York, especially, became the stuff of adventures. The Bärs rode the subway, walked along the Great White Way. No matter what the setting or context, at the core of each story lay food, presented to us in rich, detailed descriptions of its beauty and opportunity for happiness. There was the tale of the abduction of a parrot (Mutti had such a bird in happier times and regaled us with parrot stories) or "The Trip to Helgoland," drawing on Mutti's numerous ocean crossings and her suffering from sea sickness. Food, conviviality, warmth, safety; these were the treasures laid out for us. Where did she get the strength to tell us stories about a land of plenty–America, where there were bananas and oranges, neither of which we had ever seen. And she did this alone. She built for us a world where bombs had no place.

We loved it, asked for more, were sad when the end-siren wailed, hoping for new stories in the next sessions. She gave us images of a future that just may come about, someday not too far off. I remember casting glances at Mutti during these times and wondering why her voice was cracking, her hands trembling as she clutched her handbag when thunderous blasts announced bombs falling close by. Later, after war's end, when all was gone but the content of our hearts and intellect, she sat down and typed these stories. Today I treasure them.

After the raids, we emerged from the wine cellar, checked out the house and the street for damage and determined that, once more, we had gotten away. Ironically, we knew the bombs came from British and American planes, at once the carriers of death and liberation, and yet, for the moment, they were the enemy.

By now there were only certain hours of the day with electricity. Long gone were the days of maids, cooks and housekeepers; occasionally a washer woman came and once in a while, of all things, a masseuse. A few houses down the street, an elderly seamstress could make a dress out of two old ones.

For the rest, Mutti became a housewife and did so with grace and fairly good humor. She insisted that doing the dishes was good for her hands, that she liked the feeling of warm water. Always meticulous, she cleaned and polished things and seemed to take some pride in the accomplishment. Ironing, however, was not on her agenda, and I thanked Agnes for having taught me; I did the ironing.

We still went to school. Our teachers, too, showed courage. When raids came, we went to the shelter, and class continued there. We learned the small multiplication tables by sitting on bunk beds: Three times four children on one side, two times six kids on the other—what does that make?

If things got scary, we sang. We especially loved the song with the refrain:

Wenn wir gehn,

dann gehn wir alle,

zusammen, miteinander,

ins Himmelreich, ins Himmelreich, ins Himmelreich hinein!

[if we go, we'll all go to Heaven together].

Did we understand? The teachers, of course, did. Once, we had been dismissed early, and on our way home, were surprised by low-flying planes. We were running down the hill toward the village, yet still under cover of the forest that surrounded school and church. Suddenly, planes were roaring overhead, very low; we could see the propellers of those old four-engine bombers. Rows of little bombs dropped out of their backs, slowly trailing to the ground like ribbons on a kite's tail. We did get scared, but also thought this was a princess and robbers game, for real. We knew of a tree that had exposed roots forming a huge umbrella with a cave beneath. It stood near the road, and at times we had played hide-and-go-seek there. Now we thought this to be a great bomb shelter. All five or six of us crawled under these roots, huddled together and watched the bombs fall to the ground in the distance. One kid remarked how funny it was to watch these bombs emerge from the plane's rear end, "Look, they are floating in the air like ducklings following their mama!"

"Na," said another. "They are coming out like poop from a running horse!"

I don't remember whether alarms went off, but I do remember a group of frantic mothers running along the road in search of us, clutching us, crying, and rushing home. We were wondering why they were so excited; we had done the right thing.

This must have happened late in the war; I can't remember much school after that.

The Final Days

Things became desperate, and while my memories of the early days in Graz are lit with the seasons, sun or snow, the light of day, the color of flower beds, the later ones have lost all definition. It is as though happenings appear in close-up, not in a setting, the event isolated from its context. Adults stood around in groups talking gravely about things we could not comprehend, but judging from their faces, it was bad. Mothers held our hands more tightly than they had done before; many things were suddenly forbidden, and we were rarely allowed to leave their sight. Rumors went around that the airplanes had dropped poisoned pencils and toys, and never to pick up anything shiny we might find by the side of the road. Adults were silent about that; were they afraid this just might be true?

The bombings became more targeted, closing in on us and our road. There were the fearful days when I had caught the whooping cough and was not allowed in the bomb shelter. That was a rule: no contagious diseases. Long ago, access to antibiotics had been restricted to the military, and in fact just about all medications were unavailable. I spent day after day in bed, gasping for air, and during raids, Mutti gazed out the window, hoping that no direct attacks would move into our area.

Our apartment on the second floor; Mutti's piano stood between the two windows.

One day it did happen. The noise was deafening. Terrified, Mutti carried me out of bed, and together we crawled under the dining table, covering our heads with blankets and anything else we could find.

Trembling, she hovered over me, the way a mother animal protects its young. I remember scarcely being able to breathe, Mutti's panting breath brushing past my ears, her tears falling on my face. Outside, there was the deep rumble of planes flying low, the high-pitched whine of bombs whizzing by, then the detonation—a heavy blast that shook the room, rattled the windows, and blew them open. I think we both believed that we were going to die from the next bomb.

Suddenly it was over; we cautiously made our way to the open window and saw a huge hole less than a block away, a crater in the middle of our road. Pavement had been blown hither and yon, dirt was everywhere. The supply road to the Balkans, the road that kept carrying soldiers and munitions day and night, had been targeted and hit. I don't remember how many days it took, but the road was fixed rather quickly, and the convoys continued.

That day, however, Mutti opened both living room windows, sat down at the piano and let loose with a great piece of music; all her energy, her surprise at having survived, her fear, went into the effort. Down below, the neighbors who had stared at the crater, looked up and waved to the open windows.

Here was the power of one human being to tell of pain or joy in such an assertive and transportingly beautiful way, one that rose directly from the soul: "Hey, world, you are going to listen, I will force you to pay attention; here I am! I am still alive!" I marveled at the sheer guts, knowing full well that assertiveness would never be part of my approach to life's obstacles. Vati must still have been out bartering for food, for I remember him being there in the evening, trying to calm us down and help me find some sleep in the large bed.

Mutti's talent, I see now, was monumental. It had become a lifeline. Often, she turned to Beethoven Sonatas, not Bach—the spiritual heights too stark; certainly not Wagner, whose compositions she despised and compared to Nazism and bad dreams; but Ludwig—now *there* was music! How did she survive the death of her music, her career? How, in fact, did she survive all the rest of her life?

Ah, the strength that gradually grew in this woman.

In many small ways, frayed nerves would show; tensions and fear found strange, surely unintended outlets. One day, when Vati had managed somehow to obtain a bit of butter, we three were sitting at the dining room table eating a slice of buttered bread. This was a feast of great splendor, and we were feeling incredibly lucky. Now Mutti had lovely large front teeth and their pattern appeared very distinctly in the slice of bread where she had just taken a bite. I remarked how her teeth showed in the butter, and she flew into a rage, accusing me of thinking that she was taking all the butter for herself and spreading it on her slice so thickly that the teeth showed.

I burst into tears and insisted that all I meant to say was that she had large front teeth. Vati stared frozen, Mutti cried, and in the end we all sat quietly for a while.

Hunger was indeed rampant. Graz, the gateway to the Balkan fronts, had been declared a "city of last resistance." Long ago the railroad station downtown and most buildings surrounding it had been leveled, although rail lines were always repaired quickly. If we did go into town, we saw the erstwhile lovely Baroque streets with huge gaps, the ugly shells of former buildings reaching into the air like an accusation. Dust and rubble everywhere, huddled people trudging around the piles of bricks growing on the sidewalks.

All Children Evacuated

Around that time, I think, the system decided children would be evacuated and placed on farms around the countryside. Farmers were supposed to feed us and, if possible, send us to school. I, too, was included.

For a confirmation on the issue of evacuations, I turn to a devastating and thorough book by Nicholas Stargardt, *Children's Lives Under the Nazis*. And there it is: Private efforts to evacuate Jewish children to other countries, or their rescue from a fate not to be contemplated. Later, the regime, too, began evacuating children out of large cities such as Berlin and Hamburg, the focus of the earliest bombing campaigns. Finally, there was the temporary evacuation of children, and sometimes mothers with small children, in the face of "last stand" battles. The facts shake you.

What shakes me as well is the image on the book's cover: The street scene, a single standing wall of a bombed-out building, gaping openings where once there were windows and doors, stairs hanging in mid-air, pedestrians walking among piles of rubble. There no longer are sidewalks.

You see four children, a boy in the shadows and three little girls walking hand-in-hand but momentarily turning to the photographer. I instantly identify with them. Yes, that strange roll of hair on top of the girls' heads is familiar, my hands recall the softness of that hair. Their faces could have made me their sister. Yes, that *was* our world when the end came, I did not make it up.

In those late days of evacuation, it must have been spring 1945, things may have been less organized, for I know that it was Vati who took me to the designated farmer's family—or had he found them on his own and made sure I would be safe? I do not recall encountering another child evacuee.

I have no idea where my village was, perhaps somewhere toward the west, as far as possible from anticipated Russian battle lines. It certainly was in a corner of southern Austria somewhat forgotten by the modern world.

Today I think as a parent and grandparent. What did it take for my parents, with daily raids, with the sound of heavy artillery booming in the distance, to give up their child in the face of the unknown just around the corner, never knowing whether either parents or child would survive or be seen ever again? Did they trust those farmers? Were they convinced that starvation was definite and the suffering in a place of battle so huge that children had to be removed from the city in hopes of their survival?

I don't remember crying when we left. In fact, I have no memory at all of the time leading up to departure or goodbye. Had we all become stoic or numb under the bombardment of horror? Was even fear too much of an effort? I do recall, however, the brief train ride, then sitting on the front bar of Vati's bike, and finally a walk up steep hills.

The farmer family that took me in was desperately poor, eking out a living in a high mountain area with very small homesteads. Besides father and mother, who were both tiny, there were two or three children, not all theirs; at least one, I remember, was an adopted boy, perhaps an orphan—a common way for families to acquire cheap labor. It is strange that these children inhabit my memory without descriptive features while the farm and surroundings stand clearly defined and in great detail.

The farmhouse was one of the traditional kind, where family, animals and hay are kept in one long building. The kitchen had a large table in one corner, a bench and stools surrounding it. In the other corner was a huge round oven with benches where one could sit in winter and warm one's back. Father and mother slept on a ledge behind the oven under a pile of blankets and pillows. The room was low and dark, but much of life took place in the forecourt anyway, so it did not feel oppressive.

When we arrived, all the family stood around to watch me unpack. I had two possessions that were of deep interest: a toothbrush and toothpaste. When they came into view, the farmer mother asked me if she could borrow them on Sunday when she washed and dressed to go see the Holy Virgin at church. Better yet, the entire family decided to use them that Sunday. After that, I did not think I needed to brush my teeth, telling them that they could have the brush and paste as a present.

At meals, large bowls and a pitcher with drink were placed in the center of the table. Each person received a slice of bread, and the bowls and pitcher would make the rounds, bite-by-bite, sip-by-sip. When the meal was done, we stashed our spoons in our boots or pockets, got up and returned to work.

All this took place in silence, except for me: I was used to making conversation. Here, I usually talked alone, without the benefit of answers. That did not bother me in any major way, nor do I remember being reprimanded, just ignored.

However, the few answers I did get surprised even a seven-year-old. Most memorable was the day I started to talk about the moon, and how round it looked in the country sky; how it, and the earth, traveled around the sun. This was too much for the farmer who looked up from his bread and said: "Be quiet now; this is nonsense. How could the earth be round–we'd all fall off if that were the case. Of course, the earth is flat and the moon, too. Sun and moon just go up and go down."

The finality of his declaration forbade all discussion, and besides, I did not have the intellectual equipment to convince him otherwise. It shut me up for a while.

The family lived off a single small field, little more than a major garden bed, that was plowed by the lone cow in the farmer's possession. At night that cow was expected also to supply milk. We all worked. All of us hoed, raked, gathered. The sun shone brightly; it was warm, the grass fragrant. I loved all of it, stopping my work for a moment, conscious of the beauty around me, even though I could not have put it into words.

The field next to us belonged to another, very young family, and snatches of conversation flew from field to field. The neighbors had just had a baby, and since the young mother could not afford to stay at home, she brought the little bundle and parked it under a shady tree. I heard her tell our farmer mother that a good way to keep the baby asleep was to wrap a bit of poppy seed in a bundle of rags, dip it in plum brandy, and plop it into the baby's mouth. We all thought this was a fine idea; the baby slept all day. Today I realize this poor kid could easily have become a candidate for village idiot or at best a future drunk.

After field work we went home and did chores. Early on it turned out that my father's teachings with tools, and my own delight in using them, qualified me for wood chopping. I enjoyed being out under the large tree in the forecourt, where an axe was parked in the riddled top of a chopping block. There, the farmer divided a log into quarters or manageable chunks, and I followed by doing the finer chopping. Eventually, I became so good at it that I could make fine kindling. One scar on my thumb, however, proves that learning was not all painless. My use to the community thus established, I was accepted, even warmly, although familial love was not a thing expressed in the manner we take for granted; rather, it was an unspoken sense of belonging, more like a pack of lions that know they are a pride.

Outside, and built into the side of the house, was a round stone oven where bread was baked once a week. On that morning, it would be fired up with wood—the fruits of my labor—until the stones inside were very hot. Then the ashes were removed and risen loaves slid in to bake.

Words cannot describe the intoxicating smells that arose in late afternoon when the finished loaves, each about a foot in diameter, were pulled from the oven. The farm mother pressed a loaf to her chest, and with a huge knife, cut off a chunk of hot bread for each of us. Never since then has there been a bite of food more fragrant or delicious. If things were really flush, we each got a half cup of pumpkin-seed oil to go with it; that meal was called *a Jausen,* or snack. We dipped the bread into the green-black oil, drank it up when the bread was gone and wiped out the rest with a finger. I often finished the last traces by running my tongue around the cup as deep as I could reach.

I learned much during this stay. I had never been one of many children in a house. Here, all three or four of us slept on the floor of the room adjacent to the kitchen. We slept on sacks filled with dried corn husks that smelled very good. Our pillow and down cover, patterned in red and white, resembled a nest more than a bed, the mattress growing around the sleeper, and the coverlet forming a mountain above.

Sometimes we could not fall asleep right away, and we would talk, giggle, brag or fight. My range of experience was so different from the others' that I had little to contribute, and what I did send forth fell on disbelieving ears, or more commonly, ridicule. At age seven, I had learned that, in the company of others, you bring out what connects and keep to yourself what separates—a lesson in survival.

One night, the older of the boys came to my mattress and told me that he would now show me where I came from. He crawled under my blanket, started to heave around beside me and let out long grunts. Nothing else. Had he touched me, he would have encountered a fighter. I listened to him, convinced that he was nuts.

He said: "Well, you know, you would not be here if your father and mother had not done this." I kicked him and told him to go to his own bed.

I was strong from chopping wood, large by northern heritage and could easily fight him off, all the while wondering what on earth he was talking about. Everyone laughed, and soon we dropped off to sleep.

I learned other things, less earthy, as well. The village had one public school, but it was reserved for boys. The other kids on this farm did not seem to go to school at all. It was decided that I should attend the girls' school, which was run by nuns, a fair distance away over open fields. Someone must have convinced the nuns there could be little harm in accepting this child. More likely, nobody imagined there would be a Protestant, or God forbid, a child of agnostics, anywhere in the region.

In the classroom, they placed me at the center of the front row, immediately in front of the teaching nun. There was a large belly clad in black, the underside of arms in black sleeves, a chin crowned by a white head dress. Teaching, the conveyance of knowledge, went over my head, literally.

In this school, too, math was a struggle. Numbers seemed, and still seem, to have a life of their own, never fitting into the overall concept which in itself is clear—it just does not work with the numbers. At the core of what I call math anxiety, must have been the constant interruptions, changes, insecurity of once again being "new." Today I wake up from sweaty dreams, terrified there will be a math test, and I don't even understand the questions. We all have our demons.

On a small shelf in the corner of the classroom stood a miniature altar—a picture of the Holy Virgin with the Child; in front of it, the nuns had placed and a vase with flowers. Every morning, and several times in the course of the day, we had to kneel before this altar and say the rosary. I liked the repeat of the verses, the patterns of sound and meaning, bead by bead. Trouble was, the rosary and kneeling were also used as a form of punishment. If even one child committed any minor infraction of the rules, and the class would not snitch on that kid out of a sense of solidarity (a highly developed ethic, I found), the nun would make us spend our recess saying rosaries over and over before we were allowed to eat our slice of bread. If things had been very bad, there was no time at all to eat.

Not trained for the job, my knees started to ache from long kneeling. To this day, the floor boards are etched into my memory: dark, oily planks with splinters and dirt, the wood grain somehow joining the sequence of words and lines—pattern and repeat—for one prayed with bowed head over folded hands and only occasionally looked up at the Virgin.

One means of control was instilling fear—the terrible, elemental, picturesque fear of Hell. It was reserved for descriptions of both Heaven *and* Hell. Heaven, of course, was glorious—mostly there was food. But Hell—oh, the nun in front of me would go into minute descriptions of how the devil had long sharp pitch forks he would heat in the eternal fires. She described in detail just how the points of the forks would turn red with heat, then sear the sinner's flesh with a hissing sound. My classmates began to cry and whimper, calling out to Mother Mary.

Once more I realized I was different. A child whose mother had banned Grimm's Fairy Tales because of their violence and had substituted them with Oscar Wilde's stories illustrated by Aubrey Beardsley–intoxicating, and strange–such a child was ill-prepared for Hell. No one had ever threatened me with the afterlife, and the images filled me with great disbelief. I simply could not join in the general mayhem, but also felt it was important to do something to calm down my classmates.

So, trying to be very polite, I said, "My mom told me the devil is within us; he is our feeling of regret or guilt, our conscience that tweaks us when we have done something we know is bad."

There was silence in the classroom. I have no memory whatsoever of the nun's reaction, nor the children's. I do remember that at day's end, I was given a note to take home to the farmer. It said: "This child need not return to school."

Freedom! For the second time, I had discovered ways to avoid school, just as I had avoided kindergarten by screaming for days; this was growing into a useful pattern that could be repeated, and would be, again.

At length it was time for Vati to pick me up. Somehow, I must have known the day and time, and I walked down the hill along the dirt road, as far as I dared go, waiting for him. Of course, he would come; the possibility that war, bombs or death might keep him away never entered my mind; my father was a concept so all-encompassing that other forces were nil by comparison. Of course, he would come. I sat by the road; it must have been a long time; it was hot.

Finally, there, in the distance, I saw the familiar figure–Vati with his large bike. All would be well.

We returned to Graz, to our routine of air raids and to bland acceptance of the coming end. The "battle of last stand" had obviously been abandoned. We all had become numb, stoic, unable to absorb.

But absorb we did, we had to.

I am told some children of war lose speech. What has been seen and felt has no words, so why speak? Unbearable images just hide in the heart and the depth of the mind, curled together like some menacing ball of barbed wire, its ends tied to every nerve, there to lay in wait. You see scenes of war on TV, and knowing what the streets, houses will look like, what the faces of children will tell and yet not tell–it is *that* coil of barbed wire that keeps you from ever taking risks, from facing the world with confidence and happy ambition.

Today we call it PTSD. We have given a fancy name to a condition we keep inflicting on children and soldiers alike.

~*~

Back in Graz, things had gone from bad to worse, but at least we were together, all three of us. There are no photos of that time–who would have thought of photography, even if film and processing had still been available?

Hunger was a daily horror, driving everyone to deeds never contemplated. Vati's forays for food became dangerous; people were arrested, at times shot on sight. These challenges were discussed at home, and yet, my parents' drive to feed me neared obsession.

One day a neighbor mentioned that, while the police did search adults, they usually ignored children. I remember offering to get some milk. I also knew the way, having been along on a few such trips, and besides, had I not delivered my dad's glasses to his office some years ago? All by myself?

What compelled my parents to let me go, I don't know; perhaps terror clouded their rational thinking. But I took the little can we used for milk, caught the trolley, then the bus to the countryside, hiding my can in a large bag. Once at the farm, the woman poured some milk into it, and I began my return to town. Anxiously, I tried to hide in the shadow of adults, holding on to my can.

That day there was no search of the bus, no police, but I still feel the triumph, the sense of adulthood and empowerment at the achievement. I don't remember the taste of the milk. This little can–I can see it now–narrow, tall, on a rectangular base, blue enamel exterior, white interior, a bit chipped and rusty at the rim. This milk can will again play a part later in this story.

Refugees

It has been some weeks since I last returned to this text. Intense melancholia descended over my thoughts, and I could not figure out how to tell about situations that had no light moments, that just kept descending from terror into disaster and on down from there.

I have recently had nightmares of being on the road, of having to move on, of being in environments where survival and escape are always on a most elemental level such as trying to get on a moving train. Dreams take over an entire day, their reality much more intense than waking hours. Only removal to the garden will ease the numb fear. Touching something, digging, is good. Holding and rocking a grandchild is a balm beyond words.

But since life did turn out to be so good, so incredibly lucky and warm

94

with love, I will try to tell the rest as best I can. This need came home to me recently when reading *All Over but the Shoutin,'* the memoir of Rick Bragg, the poor Alabama boy, perhaps a new Faulkner, and already the winner of a Pulitzer Prize. His story centers on the redemption that comes from belonging–belonging somewhere, anywhere. In the opening of his book, dedicated to his mother, he says:

> *"I have been putting this off for ten years...because dreaming backwards can carry a man through some dark rooms where the walls seem lined with razor blades.... 'People forgets if it ain't wrote down'.... God help me, Momma, if I am clumsy."*

By this time the flow of movement on Mariatroster Strasse began to reverse direction. Whereas the singing soldiers had formerly marched from right to left in orderly formation, their tanks and armor impressive, the daily flow was now from left to right, from the southeast toward town, or what was left of the "city of last resistance." First came limping soldiers, or wounded ones on open trucks and ambulances with red crosses on them. Armored vehicles were scarce and battered-looking.

Then came the refugees.

In fact, the stream of humanity seemed to be a thick, slow-moving, river of misery as though all despair of the earth was flowing past our house from early morning, through day and night. These were eastern people (Hungarians? Ukrainians? Romanians?), short and dark, the women wrapped in black cloth or heavy blankets that all but obscured their bodies; clothes were tattered and mixed together in the way only misery can produce.

Small, horse-drawn wagons covered by half-round canvas arches, carried old people or a woman with a new baby; anyone able to walk trudged alongside in order to not yet kill the emaciated horse or cow pulling the cart. A few belongings, pots, bundles, hung off the side. Grandparents in little children's carts were pulled by women who carried their babies. There were no men except ancient ones, or very young boys. These refugees walked slowly, rarely looking left or right, but anxious not to lose their place in the column. Missing one's place in line, meant losing friends, neighbors, or relatives forever; no one remaining to help you die. The misery seemed endless, even to the eyes of a child on the front stoop, feeling so secure in knowing that upstairs was home. Today I think: Where were these people going? Who fed them? How far did they make it? How many died, and when they died, who buried them?

So, returning to my own rooms lined with razor blades, I see this eight-year-old child, sitting on the stoop of that old building in Graz, watching the parade of misery. Soon, I understood it was just a matter of time before we, too, would join the line. At the time, I did not comprehend the irony.

95

Indeed, our turn came closer and closer, the nearer the "front" was to our city. For a while now, we had heard cannon booms in the distance, but planes no longer flew overhead–there was nothing left to bomb.

Vati reported one day that he heard the Americans were advancing, up over the Alps, from Italy. He believed we should move west to meet them and hopefully be taken in by them once we could identify ourselves. He would be unable to go with us, for he had been recruited into the army-of-last-stand: Men over 60 and boys over 14. He was to learn to throw hand grenades, and with a grim laugh he pointed to his hands now deformed from arthritis, frozen into a clenched splay. Vati told us people who refused had been shot on the spot.

However, he said, he had found two men with motorcycles and a sidecar who would take us west to the mountains, to a place called Laintal, where a farmer would put us up until the Americans came. There he would join us when it was all over–very soon. My friend, Lisi Torsić, her mother, Anni, and grandmother would also go along. We would all be together.

So, one day we joined the line of misery, only we were motorized: Mutti in the side car with me on her lap, Lisi's mother behind the driver, a second cycle for Lisi and her grandmother behind the driver. Whom had Vati bribed, and with what? Why were our drivers not part of the "last stand?" Were they Yugoslav partisans who became more and more visible as the war machine decayed? Were they friends of Lisi's mother, who was, after all, a member of the Communist party and of Slovenian descent?

Questions, always questions.

I don't remember yet another leave-taking that day. It had to have been dreadful, but as always, my parents made super-human efforts to hide and protect, to make things appear very normal; we were just going somewhere, again, and this time Lisi was coming along.

This is what I remember of this trip: Slowly, we were riding through a wide plain with fields and ditches on either side of the road. It was raining, cold, heavy clouds hanging low in the sky. Around us, refugees were trudging along, hunched and bundled. Here and there we saw some soldiers, a few pieces of artillery–a human line as far as the eye could see, all trying to reach the Americans. Our motorcycles did their best to pass, at times veering onto the fields.

Suddenly there was a roaring noise overhead: closer and closer. A commotion went through the crowd, the ranks broke, and within seconds everyone ducked in the ditches. We, too, abandoned the motorcycles, lay flat in the ditch, Mutti trying to cover me with her body. Low flying planes, very low, soared overhead. I could glimpse soldiers leaning out their sides with rifles, wildly shooting at anything, left and right. Memory tells me there was laughter coming from the plane's open hatch, but I cannot imagine it to have been so. If there were dead or wounded, we did not see them, nor did we hear anything that could have suggested that. Perhaps selective memory is a blessing; perhaps these planes were no longer aiming at anything, just enjoying the sense of victory.

After moments of total stillness, a communal holding of breath, people gathered themselves together again and trudged on. Obviously, they had done this many times before.

Somehow, we managed to get to the farm in Laintal. Once again, I remember calm days, playing in the farm yard with Lisi, going for walks in the meadows with Mutti. Daily rations were meager, always potato dumplings and green salad; in the morning polenta with a bit of milk poured over it. But it was food; I liked it. All in all the days offered one of those respites that can make a child believe all has changed and danger is now over.

However, one day, there was news that the Americans weren't coming after all; there had been some arrangement by which they held back, allowing the Russians to advance.

The word "Russian" struck fear in everyone. Rumors had been coming in for months about their unspeakable brutality, a loosening of vengeful hordes that shot, raped, robbed and burned everything in their path—they were the reason for that endless line of humanity streaming west past our house. Later we would learn these Russians were themselves poor, brutalized people, men and women soldiers who had been forced from their primitive farms in deepest Russia, had endured unspeakable tortures and hardship, and if they did not advance and shoot, their officers would shoot them from behind. Simple. At this point, even if we had known, the reality would have mattered little to us.

Mutti and Mrs. Torsić must have panicked, for suddenly we packed whatever we each could carry, including a bit of food. A farm woman guided us into the alpine hills to a shed that formerly had served as shelter for herds on summer pasture, way up in the mountains. It was really just a roof over four posts rammed into the ground. A lovely stand of spruce—real Christmas trees—blocked a magnificent view into the valley, thus protecting us. During the day, we were not allowed to walk into the open field for fear we might be seen from the village.

However, Lisi and I crawled on our bellies to take in the view: the roads, our farm yard, the opposite mountains and their meadows rising up to the horizon. We were hungry, and the new growth on the spruce trees, light green and tender, looked delicious. Indeed, when chewed, it gave off a slightly sweet taste, and we were proud to have discovered something great. We crawled from the shed to the trees, lay in the sun and picked the shoots. It was fun.

Down in the valley, there was much commotion. Vehicles and troops retreating, refugees following and others advancing. Actual fighting had long ago ceased. Then, one day, we saw soldiers in yellowish-green uniforms, tiny specks moving around the village streets.

Recently, I boarded the spaceship "Google Earth" and traveled to the Laintal Valley, found the small village, the square, even the mountain pasture with the view of that valley from behind the spruce trees; I moved the little yellow fellow to the site of the meadow–and there was our view! Peaceful, charming, nothing had changed. All was forgotten.

That day, however long ago, the square suddenly became populated with running soldiers, tanks, fleeing women, images burned into the brain of an eight-year-old.

After a day or two of hiding, the farmer woman came gasping up the hill telling us to return, that we had been seen or reported, and that the Russian soldiers would come for us if we did not. So, we quickly returned to our one room in the farmhouse where all five of us slept together: mothers and children together in two narrow beds; grandmother on a cot. It was a tight room with two small windows, bare floors, two night-stands, and an old armoire where we had put our bundles.

Nightfall came and with it the disaster outside on the village square. Mutti tried to hold my ears tight so I would not hear, but it was not to be missed. There was shooting, women screaming, motors running.

Suddenly our door opened with a sharp bang. The first thing we saw was the butt of a rifle, then a Russian soldier, then another and another. Our mothers sat on the edge of the beds (of course no one had undressed for the night) shielding us girls, and silently staring at the men. They proceeded to search the room, looking for weapons or German soldiers who might be hiding. Under our beds? In the night stands? Under our blankets? All of this the soldiers roughly inspected, guns drawn on us.

Then they started to look over the folks in the room. Three women, two quite old, one young and pretty; two little girls. If you could not hear hearts pounding, you could see the tight breath both mothers drew. At this moment, Anni Torsić was struck by genius or martyrdom, certainly super-human courage. She spoke some Serbo-Croatian; her work in the Communist underground had added a few words of Russian–all of which she now applied. She was a lively woman, intelligent, attractive and assertive.

She told the men that, if they would go downstairs with her, to the farm kitchen, they could have a party, and perhaps she would tell them their fortunes from playing cards. After a quick explanation to Mutti, she grabbed a deck of cards and gently herded the soldiers out of the room. Then all was quiet save for voices downstairs. We children must have eventually fallen asleep.

Toward morning, Mrs. Torsić appeared in our door. A shadow of her former self, she collapsed on the floor where she lay in stoic silence for a long time. All of us sat quietly, unmoving; there was no energy to comfort her, to explain to us children, no strength left to hug or to console, just mute exhaustion. Annie Torsić never talked about what happened in that farm kitchen that night, never mentioned whether telling fortunes was all she had to do, but as surely as I now sit in the safety of my home, I know she saved our lives.

By the next morning the Russian troops had passed on, moving farther west. We, in turn, managed somehow to get back to Graz, which the Russians had overrun without any fighting–neither the old men nor the boys gathered to defend the city having considered the last stand worth their lives. Anyway, the Nazi officers had long ago left town.

The Stoop

We children returned to our perch on the front stoop, watching the world pass by. Now the stream of refugees took on a different look; there were Germans who fled the persecution in Czechoslovakia, emaciated German soldiers appearing from behind trees, begging for civilian clothes, any clothes, for often they were half naked, having shed their uniforms. They hid all day, and at night walked home, wherever that had been.

The streets belonged to the Russian soldiers who patrolled with drawn guns, shooting at everything that appeared to be a threat. We stayed in the apartment, of course. What did we eat? Were there any supplies? Memory fails except for a few images that will have to represent the spirit of the days, it also fails at invoking any emotion as well. Was there none? Was it pushed into deeper levels of being, only to rise when fear arises as well?

It was not long after our return that, on May 8, the end of World War II was declared. Ironically, the German surrender was broadcast from the radio station in Flensburg, the last German city to remain unoccupied by any of the allied forces. This official end of the war came almost as an afterthought; we were already living the end.

Again, I sat on our front stoop, all by myself, and that day I became an

The stoop at Mariatroster Strasse 1

adult although my eighth birthday was three days away. I remember feeling numb in body and soul, no relief, just total exhaustion. I knew I would never forget this day and this feeling, and that it would shape my entire life, no matter what happened in the future. I sat wondering what the reason may have been for all this, for whose gain, at what cost.

Every year, when May 8 comes around, I have a moment of reflection, a private memorial. Again, I sit on the stoop, again there is the limp void, the ache in the heart that is tinged with an all too fragile hope. This is how war destroys childhood.

My Russian

Of course, the end of war was just a continuation of hardships. Suffering had become a local matter, for no longer was the inner landscape conscious of war's broader wave and how it washes over humanity near and far. Life centered on the moment, survival–here and now. Any governmental structure, good or bad, that might have regulated the supply of food or security had disappeared. Furthermore, all visible traces of civic life had collapsed, and survivors tried to take matters in their own hands to whatever extent their ingenuity and resources allowed.

Probably, if most of the German men had not died fighting, and every single survivor not been depleted of energy, there would have been anarchy. Now there was just a vast vacant hole, a stillness very similar to the feeling when you wake up after having fainted–heavy muscles and nerves not yet able to take in outside stimuli, in fact, barely feeling at all, and yet somehow lacking all tension.

Within a few weeks, or months, a semblance of order was imposed by the occupying forces, first Russian, later the British. Starvation was rampant, but limited food supplies were distributed and rationed. Our street, once the life line to the south-eastern front, was deserted and remarkably intact. Evenings were silent now, no sirens, no artillery. Once our parents had determined the outdoors were relatively safe again, we children were allowed out.

It was early summer, and in the villa across from us, Russian officers had been quartered, giving us a modicum of protection since they maintained discipline over their troops. We children knew the villa's garden once had lovely strawberry beds, and lying on our bellies behind the hedges, we could see the fruit, red and luscious–but we could also see the Russian officers on their knees picking and eating them.

On warm nights, these officers sat in the garden, talking, their voices rising from behind the hedge. Before long, they broke into song: low, plaintive melodies, rich with those magnificent bass voices and high tenors, harmonies that filled the listener's heart to weeping. One could taste the homesickness that brought forth their songs, but also the depth of soul. How could these men be devils, murderers, rapists?

Soon we learned that many Russians felt like kids in candy-land. Quite a few of the simple foot soldiers from the far eastern provinces had never had indoor plumbing, or houses with electricity. And they fell in love with wristwatches. Many a soldier's ration was traded for a watch–if it was not taken at gun-point. Happily grinning men could be seen sporting multiple watches on both lower arms. If the watch stopped, they shot it, or cornered the previous owner and demanded retribution. Often that meant being shown how to wind it. They cooled butter in toilet bowls, they marched into houses, looked in the cupboards and whatever they liked, they took. And yet, it was hard to be too angry or too afraid of them. One did not expect much else of the conquering army. They, too, had barely survived, and they were now masters over a culture that had for so long lorded it over Russia, inflicting untold misery, not just in this war, but for decades and even centuries. It was their turn now, and they celebrated it with childlike joy.

In fact, miraculously, humanity sometimes bubbled to the surface, asserting itself like a gift from God in the middle of all that chaos. One such moment happened early in the Russian occupation, and it has cast a light in my memory, sending fear and terror into shaded corners.

One day, Mutti decided it was safe to let me do an errand, or perhaps she was ill. By law, children were allotted 1/8 liter of milk per week, and, from early morning on, long lines snaked their way outside the food store, each person hoping to have arrived before the supplies ran out. Mutti sent me off with my little blue milk can, the same can I had carried on my first mission for food. Once I was outdoors, she lowered the house key by a long string so that I could lock up after myself. Off I went; just as I was getting to the next building, a very tall Russian soldier, young, blond, and pink-faced, came walking in the opposite direction. He looked at me, looked again, seemed to think for a moment; then he took me by the hand. Mutti watched from the window in stark terror, but he waved to her that all was okay. She must have trusted him, and if not, what was she to do? He might have shot both of us. But instead, he stroked my hair, then lifted me up onto one shoulder and pointed to the milk can asking in sign language where the store was. I signed back in the direction of the corner.

Calmly, the Russian carried me to the small store, actually just a shed-like addition to a house. There, sweeping aside the line of waiting people, he entered the store, sat me on the counter, and pounded the milk can on it.

The dairy store today?

The shopkeeper stared, terrified, and poured the required cup of milk. He looked in, shook his head, pounded the can on the counter again and again, until the can was full. Then, in triumph, he lifted me back on his shoulder and took me home. Worried sick, Mutti had rushed to meet us, but he calmly turned me over to her, greeting politely. Then, pointing eastward, he conveyed with gestures that, back in Russia, he had a little girl who might be close to my age. Who knows how long it had been since he had seen her, if ever.

After that he came several times to take me shopping, but one day he was gone, just as he had come. Somewhere in Russia lived a man whose actions overshadowed fear and so much pain, who planted in me a deep love for things Russian. Here was a man who, I hope, made it back to his child, a man who did not have to suffer the way the Russian people continued to suffer under their leaders. If there is a Heaven for Russian soldiers, any Heaven at all, he is there.

If this one memory set the tone for life on how I viewed Russians, then another experience, sadly, did the same for the British occupying forces. They had been in our part of Austria for a short time, retreating from the eastern regions once the Allies decided to give Russia a greater share of territory thus setting up the territorial boundaries for the Cold War. The British forces had found us even more terrorized, hungry, and confused.

I remember a gang of us kids hanging out around the British headquarters in Kroisbach, in what had once been the café by the pond. There the officers took their meals and the leftovers were simply dumped onto a big garbage heap in the garden. Food, lots of good-smelling food, and we were hungry. We hung around, waited, then tried to clamber over the fence and get at the pile.

Just then a British guard came with a gun; obviously he had orders not to let us take the leftovers for sanitary reasons, so he pointed his gun at us and tried to shoo us away. We were hungry, so as soon as he pointed at one kid, the others started to close in again. This went on until he grew visibly angry, and we became scared. We never did get to the food, nor were we handed some from the kitchen.

Lake Hilmteich and café in Kroisbach

Loni Bär Stories

Dazed, we continued our search for ways to survive. Families tried to calm their children, others spent most of the day looking out of their windows, searching the street for a man or young boy who just may be their husband or son, returning from "the front" or from captivity. Since there was no telephone, hardly any mail service, the majority of returning men simply walked until they got home, or to the spot that had once been home. If it had not been bombed and the family not displaced, there would be cries of joy, or stunned greeting if the man returned missing an arm or limping on a crutch.

Our family was spared this agony, and both my parents and the Torsić family tried to build a sense of normalcy. As Mutti had done in the bomb shelters, she continued her stories about *Herr Bär, Frau Bär, Loni Bär,* bears magically transformed into humans by *Frau Nachbarin* [Mrs. Neighbor]. By now, these stories had carried us through some hard times, they were an escape to a better world.

Today, retired in comfort, pleased at how beautifully day follows peaceful day, I have time to reflect, organize papers. Going through the old black portfolio that contained so many signposts of my parents' lives, I came upon a folder with a book of stories Mutti wrote in 1945, after war's end.

The cover, now stained and yellowed, shows a watercolor illustration of a woman walking along, holding a child by one hand, her other carrying a parrot cage. Both child and parrot identify the woman as Mutti. Both figures seem to be dressed in travel clothes—hat, coat, good shoes—heading off confidently… where? They do not look like refugees; they are just on the road, as we had always been.

Cover, "The Stories of Mrs. Loni Bär"

Bound together is a set of typed sheets with about twelve watercolor illustrations. This was a Christmas present at a time when there were no presents to give. The title page has a German dedication, a poem illustrated with Christmas trees, gifts and flowers, in the unmistakable hand of my father. The poem in translation reads:

*It was in the Lain Valley, in the days of
the Russians,*

The war was over, home far away.

There, you children were much comforted

By the stories of Mrs. Loni Bär.

When you read these stories, once peace has come,

Then,

Think of me, who imagined them!

Dedicated to dear little Erika,

with great love, Mutti

The final story was "Loni in Christmas Heaven." These mirages were brought forth through "Frau Nachbarin," a generous, wealthy, imaginative person who spent her days planning new adventures for those she had taken under her wing. There is no doubt that, for us listeners, Mrs. Neighbor was my mother.

Frau Nachbarin plays the piano.

This booklet that moves her now aging daughter to tears also contains one painful image. Was it happenstance? Surely, the illustrator meant only to show Mrs. Neighbor playing for Loni, the child of the Bär family, whom she has taken into her house.

Here is the image: An elegant living room, carpeted and illuminated by lamp and candles. A beautiful woman in a winter ball gown plays the piano with grand gestures. The lady is enveloped in clear, light colors, from blonde hair to lime-colored gown and white lace. She seems to float on the melodies.

Next to the instrument, on a small wooden stool sits a little girl. Her dress is patched, her feet clad in clumsy slippers. The story makes it clear this is the Bär child, now brought to human form by Mrs. Neighbor's magic. Still, this small person remains somewhat alien and devoid of refinement. She sits upright, hands folded in her lap, listening intently. Her colors are brown, ochre, dark red. There is no question she will sit like that, without moving, for a very long time. She has been trained for that, but she also knows she will never match up, will remain the clumsy bear child.

Whatever the source

Dedication and Christmas poem, 1945

of this image, or its original intent, it speaks to the woman, now eighty years old, and once again, it confirms what the pianist's daughter had always known: There is a gulf between these two, woman and child, and it remains intact over the gap of almost a century.

Aside from Mutti's emotional strength that rises out of these stories, this one image in the booklet exposes the deep wound, an ancient hurt called "My Mother, Music, and Me." Was I alone in the realization of my position within this hierarchy? Did others notice?

Except for these few glimpses, the remainder of the year 1945 remains blank in memory, as does the winter and spring that followed. Surely, we suffered, but I do not remember.

Gradually it became clear that all of the family's investments and possessions had been confiscated, disowned, and ground up by the Nazi war machine. There was no work, and Vati's health was failing. It must have occurred to him that returning to the United States would solve all problems. He embarked on a frantic effort to reestablish his American citizenship and with it the right to travel to the safety of the United States.

Chapter 5

Coming to America

On the spring day of 1946 when Vati returned from his most recent trip to Vienna, he brought along a Care package–that object of gold and dreams. There was chocolate and sweet condensed milk so thick you could spoon it out and feel it ooze all over your tongue. I have no idea what else may have been in the package, but ever since those hungry days I have made contributions to Care, hoping that somewhere in the world there may be a child for whom the package constitutes the difference between going to bed hungry or with the memory of sweet cream on the tongue.

This trip to Vienna seemed to have been very important. Vati had again visited the United States embassy. Now my parents briefly spoke in English, their faces were grave, and their somber moods did not go away even in the evening, or the next day.

When it came time to involve me, my parents chose to inform me in the manner that had become a pattern. They asked, "How would you like to travel to America, on a big ship, to New York, where there are huge buildings with lights reaching to the sky, and more food than you can ever finish?" These were enticing images. They evoked Mutti's Bär Family stories during those long hours in the bomb shelter. These questions implied choice, although of course I had none. But since change was always presented as a grand adventure, of wonder, change gradually became a good thing in its own right.

Carefully, slowly, plans unfolded. Vati and I, both of us having been reinstated as American citizens (the child of an American citizen born abroad is automatically an American citizen as well), would go to the States, and from there Vati would try to get a visa for Mutti.

"Your wife, Sir, will not be allowed to travel since she remained a German citizen after marriage and has not yet been denazified." Those were the words Vati had brought back from Vienna.

Here my thoughts return to my mother. How would she, still starving and freezing, endure the separation from her husband and only child? How would she survive for what would become four years before we were reunited? How to meet her child, by then an adolescent?

So, to be allowed to leave, Mutti would have to be *"entnazifiziert"* [denazified], a process perhaps similar to brainwashing, ridding the person of previously held beliefs before being allowed to travel to the States. My own mind, however, equated it with being *"entlaust,"* cleaned of head lice, a treatment we had endured frequently during recent years. Of course, I had no idea what the actual process was to be, nor can I today envision what kind of interrogation Mutti was to go through, what kind of mental retraining would have been thought beneficial for a woman who had been hiding in Austria and had a spotty *Ahnenpass* [ancestry passport], a document you had to carry with you, establishing your pure Aryan ancestry, or lack thereof. All that had been dangerous yesterday was now a safe ticket; all that could have gotten you into camp then, was now a desirable attribute. Where did we fit? Again, it was a struggle for balance of mind and soul.

Unable to gauge the emotional cost of separating the family once again, perhaps unwilling to do so, my parents focused on the minutiae of logistics. Mutti, who had grown from the indulged artist into a stoic trooper, looked at my shoes that had lost half their soles; there was nothing to be done about that, but she declared the child would have to have at least one dress for the trip. From among Vati's clothes she picked a pair of Knickerbocker britches, took them to a seamstress who made me a dress by turning the material inside-out. Out of some other materials on hand they made a blouse, skirt and apron into an Austrian *Dirndl* dress, fine enough to be used for the new passport photo that would guide us to America and for one melancholy family portrait, our three heads leaning together, our faces thin and sad.

I remember the trip to Vienna by train, I do not remember the farewell from Mutti—too big a dish for a child's brain to absorb, much less retain.

The next image that comes to mind is bombed-out Vienna: hollow buildings, mountains of rubble lining the streets where gutters had once been, gaping holes to the sky where windows had once opened from fancy apartments.

The few people in the streets were women, mostly old, scurrying to stand in line for hours, hoping for their weekly ration of potatoes, a bit of bread. The men were old or had missing limbs; they teetered along on crutches, the pant leg of the missing limb folded up and pinned on the side; one empty sleeve tucked into a jacket pocket where once there had been an arm. Slowly these hunched figures went by, their shoulders pulled high; they did not look up, hugging the sides of the buildings as though the middle of the sidewalk belonged to someone else.

Vati and Erika; passport photo for the big journey, spring, 1946

Repeatedly, over the years, I have revisited the film, "The Third Man," which better than words shows the setting and the spirit of those days: clawing, trembling life emerging from the ruins, trying to find a way to keep going, living on memories of a genteel and elegant past, fear and danger lurking in every doorway or creeping around corners. There is the scene where an old woman answers a doorbell. Her apartment has no heat, no electricity; she has wrapped herself in a coverlet to stave off the winter cold—but it is made of fine damask silk.

A civilization had been thrown to the winds. No one at the time could envision the rebirth; no one would have been so crazed as to hallucinate about the luxury, hedonism and internationalism that would rise in the late twentieth century. No, this was the end, and just as the population had passively stood by when this civilization was taken over by fanatic hordes, so they now stood by and considered all this the way one considers a natural disaster. No, it had not been their fault, nor caused by their lack of political awareness and participation; it had swept over them like a force of nature, and had they been asked, they would have told you that they had "gone into inner exile."

The next thing I knew, Vati and I were on the Orient Express from Vienna to Paris. The name of this legendary train called forth red-hatted porters, Pullman *Wagons Lits* (sleeping cars) and steam-filled cast-iron stations. Still sporting the fancy compartments and inlaid wood walls, it was now battered, torn, scarred and rattling. The cars creaked on rails that had been bombed and repaired a few times too often.

Vati enriched these sights with stories about the stops along the route:

Constantinople, Budapest, Vienna, then Paris. He painted lush images of adventures and luxury, the proof of which lay in the elegance I could still see–yet one more lesson in the intoxication of the new. This was my formal education, never mind schools.

The train was full of folk like us: Americans who had been trapped by the war and gathered together by the hastily set up consulates; there were stateless people or refugees who for some reason or other had obtained permits to go to France, and from there to somewhere else–the United States, South America, perhaps, or Australia. Who knows? The American Embassy in Paris had a hotel where all American stragglers were housed until they could be sent to their destinations in the States.

My only memory of Paris, of the Champs-Elysées, was a peach. Vati and I were walking down the avenue, itself looking worse for the wear of war, but fruit stands lined the sidewalks in colorful abundance. Vati bought me a peach, and with the first juicy bite, all the promises came true. I embraced the idea of adventure, of travel and change; accepted it whole.

Soon we were assigned to a group of travelers and taken to our ship in Le Havre. As had happened a hundred times since D-Day, converted ocean liners transported American troops to Europe to fight and often die. Ships disgorged the soldiers and took on the stragglers.

It was late afternoon when we encountered our ship, the *George Washington*–the largest hulk of anything metal I had ever seen. Now I know that she was an aged ocean liner from 1909 that had been re-commissioned out of mothballs for troop transport. There she lay in the Atlantic, just off the docks, and a sloop bounced us over to the gangplank for a terrifying climb along the side of the ship, all the way to the cargo deck. This climb was surely the source of my returning nightmares that involve swaying ladders.

The *George Washington* had long ago been stripped of its cabins, dining rooms, and bars. There were only large halls with bunk beds everywhere, three high. The ship's halls were divided into dorms for women and men. I was placed with the women, Vati, standing at the door, pleaded with a lady to please look out for me. To my joy I got an upper bunk, smack up against the metal ceiling. The weight of male bodies had stretched the mattresses and springs into nests, like hammocks. Today, I shudder at the realization that these bunks resembled caskets that shipped young men to battle, human cargo of death. The mind boggles at the thought of young boys from Nebraska clutching the tiny pillow at night, unable to sleep, homesick and scared to death. When, in turn, I clutched my pillow, I was unaware of the tragedy but yes, I was homesick, too, and for a little girl of nine, away from home and any acquaintance, the nest held great solace.

At night, the smell of ships–that mixture of oil, steam and salt–permeated hallways and dorms; the gentle sway of waves added comfort; the engine's rhythmic stomp pounded out time and brought sleep.

Earlier, at the hour of departure, Vati had explained that we ought to go on deck to watch the departure. It was a gray July evening, the air a mix of fog and salt. On shore, the frenzy of harbor life played out–the clatter of cranes, trucks, shouts. Slowly the engines revved up, the stack let out three terrifying hoots of farewell, and we moved off. I sat on Vati's lap. He held me tight, looked back to land, deep in thought, his inner focus making his eyes look like frosty steel. Perhaps he was quietly taking stock of the lashes fate had dropped on his life since he last traveled in this direction. Were the regrets rising from the past larger than the anxiety of what lay ahead?

As land gradually retreated, he woke up and said: "Take a good look; you are leaving Europe behind. Say goodbye." At this moment, we two became a team. Over the years, the balance of our positions would change with my growing maturity and his failing capacities, yet our deep connection never diminished.

It used to be, before the days of hedonistic cruising, that every traveler on board a ship had a companion: Fate. As ships cut from land, they made tangible the cutting of ties. With the receding coast went one's old life; a choice had been made, for better or worse. Mostly, this choice was irreversible, for few of the millions who emigrated to America ever came back. They rarely wrote and never again saw their families, ever.

After five or six days at sea, our ship pulled into New York. Vati and I had come on deck early to take in the drama of a ship's arrival. There, still at a distance, rose Manhattan from the mist–so solemn, so delicate, as though a precious necklace had been suspended between water and sky, cushioned by rose-golden clouds. Morning fog still hiding its footings, the skyline of New York City rose like a vision: elegant, narrow towers ending in numerous turrets reminiscent of elongated church spires, their close grouping giving the tip of Manhattan its fragile appearance.

Herman Melville opens his book *Moby Dick* with a description of the city hovering over the water, its machines pounding out a new era, asserting the growth and power of the New World–hard facts of iron and steel, of squalor and poverty or backbreaking labor. A symbolic presence.

A child does not see the world in this manner. There is no previous knowledge or association that could color the scene or pass judgement. Manhattan rising from the mist that morning was a vision, incredibly beautiful, unreal and fragile, hiding the hard facts of progress.

That morning in the mist, it was all image, it was all promise... If the hard facts of life would bring defeat, that might come later. If memories or regrets caused Vati to shed inner tears, he did not show it.

The American Family

The unreality continued during the excitement and noise of disembarking, of finding the relatives, of gathering luggage, hundreds of people hugging and talking all at once. I was introduced to Tante Stina, to Onkel George Warming, cousins Sophie and her son, Curtis, people who would warm my later life in America–and still do.

The American family, gathering on the Astoria rooftop, summer, 1946

A faded photo shows Vati and myself with these much-loved people, joined by Vati's youngest brother, Onkel Hermann, Tante Edith, their daughters Carol and Greta, thoroughly Americanized folks.

My father's sister, Christine, and her husband had immigrated after World War I at the invitation of Vati who had given my uncle a job in the construction company. The Warming family made America their life. They never followed the migration of Germans from Astoria to the suburbs of Westchester or New Jersey; they worked hard but clung fiercely to a sense of family and interdependence.

On our first day, Onkel George, a bear of a man with the gentleness of a kitten, took a good look at me and said: "This child needs shoes. Let's go."

We piled into his car, made our way downtown to catch the lights of the Great White Way. We drove up and down Broadway, pointing out the theaters, the Camel man who blew smoke rings into the street, the buildings that seemed taller than the world itself–the lights! Then we stopped at a shoe store. I was fitted with a pair of white leather sandals, the most beautiful things I had ever seen or smelled. Too good to wear, I hugged them all day and slept with them all night; shoes, the beauty of which, the luscious leather smell of which, the elegance of which painted my memory of this giant man, Onkel George, in colors of gold, rose and love.

Such wonders were repeated with ice cream cones, a trip to Coney Island (have you ever ridden the spinning bag merry-go-round with a hot dog in each hand?) and later an outing to the waves and crowds of Jones Beach. I remember it all as a great adventure, but the family must have looked at that scrawny, starved kid, wondering what to do.

Cousin Sophie was a proud, beautiful young woman, a designer of fancy hats for a fancy store on Fifth Avenue called Bonwit Teller. She would take the subway to work, wearing one of those hats; sometimes they were huge wheel-sized, or tiny caps with feathers or birds on them. Usually all kinds of things bobbed on those hats as she walked on her high heels. And, at six feet tall, she was quite a scene. Besides that, she was a skier, a camper, and a bit of a dare-devil who loved to have a good time.

Always a lady of great courage and good humor, she has been a favorite of mine for a long, long time. It began when she made me a bathing suit of white material with large black polka dots. It was the most wonderful thing I had ever received, and I loved her from that moment on.

All these experiences were like a repeat of Little Orphan Annie having arrived at Daddy Warbuck's house. One "Oh, my goodness" experience after another: ice cream and candy, toys and new clothes. The streets of Astoria, Long Island, were lined with cozy houses, no windows missing, kids playing new games on the sidewalks. I thought it was very pretty, even if today it is a bit of a stretch in terms of urban beauty. But, there was Angelo's fragrant pizza place, right as you got off the metal stairs from the elevated station. Standing in his intoxicating hole-in-the-wall was smiling Angelo with a paper hat on his dark curls, pulling from the oven pies dripping cheese and fat. You ran home, carrying this treasure, to make sure it was still hot, the cheese runny. The kids on the stoop looked longingly at the box.

The corner candy store sold lollipops and jellybeans—color, sugar, texture never before experienced by the tongue. There was the toy section of Woolworth's, and the deafening sound of the elevated subway rattling by the apartment building day and night, all new all good, bombarding the senses.

Every morning I had to check out the barber's entrance with its rotating column: spiral—red, round-and-round, circling up, up, up, an experience that left me in a dazed state of disconnect, a constant high that was almost impossible to sustain, much less to absorb, and yet everyone did their best to make my life one large birthday party.

Best of all were the weekend outings on Onkel George's boat moored

The "Christine" on Long Island Sound

under the Whitestone Bridge. Tante Stina packed fabulous food: cream cheese and jelly sandwiches, and Coke. All the family, even cousin Sophie and her three-year-old son, Curtis, and Queenie the dog, would ride into Long Island Sound, stopping at little sand spits or islands to swim and picnic, the boat gently rocking on the sunny sea. I lived for these weekends.

If Curtis and I had been especially good, Onkel George, with the patience of Job, would roll out the Packard, load us in the back and trundle off into deepest Queens (I think). There were miles of Quonset huts on dusty unpaved roads—the housing for returning GI's and their young families. The roads had become rutty and worn, the surface like washboards, with tiny ripples making car wheels bounce and raising mounds of dust in our wake. The Packard had no suspension to speak of and would have been a classic had it not been so worn. Ever-patient Onkel George drove at top speed along these roads, back and forth, back and forth. The ride surpassed anything Coney Island had to offer. Curt and I bounced in the back seat like two screaming rag dolls, forever demanding "do it again!" until enraged occupants emerged from the Quonset huts, shaking their fists and waving the dust from their faces.

With Tante Stina and a guest on a sandbank

Other gems of memory include adventures of wild release—yelling, laughing, wind-in-your-ears running—emotions of childhood almost forgotten. I remember studying American children for their joy, their release of emotion, their demand for "fun" and considered them like you would ponder a hitherto unknown species. I knew none of this would ever be possible for me. I was outside, fascinated, keenly aware of my compressed stiffness.

America was the great adventure, the perpetual ride on a merry-go-

114

round, and Tante Stina was my anchor. She remained that until her death at age 105.

There exists an August 1946 letter, the first Vati wrote to Mutti after our arrival. As always, he called her *"Muttchen"* [little mother] and painted a picture of our arrival, of my cool acceptance of change, of the wonders. He described the greetings and acceptance of old friends who found work for him and smoothed the path. Of his daughter he said:

Erika and Tante Stina

> *You ask about Erika's impressions. The thickest of crowds in Paris were her favorite, the stands on Montmartre... Here in New York, it is chocolate ice cream that is more important than the gigantic buildings and the traffic... She regrets that Mutti cannot see all this, but let us be glad that she is not all too sensitive and does not show homesickness.*

I greet and kiss you, your Old Man."

Tante Adele

Another encounter in this New York setting was with Tante Adele, Mutti's elder sister. As mentioned before, she had lived in the States since the early years of the 20th century.

The years of the Depression and war must have been difficult for her. She had faced great hardships, and the search for jobs led her to move from coast to coast. Still, she spent her life and available funds in service to the family. She helped her European relatives during the war, sending food package after food package. I often wonder, did she, herself, get enough to eat?

With Tante Adele, Mutti's eldest sister, living in New York

By that time Tante Adele had long been divorced from Stephen Naft.

In 1946, I spent occasional weekends with her in the city. I recall a short, rotund woman, old beyond her years, dressed in coat and hat so worn, they had taken on her body's shape, hanging and bulging as did the person inside. Handbag and shoes were so shabby even a nine-year-old could notice.

Tante Adele's energies, however, were undiminished. We walked along Central Park to the Metropolitan Museum with promises that we would later go shopping for dollhouse furniture at Woolworth's. This was followed by lunch at Horn & Hardart, that shiny temple of aluminum counters, red seats and luscious morsels behind little glass doors.

At the Met she so loved the huge Rubens paintings in the stair halls that we stood there, studying them for long stretches of time. She pointed out the dapple of sun on luscious nude skin, sunlight on trees and meadows. She gave words to the images of glowing sky that illuminated a pastoral landscape, a place of delight recalling an ideal past. She recited to me the names of the Greek and Roman gods there cavorting.

There was the magnificent *Feast of Acheloüs*, where a river god explains to Theseus that a distant island is in fact his former lover, Perimele, transformed by Neptune, so she can forever remain within the river's embrace. Was Tante Adele, whose marriage to Stephen Naft had ended, reliving love that was no longer hers, and perhaps had never been?

How about *Venus and Adonis*, where Venus, accidentally pricked by one of Cupid's arrows, falls in love with the handsome hunter Adonis? This world of beauty and grace must have offered solace to a soul so bleeding from the wounds inflicted by a cruel world, the killer of dreams. Were these places and images of delight her soul's refuge?

Perhaps that is why museums often have those temple fronts and numerous white steps. You have to climb in humility so that you may be purified, elevated and consoled before you enter the holy of holies, a place of escape and delight. Why do I remember that? Were these lessons seeds that grew into a lifetime's pursuit of art history, of spending decades in museums in the service of art?

The Fishkill Family

Vati's youngest brother, Uncle Hermann, lived with his wife and two daughters in Fishkill, New York. They were the family standing with us on the Astoria rooftop for the group photo. Uncle Hermann had been the third sibling emigrating to the States.

Under the tutelage of my two cousins, I learned about the life of the suburban American child: station wagons with a gaping back section, coloring books and crayons strewn about, so we could be busy on our way to Bear Mountain or Hyde Park.

There were paper dolls to dress and dolls whose hair needed combing. There was whispered talk of lipstick and hair curlers. We sang Stephen Foster songs in that car, ate in that car, fell asleep on the way home–outrageous! I joined in hesitantly. Landing on the moon could not have been more alien, even if the language barrier had not existed.

However, nobody ever asked about our experiences in Germany, as though that were too painful a subject to touch. Everyone seemed to live in tacit agreement that it was best for this child to erase all earlier experiences, to cure me with silence, forgetting and fun, fun, fun.

Nobody asked me about Mutti or brought up the subject of our separation. Everything was new now; this was reality. The past, if ignored, might cease to have its power and should be shed as quickly as possible. This, of course, does not happen. Soon the excitement becomes commonplace, and the void inside demands to be filled–ask any newcomer. It is in fact the experience of immigrant life, repeated a million times.

Westchester County

Soon, indeed, the reality of American life took over. Actually, it was the general, international reality of children's lives that I knew too well, and from which no adult can provide protection: the condition of the outsider, or simply the kid who must function within the community of peers.

Vati had found work somewhere, and since Tante Stina's apartment in Astoria was too small even for the family, we moved to the suburbs, where an uncle and aunt had a nice house and a delicatessen. He was Vati's cousin from Wyk auf Föhr, the North Sea island. The couple was childless and agreed to look after me during the week while Vati took care of me on weekends. Their house was at the end of a pleasant cul-de-sac leading to a branch of the Long Island Sound. There were wild ducks, small boats, and lots of open space in which to play–quite the American ideal. And as long as adults surrounded me, I was safe, looked at and treated as this oddity who needed to be pitied and clucked over.

But once outside, things changed. My English was poor but passable, tinged, of course with a heavy accent. The kids in the neighborhood knew this accent. They had heard it in news reports and from games that reenacted the war. Now they had a real Nazi in front of them, and groups of kids danced around me screaming, "Nein, nein, nein..." the only words, I am sure, they knew. I remember standing in the center of this circle and feeling rage mount in my innards, fury I

Uncle Thomas feeding the ducks along Long Island Sound

had never experienced before, combined with a dogged sense of pride that would not allow tears or defeat.

I knew I was tall; I knew I was strong. Chopping wood in the hills of Austria had done good things for me. So I flung my fists in all directions, violently attacking anyone who came near me, a bloody nose here, a pulled set of braids there, shins kicked, bellies boxed, rolling on the ground. I took little damage, for I am sure the pleasant suburban mommies had taught their kids to be nice and non-physical even if they were verbally abusive. This fight was new to them; the circle widened, the kids ran home to tattle, and soon the phone in our house was ringing. Aunt Maria had to do some explaining.

Help came from a corner one might have least expected: a Jewish girl whose home was a few houses up the street. Had she suffered similar treatment herself? Had her folks told her about what had gone on in Germany? I don't know where in the cosmos of war's horrors they placed us, or whether they just had kind hearts, but they invited me in, showed friendship and soothing companionship that was not a threat. The little girl's name is lost to me; I think it was Sarah, but never will I forget the warm words and the protective friendship she and her family showed in the weeks and months afterward.

Jewish life in America had another attraction for me. I must have been homesick and exhausted from coping in a new language. I loved to flop on my belly in front of my aunt and uncle's fancy radio cabinet and, after playing with the dial, found a program in German–funny German, but German nonetheless. It told stories, sang strange but enticing and comforting songs, added jokes. I loved it.

Aunt Maria, hearing the broadcast from the kitchen, rushed over with an angry face and turned off the radio. There was no explanation, just an order not to listen to this show ever again. Later, I overheard something to the effect of "Jew program" but it meant nothing, so the punishment made no sense. As a result, I learned to hide this cozy interval, reserve it for evenings when both aunt and uncle worked late at the deli, and I was home alone.

All players in this story are dead now, so I can tell about my deep dislike of living in that house. Instant parenthood must not have been easy for this aging couple. They worked very hard in their deli, surely had faced some discrimination as Germans, both of which may have accelerated my uncle's alcoholism and Aunt Maria's bitterness.

Uncle Thomas would take me for rides in his shiny, new, powder-blue Dodge. I liked him; he was always friendly, but not predictable. Sometimes he would pull up to the curb in the village and tell me he'd be right back. I sat and sat, until, an hour or two later, he came out of the pub, rolling rather than walking, but in a jovial mood. Somehow, we got home, only to be greeted with stone-cold fury by Aunt Maria, who had spent the day washing the porch or waxing the kitchen floor.

For my part, I got back at her by being unspeakably messy, leaving roller skates in the driveway over which she regularly fell, or reading all night by flashlight. I did not clean the floor of my room, which she tested by making me slide under the bed in a dark dress and then pointing out the accumulated dust on my belly.

On weekends I would tell Vati of my dislikes, but what was he to do? He lost one job after another, finally having to commute to Falls Church, Virginia, during the week and coming home only on Friday evenings. From about 4 o'clock on Fridays, I would hover on top of the hill beyond which I was not allowed to go, waiting for him to turn the corner. When the tall figure came around, I raced with all the speed available to me, jumped into his arms to greet him, and for two precious days all was well. In the morning I would go to his room, crawl in his bed, and he would tell me stories (the same old stories, chords of warmth for the heart).

We would take the rowboat out to the Sound, fish for eels, or take the train into the city to marvel at Grand Central Station or Fifth Avenue. Often, we ended up with Tante Stina, the highlight of any trip. How, I ask myself now, was that man able to entertain a nine-year-old child who had pined for him all week when he had spent the time stressed in a city far away? How did he manage, without rest, and no quiet at the end of the week, just more demands on his energies and fading health. I never sensed the hardship, it was just love.

Once in a while he read me a letter from Mutti that had arrived during the week, but he spared me the details. He read just the greetings, not her account of being expelled from Austria with one day's notice because she was

119

German; of having to make her way to the relatives in the North, sick with diphtheria and out of money. Since all of our accounts had been blocked, Mrs. Torsić, our friend and fellow refugee in Graz, gave her what she had. She promised to guard our apartment, which she promptly turned into the communist headquarters of the city, the safest thing to do. I listened to Mutti's words in that letter and hung on to the promise that, soon, Vati would find a way to get her out of Germany. I don't ever remember crying for my mother.

Oh, and then there was school. That fall I would have entered fourth grade, but I was placed in third on account of the language. I confess I have no memory of third grade whatsoever, except utter boredom and a somewhat arrogant disdain. By the time Christmas came around, I must have learned enough English to be moved to fourth grade, Miss Brady's class.

If instruction took place, it was not the kind I knew from early years–math, reading, writing, discipline. Learning, intense learning, happened on the social level. Teachers and students operated in a sphere that was semi-adult, verbal, sophisticated, as could be expected from offspring of a community where many a dad was a CEO, and moms were products of the Junior League. Miss Brady was young and pretty. She had a mass of very curly blond hair and lovely red fingernails which she studied intently and for long minutes during class. Kids flirted wildly, and Miss Brady flirted with the handsomest and most mature boy in class. I remember observing all this in helpless amazement.

Once energized into action, we spent days organizing ourselves through vote into some kind of body politic–president, treasurer, vice president, chairman, everybody else trustees. However, whatever this body was to do after having been formed was never articulated, nor did we carry out any project. The effort's emptiness struck me as very disappointing.

But there was one more very important experience: cousin Helga and her sister Katie, were the daughters of Uncle Thomas' partner in the deli. Helga was a year older than I and, in my view, hovered in a celestial sphere of perfection forever out of reach. She was pretty, self-possessed, had long blond curls that were wound around sticks to form ringlets. She wore just the right ribbons in her hair, just the right bouncy skirt held up by a multitude of petticoats, just the right saddle shoes. She had an adult woman's way of judging the world and expressing her findings with an air of finality.

I venerated her.

She was the queen of cheerleaders, the dream of Hollywood beauty, and even a short word from her made my day. When invited to their house, I followed her like a puppy but never dared look into a mirror that would show the two of us at the same time; the contrast was too devastating: the goddess and the angular, hemmed-in kid with a frown, mousy hair and clothes picked by an old aunt. I could not stand to be in her presence because I felt judged and somewhat rejected, but I also could not stay away. This was my first conscious experience of inadequacy, and it stuck, became part of a permanent state. Sadly, I have never seen her as an adult.

Helga, perhaps more than any other experience of that year, represented the strange, intangible, quality of life in America. It is a platitude to say that coming to America is like entering a technicolor film after knowing only black-and-white, but that is exactly what it was. Dream-like, fast moving images in high-keyed, ravishing colors, pleasures, ease, enticing possibilities all piled one upon the other.

But when you reach out, your hand comes up empty–it is all image, as though one were driving in a car, seeing the scenery through glass, like a movie, never to be touched, smelled, sensed–a disconnect lacking three dimensions. This feeling was vague and without words in my first American experience but was repeated again when I returned as an adult, and it has remained with me, confirming the sense of outsider. I see it as the difficult challenge of life here; it is like moving in a vacuum which it is up to you to fill. If you don't, the failure is yours alone, there is no fate that imposes its limitations upon you and asks you to make do under circumstances beyond your control. Is that why failure to succeed is so much more punishing here?

Not that I would have noticed in this oblivion of childhood, but life for Vati must have become increasingly difficult. He lost another job to younger engineers with more up-to-date training. Living with relatives for such a long time, by then almost a year, being deeply in their debt in terms of caring for me, and finding me unhappy in that setting was surely a burden to him. Besides, his health must have begun to give out, and the prospect of getting Mutti out of Germany had become ever bleaker. And if he did get her to come over, what would we have had to live on? I ponder this situation now, as an adult, and feel cold terror.

I look at the photo of Vati and me, taken in the driveway shortly before our departure. I see the drawn face, the lack of any energy or will, the deep-set eyes unable to smile, deep creases running down on either side of his mouth–the image of a beaten man. I also see a little girl leaning against this man, finding some comfort in the closeness but also showing a troubled face. By then I had spent many days in bed, sick with stomach troubles, vomiting frequently, unable to eat, causing more work for aunt and uncle, more worry for Vati. Doctors called it a "nervous stomach, gastritis" and gave me belladonna.

All I know is that one day, sometime in the spring or early summer of

1947, Vati came to me with the question: "How would you like to travel to Africa?" He also mentioned in passing that the doctor had told him he needed

to move to a hot, dry climate, and that another option was a job in the oil fields of Venezuela (the latter stated with little enthusiasm). Africa seemed fine by me, especially once he began telling me about his friend's plantation in the mountains, about the animals, the long ship journey to Angola.

Soon, again, we sat on deck, off to somewhere. This time it was the *Tamerlane*, a Norwegian freighter. We were saying goodbye to Tante Stina, Onkel George, and Tante Adele whom I had learned to love and whose life in New York remained rife with poverty, abandonment, and loneliness.

Giving up on America, summer, 1947

Beside us there were ten other passengers, including some children. All of them were missionaries going

to various posts in Africa. The journey would take about three weeks, stopping at most harbors along the west coast from Dakar to South Africa, unloading and taking on goods along the way. We were on our way to Fazenda Lunda, the coffee and cattle plantation in the mountain region of central Angola. Vati's friends, the Gärtner family, had invited him back to help build more structures on the site.

Travel, the sea, change; again, we lived in abeyance.

The family seeing us off on board ship

Chapter 6

Angola

Living in Abeyance

For months now, I have stolen time to travel on "Google Earth." I surf over Africa, scan the mountain ranges of Angola, search for the Benguela Railroad, zero in on towns the names of which are burned into my heart–Lobito, Benguela, Ganda, and Chicuma. I am looking for Fazenda Lunda, the huge coffee and cattle plantation on the Benguela plateau.

Flying over the dried highlands, I see settlements, roads, lines of vegetation that suggest sources of water, and if the tiniest of lines crosses such a feature, I believe it to be the very mud passage where our truck always got stuck, and we labored for hours, digging it free. Surely, this road will lead to that barren mountain, fragrant with burnt grass, on the slopes of which lay the plantation: the main house, hidden behind orange trees; the little bedroom houses, the kitchen buildings, the dairy and the endlessly long stables that housed up to 300 head of cattle. All buildings were made of the same mud brick, rough textured and of a color suggesting they had been created from the very earth around them, of the dust and smoke delivered by the African wind.

As I scan, I search for the miles of pasture, the square coffee fields, the woods by the house where we cut our Christmas tree. Again and again, obsessively, I try to see detail, only to find that the railroad track abruptly ends in the bush, that the roads lead nowhere, that Ganda has few remaining houses, and Chicuma is but a dusty blur in a valley.

And then terror comes to me. I remember that this central area along the rail line was the heart of the endless war that followed liberation from Portuguese colonialism, one side financed and supplied by the United States, the other by Russia–a distant, cruel theater of the Cold War. I know that all those who once lived there are dead, black and white, and those who remain must be starving.

And again, my Africa sinks back into the den of dreams. That which is visible now does not resemble the magic I have harbored for so long. The world I am about to describe to you cannot be found there, and memory becomes all the more precious.

I have to give up "Google Earth." Tomorrow I will.

On a sleepless night many months ago, I rose to write the section on Africa, a task I had feared and put off, circling the computer like a leopard the snake. Before my mind's eye lay beauty and suffering so intense it was fearful to recall. Later, floating in the pool, the Atlanta sun warming my back, and my much-loved garden surrounding me in a visual feast, I still could not shake the images. They were more powerful than physical experience, more real than reality. So, once again, the only way to recapture the past is to examine it.

~*~

It must have been June or July of 1947, when our ship, the Norwegian freighter, the *Tamerlane*, pulled out of Hoboken, New Jersey. I was ten years old. Vati was fifty-seven, an ailing man at the door of old age. How come I had never noticed that my father might well be my grandfather, that the walk of those long, thin legs had become lumbered? Or was it just *our* life, *our* situation, and hence normal, not to be questioned? The few photos taken on board when our New York relatives saw us off show a still-handsome, even dashing, man and a little girl too antsy and energetic to pose.

The family saying good-bye on the Tamerlane

We look different from the others; I flatter myself into thinking that Vati and I looked freer. The relatives carry with them the distinct appearance of 1940s America—conservative clothes and hats, faces a bit worn by the quotidian of life.

If the decision to take a ten-year-old child to

124

unknown challenges haunted Vati's thoughts, he did not let on. Perhaps the dream that looks for greener grass on the other side of the hill drove him to the site of his 1937 adventure–or was this trip born from desperation? Had he thought through the prospects of a sick man in the middle of aboriginal life, hundreds of miles from a hospital or even a doctor? Had he considered schooling for me? Did he know how his friends' lives had changed since his visit? It was now exactly ten years and another world war later, one hundred in experience and struggles since last he had seen them.

And how about Mutti, left behind in Germany, had he asked her?

~*~

Anyway, we were on a ship, and for the duration of this interval on the ocean, all was well, all was held in abeyance for that brief period of respite hovering between an unbearable past and an equally terrifying future. Motion is healing, restful, liberating, even if only temporary; loving life in abeyance, is loving that gap.

I think all three of us, Mutti, Vati and I, secretly lived for this state between things. You move on; you do not stand and fight. Fighting, we had learned the hard way, leads only to death. But the next turn in the road may bring something better. Never were the words in Herman Hesse's poem, "*Stufen,*" [Steps] truer: *Und jedem Anfang liegt ein Zauber inne, der uns beschützt und der uns hilft, zu leben...*[...and every beginning is inhabited by magic that protects us and helps us live...]

We moved along, and things would be fine. Abeyance allowed us to sense what the poet, Emily Dickinson calls, "rowing in Eden."

Rowing in Eden

If America, for me, felt dissociated, Africa was tangible. I have talked with many a traveler–never mind people who spent their lives there–and sooner or later the words "magic" or "dream" will come up. Africa grips you, invades your soul, and never, ever, lets go. Is it the thrill of experiencing an exotic, visually enticing environment that offers a glimpse of what used to be called "the primitive," or is there true magic?

These thoughts bring up the painful question of Africa and whites. Do we have even the right, or moral permission, to love Africa? Are we not, through this very act, claiming it for ourselves yet again, robbing Africa and its inhabitants of an emotion rightfully theirs? Africans' love of their homeland drove them to fight, suffer, and finally prevail over colonial oppressors, and this warmth shines from their faces, whether in Angola, in Europe, or in the States.

Nelson Mandela's face brings me to tears; the South African play *Wossa Albert*, performed by two Africans at Washington, D.C.'s Arena Stage, was like a homecoming–those smoky voices, the movement of bodies, and most incredible considering the circumstances, the capacity for humor.

African music, too, touches a deep wordless chord, even the spoken word does. *Umbundu* and *Shona*, languages of West and East Africa, share the refrain of many a song wafting from the settlements or from the kitchens when the day's work was done; it is a lament,

ma-i-we, ma-i-we, ma-i-we...

Dreams have taken me back to Africa a hundred times; I have walked the hills, smelled again that mountain air laden with burnt savannah, flaming red at sunset. I have seen the herds stampede down the next hill in a cloud of dust. Over and over, I set out for Fazenda Lunda. I turn into the foothills, enter the cover of vegetation. I know the way, yet my dreams never let me arrive....

~*~

I knew nothing of such dreams or of the deep impact Africa would have on my life on the day our ship, the *Tamerlane*, pulled out of New York harbor. Slowly, we entered that netherworld of water, sun, and soothing waves on the South Atlantic between New York and Dakar. Day followed day of sun and sea, solitude and the routine on board. Vati pointed out the ocean's changing colorations, explaining that the deep-green water was filled with seaweed drawn across the Atlantic by the Gulf Stream. Soon we saw flying fish with wing-fins so strong and agile they would jump on board, their scales glistening in the sun like shooting stars.

Then, in the increasingly warm evenings, all twelve passengers, young and old, gathered on deck. I believe most of them were missionaries destined for many places in Sub-Saharan Africa. The stories they exchanged betrayed their hopes and determination as well as their total ignorance of what lay ahead; even as a ten-year-old I could guess that.

Stories were followed by songs–old American hymns or Steven Foster songs dripping with sentiment like moss off a Live Oak. Wrapped inside these sounds was a taste of the racism, benevolent or not, about to be bestowed upon the natives. Did these good people sing to shoo away doubts rising from the night ocean and from the inexorable progress the engines pounded out second by second? We children, no more than two or three, listened quietly. Today I remember these very American, very middle-class and somewhat provincial folks and know they were ill prepared, even if they had brought with them their Bibles and the contents of an entire PX.

When land finally emerged, we hung on the ship's railing not wishing to miss the exotic panorama of the harbor towns along the African west coast–Dakar, Accra. Lagos, Takoradi. In port after port, we watched the unloading frenzy. In the Muslim, northern regions, hundreds of men, tall and gaunt, milled about the docks, dressed in billowing blue or white robes and small caps. They rushed about, shouting, gesticulating. Yet somehow, they made an organized operation out of all this: Cargo did get off the ship, the cranes did turn to the empty truck without killing the bystanders, and traffic did uncurl itself.

Just beyond the dock were a few shabby public buildings and narrow streets with faceless houses, their colorful colonial baroque having long ago succumbed to the all-pervading dust and neglect.

Farther in the distance, minarets delicately rose in sun and twirling sand. Then, suddenly, a sing-song voice arose from there. In an instant all movement stopped. The crane was left in mid-air, truck motors kept running. Out from under the workers' robes came carpets, and within seconds the entire dock was covered with prone men in prayer. After some minutes, the rugs would disappear, the commotion took up where it had left off, and the cranes began to move again. This scene was repeated several times during the work day.

Farther south, the continent gradually changed from the Muslim, and Arab-influenced, world to that of central Africa. The scene changed. Dock workers now were very black, smaller and poorly dressed. The commotion was the same, but no one prayed. White supervisors were much in evidence, rushing around, ordering workers in harsh voices. Young men rowed up to the ship, asking passengers to throw coins to them, for which they would dive.

In harbor after harbor, conditions became increasingly primitive, undeveloped, and poor until they would reach their height (or depth) of deprivation in the Congo, at the time still called Belgian Congo.

On freighters, the

Diving for coins thrown from deck, Takoradi (?)

accommodation and food were first class, the service excellent. The few passengers sat at the captain's table. One night he announced the ship had been ordered into dry dock in Matadi, a city some miles up the Congo River. It needed paint, and the work would take one week to ten days. Since the constant hammering on the metal hull would give everyone migraine, the captain had arranged to put us up at a hotel in town. Now, when traveling on a freighter you have to expect such things; you are warned ahead of time; there is no real schedule of arrivals and departures—it's part of the adventure, and the Congo promised that in rich measure.

If you watch the movie "The African Queen," you get a feel for this African river. The scenes are an archival treasure showing the original state (embellished, of course; it's Hollywood doing the filming). They capture the lazily oozing fluid rolling in a gray-brown mist of heat, vegetation, water, sounds—all coming together as the engine pounds out its rhythm against the current. The boat's noise scares birds out of trees; animals you can't see, but hear, drop off the shore into the water; local inhabitants drift by in canoes. Most of all, you become aware of mud—mud in the water, mud on land; it covers everything. The heated sky itself takes on a brown-yellow tint, almost threatening. If you stop, it may envelop you, smother you, desiccate you.

After a day or two of chugging up-river, we reached Matadi. The hotel was an interesting structure, a few stories high, with a triangular courtyard ringed by balconies that led to the rooms. The restaurant was in this inner courtyard. I just learned that this hotel, once glamorous and famous, is still an imposing landmark, rising high above its low-rise neighbors.

My only other memory of Matadi is a first, devastating encounter with colonial brutality. Belgium is a tiny multi-ethnic country, long ago thrown together as a buffer between France and Holland thus destined to have been the battle ground of all European wars. In Africa, these people found themselves the masters of a region so vast the thought of controlling it must have compelled them to mask their fears with a reign of terror. Also, the financial needs of King Leopold II were monumental.

Vati and I saw the ugly face of colonialism on our first walk through town. Here was a bustle of street life, vendors crouching on the sidewalk, hawking their wares—mostly ivory (the little ivory crocodile on my shelf comes from there). Then, all of a sudden, a large white man in tropical garb, khakis, helmet and all, strutted along the sidewalk. Like the Grim Reaper he swung his whip before him, clearing his path, commanding all locals into the gutter or against the walls. We, too, stepped off the sidewalk. Had he not expected us, or was he just in the throes of his power trip? I asked Vati, and he tried to explain, but could not.

128

The next memory is entering the lovely bay of Angola's capital, Luanda. Situated behind a half-moon spit of beach, the city and its lights glimmered like a string of pearls as we approached it in the evening. We unloaded cargo and next morning continued on to Lobito, our destination. From there we were to take the Benguela Railroad to Ganda (or Villa Mariano Machado to the Portuguese, a name nobody used).

The Benguela Railroad, if I am not mistaken, is the other end of the trans-Africa railroad long ago built by the British and so prominently featured in the 1985 film, "Out of Africa." Here again, a movie is the only way to see what it was like: this toy train, by today's standards, crawling along a track hacked out of the bush, laid across plains, deserts, and over rivers–a fragile and yet powerful assertion of white manifest destiny. Every image in that film is accurate; it meshes with memories, even the sandy heat.

Our ride on that train must have taken some time. Along the way, there was little in terms of settlements. Occasionally native children, leggy and thin, wrapped in long cloths that rarely covered their distended bellies, stopped to see us pass by; so did herdsmen and their animals.

Evening came; our engine was powered by steam from a wood-burning furnace. I know because at times the train stopped, and men loaded wood from huge stacks placed along the track. Then they fired up the kettle again, and we began our ascent into the highlands. In the dark of night, a million sparks rose out of the chimney, flying into the sky like so many stars that had run away from the firmament, a fiery Milky Way that wished to compete with the one up high. Aside from that, the view out the window was one of total darkness–no lights that would have signaled settlements.

I think we arrived in Ganda early in the morning, and all I see is a little girl screaming and crouching in the dry dirt next to the train, because, while I climbed out, my little suitcase of treasures had popped open and paper dolls, dressed in the latest, home-from-the-war fashions, had dropped onto the tracks. There, in the dirt, lay the wasp-waisted all-American blondes with their prom dresses and beach outfits, their wide skirts and wonder-bra tops. I picked them up, surrounded by a circle of onlookers. The train waited; we were, after all, the only white passengers to have gotten off that day.

Memory leaves a blank, but this must have been the moment we first met Christel Gärtner, then about 22-years-old, the daughter of Vati's friend, Carl. The family had settled in Portuguese Angola after being expelled from what they still called *"Deutsch-Ost,"* or German East Africa. As they told it, the Portuguese were the only colonists willing to take in German war refugees, enough of them to form a small but far-flung community.

The Gärtner family visiting Langenhagen, ca. 1936

Over the span of years, the Gärtners built up a sizeable plantation, Fazenda Lunda, even though their hearts and souls were tied to the old colony. Stories of East Africa were nightly entertainment, and memory was kept alive by, for instance, naming each of the hundreds of cattle after rivers, mountains, and towns— the better the cow's pedigree, the more important the name. One of the finest, a half-Holstein, was named Harare.

Christel was an African, if ever a white person could be one—unthinkable anywhere else. She was bound to Africa; it was the core of her existence. She never had formal schooling; all she needed to know she had acquired by working alongside her parents, reading what interested her, doing math by keeping the books, learning science by operating the only first-aid station for miles and miles around, and building up a butter-and-cheese dairy in Angola that weekly sent fresh butter and cheese to Ganda. Never have I met a more creative, resourceful, broadly educated person.

Many years later, in the mid-fifties, she visited us during a rare trip to Europe. She came all the way to Flensburg to see Vati and me, and reported

Fazenda Lunda, 1940s

on raids, killings, and war in areas distant from Lunda. She also told us she had been offered a position at the Tropical Institute in Hamburg as a practical advisor, should she decide to leave the farm.

But, when we said goodbye at the train station, she hugged me, looked at me through her thick, bottle-glass spectacles and said, "Can you see me in a city, not in Africa?" We both shook our heads, and she quietly boarded the train.

Among my papers is a letter she wrote to Mutti shortly after my departure for America in 1960. She wrote in a clear, elegant hand, a hand one would expect from a writer, not an African farmer who had repaired many a truck; she thanked Mutti for a gift of books, among them *Kon-Tiki* by Thor Hyerdahl:

Christel and a visitor, ca. 1950

"Oh, if only one could take such a journey on a raft, or a trip on a camel or some other 'old-fashioned' means of travel. I think Erika too might have such dreams; in the past, at least, we often made plans like that, and now she has taken the first step with her move to America and into new fields of study."

Then her thoughts turned to her farm, and she continued:

"Thank God we can still live in peace here, and in today's world that is the most valuable thing one could wish for. For how long, we ask ourselves, will this be granted?"

All communication broke off after that, and we never heard from her again.

Here I digress again, for I must tell you about a book that has pride of place on my shelves: *Gross ist Afrika* [Great is Africa], by the German travel writer, A.E. Johann. It is very much an old-fashioned, condescending, ode to Africa-the-dream-of-the-white-man, to noble savages and so on.

But there is a chapter I have read a hundred times. It is entitled "Courageous Girl in the Highlands," and it tells of the author's visit to Fazenda Lunda a year or two after we had left. Johann spent some weeks with Menina, the name the black population had given Christel (I think it means Miss. Everyone had a nickname, mine was Camia—no way of knowing what it meant).

Johann's chapter starts with these words: "In the colonies, the good get better, the bad get worse."

He tells of the harsh, almost inhuman, effort of carving an existence out of the land; he describes the ravages of disease, of poisons, of crushing debts, crop failures, termites, droughts–obstacles that often took the lives of those who built the farms. He talks of women prematurely widowed and left struggling on large plantations, miles from towns. There, surrounded by a few native workers, they try to maintain the properties since that is all they have, and eventually they die very much alone. He describes how despair and alcohol make monsters out of those who do not have the strength to prevail.

And then he turns to tell the story of Menina, one of the very best. He evokes all of Fazenda Lunda; its setting: the old veranda with the fireplace where we used to sit at night; he mentions the set of steps leading from there to the main court of the complex, where the sick and needy were sitting from early morning on, asking for help. On the day of his visit, it was the "Flower-Shepherd" who needed care.

Christel treating the "Flower-Shepherd" ca. 1950

Surprised recognition and pain of loss rise in my head and heart, for I knew this boy whose job it was to keep the birds and insects away from old Mrs. Gärtner's three gardens. The story tells of how Flower-Shepherd shows up with a raging fever pleading, "Menina, help me," and how Christel hears the rattle in his chest, guesses on pneumonia, and administers penicillin.

The story continues with a ride to the cattle stations, fording streams, hearing about losses of livestock, efforts to rescue one of the precious half-breed Holsteins that broke a leg and had to be shot–by Menina of course.

At night, returning to the farm, the old truck developed a strong rattle that Christel would have to fix in the morning. Once home, they found more sick natives at the wall, more problems, and the Flower-Shepherd only marginally better.

It's all there, just as it was, and how it has been locked up in my heart for years. Even a photo of Menina is there, in her khaki shorts, white shirt and short dark hair, so I know I'm not making this up. I, too, have a few faded photos.

~*~

Upon our own arrival at Lunda, the greetings must have been celebratory for there were great hopes on all sides. The Gärtners were desperate for expert help in building the plantation, and Vati was desperate to build a life for his family. And so we sat in that truck, slowly snaking our way up the hillsides to the height of two thousand meters with vistas spreading in all directions. No one knew where the property ended; no one cared.

On that first ride, I probably sat between Vati and Christel in the truck's cab. Later on, my place would always be in the back of the old Ford, standing up with my hands on the cabin roof, the wind in my hair (thirty miles an hour was breakneck speed on these roads, and it seemed to me we were flying). At night, I would lie flat on the boards contemplating the night sky lit by stars of outrageous intensity, greeting my friend, the Southern Cross, the constellation Vati had taught me to identify the day our ship approached the equator.

Once settled, our life fell into a routine of hard work for Vati, and total freedom for me. The elevation made Lunda safe from the Tsetse fly that brought the sleeping sickness and also from the Anopheles mosquito that carried malaria. We needed no mosquito nets at night, no daily quinine, only a tropical helmet during daylight.

Lunda was a jumbled aggregate of small brick buildings surrounding the main house to form an irregular, sprawling yard crisscrossed by dirt paths and minimal ornamentation. The kitchen building was some 50 yards down a path, the dairy next to it; guest houses dotted the periphery, and around it all stood the long stables. Compared to the conditions at Vati's first visit, this was imposing.

A herd of dogs and an army of cats were to safeguard us from hyenas, leopards, snakes, mice and rats, in that order. Sometimes they lost these battles, as they did the night the dogs cornered a leopard on the stoop of Vati's cottage, creating a horrible, howling racket. When day came, two dogs were dead, others a bloody mess, the leopard gone.

If Vati was disappointed at the sight of his friends, he did not communicate it to me. Rather, he attacked the building projects, setting up workshops, digging clay pits, molding bricks and roof tiles, one by one; he set up a carpentry shop, trained the native workers, laid out the foundations for new structures. The basic facilities had been there all along but had remained unused and in disrepair for years. For a man who had once built part of the

Fort Tryon subway in New York City, this was going back to basics, but he seemed to relish it, and in the beginning, I was his constant side-kick.

Christel was enlivened by the new energy. Her father, by contrast, was a human shell. Always clad in white tropical suits and helmet, he walked the compound with halting Parkinson-wracked steps, trying to steady his body with a tall staff. To me, his tiny steps and sputtering speech made him threatening and unpredictable, like some Biblical prophet or an avenging god. He was the authority in name only. Daughterly love alone caused Christel to seek his counsel, but he no longer could participate in running the farm in any way.

Christel's mother, the old "Señora," was of no help. Perhaps she had spent too many years under the tropical sun without a helmet. Tall and thin under her giant straw hat, she saw things, heard things, and suffered from *Maculus*–either a germ or a demon that she described as entering her nose and causing great discomfort in her brain. With gaunt, spidery fingers she would point to her nose. She told all who would listen: "This is how they enter, here, up through my nostrils." In spite of all this, the *Señora* ran the kitchen and gardens with gentle authority.

Until Vati and I arrived, the three-some had run this endless spread of land with the help of one white man, Hendrik, a Boer–bony and gaunt as though the African sun had dried him out. He oversaw an army of conscripted contract workers and other black employees. He, too, had fled into exile, first after the Boer War from Transvaal in South Africa, later from the former German Southwest Africa, now Namibia.

I loved Hendrik. He spent years trying to teach me to say "good morning" when I first saw him at breakfast. Why did I keep forgetting? Still, when I hung out around him, perhaps at cattle-calling time, taciturn Hendrik would sing for me, his favorite being the Boer anthem about Sarie Marais, the girl beloved by a soldier.

"*Oh, breng my t'rug na die ou Transvaal, dar woon my Sarie Marais...*" [oh, take me home to old Transvaal; there lives my Sarie Marais].

Hendrik would croak more than sing, but to this day I can hum the tune; it spoke of war, of loss and of loving someone, it spoke deeply to an 11-year-old girl without a mother. On weekends he went home to his wife and eleven children, none of whom I ever saw. This was the extent of white stewardship of Fazenda Lunda. Just how much this differed from what Vati had seen in 1937, I don't know, and he did not let on.

What about Mutti? Thoughts would occasionally be awakened when the rare letter arrived. Vati read it to me, conveying Mutti's longing for us, her thoughtful concern for the future, even her efforts to learn Portuguese in preparation for her eventually joining us. Resourceful as ever, she had found a Brazilian person who was willing to teach her, and her messages were full of hope for a reunion, even the adventure of Africa. One letter remains in memory. She talked about the couple's bond in spite of all obstacles, listing the things that bound them together. And there was one sentence that struck me: "And," she wrote, "it was in August that our child was created..." Many years later I learned to count out nine months.

Did she not tell us until many years later that she had contracted diphtheria and almost died, that she was forced to live with in-laws she had earlier disdained and who now made her suffer for it?

~*~

Is it possible that the process of living runs in simultaneous spirals, both contracting and expanding, sinking into desperation and rising to great exaltation at the same time? It must have been like that, for while Vati's existence entered an ever more narrowing coil, his health rapidly deteriorating, down, down, down in physical pain and lack of options, the spiral of my life broadened, expanded, opened up to experiences beyond the tight bond of the two travelers.

As life on Lunda became a dream for me, and a nightmare for him, our paths also separated. Things were experienced without Vati having provided them. Here, for the first time, he became a marginal figure in my daily life—a thought that today fills me with guilt for I believe I did not help him enough when he needed me.

Daily life on the farm was a heaven of total freedom, total security, and an abundance of experience. I had a small, spare room of my own, very few clothes that needed to be put on in the morning or shed at night, a shirt, a pair of shorts; no supervisors, no routine, no chores or disciplines (did I even brush my teeth? I don't recall). Soon the last pair of shoes from America was too small, so I went barefoot just like the local people, and gradually the soles of my feet

Erika feeding the horse, with its keeper, Custolli, looking on

became as hardened, cracked, and solid as theirs.

Yes, I was alone–certainly, but not lonely. I lived in sweet solitude, my treasure to this day. There was not a child within hundreds of miles (no, let me correct that: there were black children, but they were never allowed to play with a white child). However, there were animals–uncountable cats, dogs, and other strange critters on the ground and in the air. There were fat, black millipedes that would wind themselves into a neat tight circle when poked with a stick. One could check out the gardens where every day another kind of fruit ripened on the trees, waiting for my morning rounds of harvesting and stuffing myself. Utterly safe in this environment, I had hours to wander up the mountain rising behind the farm, or down to the streams.

On those walks I heard wonderful, natural sounds, smelled the sunny grass, caught delicate trails of smoke from fires in far-away savannahs; I found plants that invited all kinds of play, such as the seed-stage of a certain flower that grew off a thick stem to look like a doll's head with shiny long hair. I could sit for hours stroking that hair and trying to braid it, then making some kind of clothes out of leaves and grasses for this imaginary doll. To this day, I am convinced that solitude and time are childhood's great treasures, and my heart aches for children whose daily schedules would put an adult into stress.

Farm workers and Custolli under the "reading tree"

Dangers, if there were any, did not make themselves known. Yes, I had been warned not to walk in dense grass without singing (which supposedly chased snakes away). Yes, I had been told about sand fleas that invade your toes, lay egg sacks under your skin and gradually infect your foot. But none of that kept me from exploring, or best, climbing my favorite tree where I had a seat between branches, a seat that was better and more comfortable than any chair– and more peaceful. There I read a German translation of Conan Doyle's collected works which I found in the living-room cabinet; also, my lifetime favorite, Alexandre Dumas' *The Count of Monte Christo*.

When all was done, or boredom set in, I could always check in with

136

Christel. In fact, I quickly became her shadow, eventually her helper as I learned to take on small chores. Sometimes we would head out to check on the outlying herds; if we drove, I could help push the truck when it invariably got stuck in a stream or rutted mud road. If it was coffee season, I could count the pails of freshly picked beans so the pickers could be paid; the beans were then dumped on a huge cement surface the size of a basketball court, where they were raked about until the shiny, colorful berries turned to shriveled nuts. Eventually, they were bagged and sent off into the world. Somewhere–in Portugal?–they would be mixed in with fancy, more aromatic East African varieties, serving in effect as fillers.

As mentioned earlier, one of Christel's morning chores was to greet and interrogate the row of sick people who invariably sat by the front door–mothers with very ill babies, men with huge sores on their legs, or young people with high fevers, just as they are recorded in Johann's Africa book. My job soon became the bathing of wounds, then applying salves which we made ourselves out of crushed Sulphur pills, Vaseline and iodine (I think). Finally, I became expert at applying bandages. I remember my intense satisfaction when these wounds healed after a series of treatments. Christel reserved for herself the care for contagious patients and the dispensing of injections. Small wonder neither of us ever became infected.

Then there was the afternoon chore of passing out the daily rations to the workers who started forming a line at the storage building–thirty or forty men–thin figures wrapped in brown shawls which they wore over their day-time garment, a pair of torn shorts or pants. From behind an open window of the storage building, we poured a jug of corn meal and one small can of uncooked beans into a tin dish stretched out toward us. That was it. On Fridays the diet was "enriched" by a dried piece of Cod, called *Bacaljaõ*.

Did it ever occur to me that this was all the food deemed necessary for a working man? That's how it was. I never questioned it. Only once did I ask about whether the people ate meat the way we did, and I was told that, yes, at Christmas time some cattle would be slaughtered and the meat distributed.

In the evening, once the food had been handed out, the workers disappeared to their small huts on the periphery of the farm, or to larger villages nearby. There, a secret life was played out. Did whites stay away out of respect, or out of fear? One could see the light of open fires, smoke rising from the valley, the setting sun painting the bare hills a golden red.

Then, lovely singing wafted over the hills and through the bush. Oh, the music! Whether it came from the villages or when sung by my two friends, Custolli, and Manuel, it was melancholy, joyful, and soothing at the same time. Sometimes a small group of house workers joined these two on the stoop, playing a small gourd instrument that brought forth zither-like sounds. And they would sing–laments of longing, of pain, or celebration: "ma-i-we...ma-i-we...ma-i-we...." trailing melodies, voices like velvet, gentle and sweet.

Being a child, I had a somewhat easier way of communicating with the people. In the scheme of things, a child fell somewhere between the white authority figure and a companion, although one kept at a distance. The local population spoke Umbundu, a Bantu language, mixed with some words of Portuguese. Soon I could make out snatches of sentences and communicate. The farm workers did not speak to me, nor did they smile; rather, they averted their eyes as though making contact were dangerous or unbearable, perhaps both. Often, when spoken to, they answered in barely audible murmurs. Many of these workers were conscripted "contractors" who lived on the farm for one year of forced labor. Their families were heaven-knows where. This was the unspoken part of African life, the part that separated humanity from inhumanity. One quickly looked the other way. There were places I knew not to visit–had someone told me that it was out-of-bounds, or was it that tacit understanding shared by colonialists, the same understanding that made a white American child know not to stand in the black line at the ice cream store?

Only to Christel did they speak freely, in fact I soon came to believe they considered her some kind of local saint, or benign ruler gifted with special powers who could be trusted to help; it was a mixture of love and respect tinted by awareness of a great gulf, one however, that did not bring with it fear but awe. You could hear that deference in their voices–not the flat, distant voice generally used for communication with whites, but an easy, gentle, intimate one, reserved for free speech. Fluent in Umbundu, Christel, too, spoke in warm tones, knew the names of all, passed out a ready grin or small joke that would bring a huge smile to the person addressed. Perhaps enough sick babies had survived, enough fevers fought, to give Menina the status of medicine woman and healer, even if her skin color was not right. And it was well known that in times of drought, Fazenda Lunda would pass out food.

My conversations were limited to those with Manuel, Gabriel or Custolli, who had been at Lunda for years. Within the black community they occupied a place of privilege and wealth but might also have been subject to a certain amount of suspicion, as though through their intimate contact with white life, they had themselves taken on some of our color.

They spoke, they joked with the white members, at times confided certain things, and strangely, they expressed loyalty, perhaps because they knew their status depended upon it.

They, as I, had a mixed status. And I must admit, I soon understood this and exercised my power with relish, never stopping, nor being stopped, to think. Through this system a white child could make a black adult jump at her command. How often did I sit on the veranda steps, yelling *"Owawa yategotá!"* [hot water] at the top of my lungs all the way down to the kitchen, and know that within minutes Manuel would appear with a wash basin of warm water? That's how it was done; it did not seem strange.

I believe the Gärtner family were indeed kind masters; never did I see punishment or hear harsh words; but of course, their kindness was played out against the backdrop of Portuguese despotism. The Umbundu's conditions, however, were as close to slavery as they had been in the States, and no one questioned that. Life for the black population was ruled by fears, some of them the demonic ones that had their roots in ancient experience, others imposed by the Portuguese colonists who governed this land through harsh punishment. Servants would allude to it, telling me with a laugh and a rolling of their eyes that, oh, Custolli had done something very bad, he would be sent to Saõ Tomé. Only later did I learn this was a penal colony on an island near the equator, whence no one ever returned, having died of malaria or yellow fever. Or, when referring to small infractions, the men would say that surely, this guy would be hauled to the nearby village of Chicuma, where the *chef do posto* (perhaps the local constable) would dole out a lashing. Thus, order was kept, even though I never saw punishment meted out.

In general, our existence there in the depth of Angola, was insular: A few German neighbors, hours away by truck, a rare drive into Chicuma where a small general store stacked the few items we could not produce ourselves. Rarely did the Portuguese world enter into daily life.

There were the rare visits of two lovely young women from Lobito, Faruka and Maria Elena, and a lunch with some official, a polite, rotund gentleman who sat next to me at the meal and poured olive oil over every inch of my food, telling me, in Portuguese, that this made it go down so much better. Then he taught me to peel an orange with knife and fork, an art I master to this day, when called upon, because, in his words, "One does not touch with one's hands what one eats."

~*~

In general, work on the farm followed a rigid routine from morning to night; tasks demanded by the hour of the day.

For me, age eleven, barefoot, shirt and shorts my only available elegance, every day happened like a wonder, every hour carried its own miracles. One of the highlights, not to be missed, came early evening, when the sun became gentle and golden.

Intense drama unfolded when the herds were called back to the stables for milking. In the sparse savannah of the highlands, these skinny, almost wild, cattle produced a laughable amount of milk beyond that which was first reserved for their nursing calves. To produce the bounty of about six Edam cheeses and a few pounds of butter a week, it took hundreds of cows.

Hendrik was in charge of these herds as well as the milking staff and herdsmen, many of whom were Maasai–tall and gaunt, with unbelievably long legs and the bearing of kings. It was said they came from the east. They appeared untouched by the cruelty of oppression; they wore their long hair, cloths and jewelry with pride and a certain look of superiority they bestowed even on the whites. Whites in turn showed a modicum of respect, perhaps knowing that without these men the herds would not function. The Maasai were in a class all of their own and inspired me with awe and jealousy, although not a one ever deigned to speak to me. For them I did not exist, and had I stood in their path, they would surely have run me over, at least that was my impression.

A senior, Maasai, herdsman

The herds near the house numbered about one hundred or more cows that had recently calved. While with milk, they grazed on the lands around Lunda and spent the nights tied to the sidewalls of their stables. Their intimidating horns, at times as long as two feet each, would make passage down the center aisle a challenge to plain courage. Being gored from both sides always seemed a real likelihood to me, although the herdsmen and milkers appeared to have no fear.

The task of getting the cattle to stable in late afternoon called for Hendrik's and the herdsmen's artistry. As the sun painted the mountains into a red-golden miracle, and the sky turned clear and cool, I knew to find Hendrik who stood on a promontory just below the stables, overlooking the valleys to his right and left, the way a ship captain searches the ocean from top deck. Aching to participate, I was not allowed near the stables. Hendrik, always dressed in white shirt and pants that fluttered wildly around his gaunt body, stopped singing and sternly insisted: "Stand here, next to me, do not move!"

Suddenly, he took on a momentary aura of magic, like some prophet or impresario. Down below, three or four different herds lingered, waiting to be driven into the stables. Their impatiently stamping hooves created clouds of red dust; the wind carried them uphill from the valley.

Then, suddenly, Hendrik would wrest from his narrow chest the most incredible yells, or better high-pitched yodels, that could curdle one's blood. Each one was different and known to one particular group of herdsmen. It was their signal to proceed up the hill and thus prevent a stampede—usually. It was most exciting, but also dangerous, to watch this cloud of dust, hooves, and horns rush up to the farm. Ten minutes of general chaos—yells and moos, and the cows were chained to their spot in the stables. Only then was I allowed to move from his side.

Then the next herd was called. The herdsmen and milkers knew their animals, and nobody ever seemed to get hurt in this bedlam; it was a masterpiece of logistics, and in another world, Hendrik would have been a cop at Times Square or even an air traffic controller.

Milking these cows was a task handled by teams of two men. First, the calf was brought to its mother to "start the milk" as they called it. I never understood how they knew which calf belonged to which cow. Then the milker would do his thing and bring the bucket with the result of each milking to the dairy. There, Christel (and I, of course) recorded the amount and dumped it into the bathtub that served as cheese vat or poured it into the manual centrifuge to make cream for butter. Nice, round Edam cheeses rested on surrounding shelves, some still yellow and drying, others coated with red wax. An acid but pleasant smell of sour milk permeated the dairy, and water always stood on the concrete floor. This milking ritual took easily two hours, for when we emerged from the dairy, it was dark—night coming fast in Africa.

Come Friday morning, butter and cheeses were wrapped in banana leaves, packed in boxes and carried to Ganda on the heads of the regular spear-carrying messengers who returned on Sunday morning with the mail. I remember marveling at the messengers' weapons (needed, I was told, since they would cross the territory of several not so friendly tribes) and was in awe of the fact these men would complete this weekly round-trip of one hundred-and-twenty kilometers in exactly three days.

Waiting for the milkers was the serene part of the day when Christel finally had time to pay attention to me. We would talk, and we became friends. There was no adult for her to communicate whatever may have been in her own mind, that private life to which we are all entitled; there was no such place in her harnessed existence. Neither mother or father could be counted on for human exchange. Christel's conversations surely went way over my head, but I was proud to listen and venerated her even more for the honesty of her attention.

When there was nothing to say, we played the recorder. Patiently she taught me, and soon we were able to play a little Bach, some folk tunes from music sheets she must have hoarded since childhood.

Oh, how I loved the triumph of being able to create sounds of my own, far from Mutti's piano. The recorder, like my books, often accompanied me to my perch in the tree where I sat, like Pan, playing to myself and the herd of mangy dogs, the uncountable cats, and the fat old turkey who mirrored himself in the dairy window, never tiring of his reflection, until one day he died by keeling over on the spot.

Remember the carts pulled by a train of oxen in the film "Out of Africa"? We had the lumbering, slow creatures, horns longer than a man's arm, eyes dull, any sense of animal pride long ago expunged from their being, their heads tied to a bar immediately behind the tail of the oxen in front. The driver cracks his long whip, the noise and sting of which barely setting the train into motion? The dust? The drama? Yes, we had that too, for beside the aging Ford truck, oxen were the mode

An oxen train on the farm

of transport. Again, the oxen drivers knew how to control this accumulation of beastly strength. I gave them distance; feared them.

~*~

Writing this text (mostly in the very early hours of morning) is of course a journey, an intense second life or undercurrent of the normal day. I still work on my art history research project, still carry on that small consulting job here and there. I still vacuum the floors and shop for dinner. Half of me lives in the present, but the other half is removed to images of the past. It is a healing and yet disturbing process; it evaluates and lends new meaning to events.

Is that good? I don't know; some memories have suddenly lost their innocence, and some of my parents' actions have had to suffer the judgment of a now-fellow adult.

How do I explain what a privilege this process is in late years; it is my husband's greatest gift to me. He allows me the time and leisure but also musters the tolerance that lets me dwell in that other place he does not share.

So, recently I revisited the small photo album that Christel had carefully stitched out of grass-cloth and painted with a scene of two giraffes. It was her goodbye present, some photos of Lunda and its great vistas.

There also are photos of our leisure activities, for in Africa, without radio, newspaper, even electricity, you provided your own entertainment. And strangely, these photos bring up a side in Christel that could not be recognized since her daily life was that of the farm's CEO. Yet, this young woman of about 22, was in essence still a teenager wanting to play and have some fun, or did she organize our little theatrical events just for my benefit and that of the occasional young visitors? Anyway, photos show our performance of a foursome Rococo minuet. Dressed up as fancy 18th-century dancers drawn from our best resources, we performed in one of the gardens before the other adults during Sunday afternoon coffee.

I remember weeks of anticipation, preparation, and excitement. Sometimes, a young woman visitor, the daughter of Swiss Baptist missionaries who lived a few hours away, played the accordion. The visiting children had been brought from the coastal lowlands, seeking health and cool air. Sadly, the young boy, one of the dancers, died shortly after this visit, unable to recover from yellow fever.

Sunday afternoon dance performance with visiting children

Who Needs School?

At some point, someone had the idea I needed school and, indeed, there was one in Angola–a boarding school that served the few remaining Germans who had settled there in the aftermath of World War I, a subculture within Angola.

These German settlements were far flung and too distant to constitute a social circle, no matter how spare. We had a few "neighbors" if one can apply this term to the one farm barely visible in the far mountain ranges. It was the

143

closest but least connected to us, owned by a former big-game hunter and animal catcher for German zoos. He looked like Hemingway—a massive, burly man whose cottage was all zebra and lion skins strewn on the floors, thrown over chairs, and hanging from the walls. Antelope heads with huge antlers and glass eyes peeked out from between the skins. There were guns and booze, and, hidden from view of the visitors, a black woman whose work in the next room could not be ignored. He probably embodied the African mystique as it lived in the daydreams and fiction of certain Europeans; in fact, his was a desperate, lonely exile, and everything about this man, from his voice to his massive boots, scared me to death.

Other neighbors included a widow, alone on a farm, who lived in constant terror of being poisoned by the natives. Once she told me she was sure her doorknobs had been painted with poisons that were smeared on the tips of spears and were so strong that casual contact meant death; another time she was convinced poisonous snakes were hidden in her bedroom. Poor soul; she was probably the only one who clearly saw the future as it was about to begin.

Erika dressed up for boarding school

Judging by these examples, the Germans served by the school were a disparate lot, some the adventurer descendants of German noble families, others expats trying to survive. Yet their numbers, spread over hundreds of miles, were substantial enough to fill a school of about 40 children, age 8 to 14. I can imagine that under Hitler it had been supported by funds from the "motherland" for propaganda purposes.

The school, a former farm, consisted of a dormitory, a classroom building, playing fields, even a pool (make that a swimming hole) and a dining hall, the main house having been converted to teacher residence. All in all, it was a pleasant layout on a lovely hillside. There was a director and his wife, both educators, and two additional teachers, a young blond man, and a pretty Portuguese woman placed at the school by the colonial government to satisfy the rule that Portuguese be taught as a second language. By 1947, however, this school had fallen on hard times, having to subsist on tuition and occasional gifts from wealthier planters.

Now, this far in my academic record, school had not been a major success: air raids in Graz; nuns in the mountains, boredom in Westchester County, and no matter where, there always remained the painful chore of having to fight one's way into a new social context. I was most reluctant.

But the day came when I was loaded onto the truck. I can't recall whether Vati was still well enough to bring me, but I doubt it; I would have remembered that.

The dormitory had two rooms, one for boys, one for girls. Numerous beds lined the walls, each with a mosquito net. This little tent and the immediate few square feet surrounding it, were one's private sphere. Some girls had decorated their areas with photos of pets and family, I had nothing to put up.

To describe our day-to-day lives, Miss Hannigan's discipline in the musical "Annie" comes to mind. We were told just how to fold our clothes over the end of our bedstead, just how to make our beds. Still today, I cannot put down a pair of shoes without lining them up exactly. Order in the room was maintained by a supervising teacher and a student militia, a rotating honor job earned by the orderly and pliant. Once, when I lied that I had indeed brushed my teeth, and the teacher found my brush to be dry, she slapped my face, and it burned all night.

In general, I failed at all routines. After all, I had just gotten used to having servants do all my personal chores, so I never made my bed, never put away my clothes. For punishment the militia upended my mattress and threw all my things the floor. I, in turn, slept on the bare mattress and did not pick up my stuff.

This battle was nothing compared to the chore of fitting into the strictly organized hierarchy of school mates. There were little runners-along (mostly the youngest kids), girly cliques that played with dolls and wallowed in catty gossip, and finally the ruling mob of the biggest boys and a few athletic girls.

All categories were dangerous in their own way, for they could hurt you with taunting or plain old beatings–and after a few days of circling around me and checking me out, all three cliques made these things happen.

The catty girls could not be changed, for girls of that bent grow up to be just that. Taunting by the "big guys" came next; it led to beatings–the most elementary and direct of social encounters, and the most significant within the power structure. Just as in America, I found myself surrounded by a circle of kids poking at me and pulling my hair, except this time the taunts were in German. (Had I acquired an accent?) In my rage, I lunged at one of the boys, pounded, kicked, bit as best I could. I remember rolling in the dirt in a mean wrestling match. As it had in earlier encounters, my strength came as a surprise to the bullies. Indeed, I was eventually invited into this elite club, an honor declined, a status I retained. To this day I am proud of my physical strength. Even illusions of strength can be protective.

Scornful of the lot of them, I was saved by a tiny group of two or three girls called the *Leseratten*, the "reading rats," those who preferred to spend off hours lying on their beds and reading, in effect remaining outside of the social structure and quietly escaping into another world. Now there was a place I could appreciate, and what little friendship and support boarding school offered, came from that corner. We passed books back-and-forth among ourselves, yet rarely talked–too busy reading.

In this God-forsaken corner of the earth, in an environment of decay and neglect, one would expect little in terms of education, but the miracle of good teaching and good learning happened. The multi-age learning groups were small, concentration was demanded, and teacher-student interaction was generally friendly. We did not mind the daily chore of school. Here we learned the structure of language from the Portuguese teacher, Irene, who taught us conjugation and the tenses; here we learned what was a *dativo* and a *genetivo*. We had math, science and literature, memorized poems. Best of all for me was the rigor, the intense focus and concentration that were demanded–a gift, or attitude, that proved helpful all through life.

And then there were long hours of recess, swimming in the pond and endless games of robbers and princesses. Our range of play was limited only by very strict orders not to go beyond the campus confines for there were snakes, leopards and hyenas. Since we could hear them at night, we knew this was not just an empty threat cooked up by the adults. Attack by the local population did not seem to have been a concern. Here, too, the colonial structure of fear still worked well.

Perhaps there was private funding and some support from the Portuguese government to satisfy the law of general education, but oversight never became apparent to us students.

There was one exception to this general neglect: The Portuguese health department saw the need to vaccinate all children for smallpox, so one day a doctor and nurse appeared. We were all lined up outside the dormitory, and the officials walked along the line hitting each child in the thigh, one needle for all of us, the syringe refilled after each use.

The reason I remember this and remember being shocked, is that I had watched Christel numerous times at our little health station in Lunda. We had an old set of needles and syringes, carefully packed in a metal container, and whenever she had to give a shot to one of the many sick people, we unwrapped the sterilized box, touched the needles with the sterilized tweezers. After use, it was my job to re-wrap and boil all equipment.

Here, at school, all adults stood and watched a single needle being used.

Memory tells me that all other children did okay under this treatment; perhaps long exposure to Africa makes you immune to just about anything. The new kid was not immune. Within days, my thigh became red, ridiculously swollen, and painful. Since the "doctors" were long gone, there wasn't much to be done except wrap cool cloths on my leg and put me to bed. Did anybody bother to notify my father? Did anybody worry that I might die? In Africa death is all around, a constant presence that creates an almost casual equanimity, the natural selection in the herd. In Africa, we are all the same.

In general, I hated the place, with my most intense rage centered on the lack of freedom and adult companionship. Of course, there were good moments, too. One was my garden, a small plot where any child could plant seeds or cuttings from the main garden. I grew radishes, carrots and carnations, the very first experience of sticking something into the ground and seeing it grow. This point was very important to me. Today I am privileged to dig a hole, set in a plant, water it, talk to it, watch it bloom. My garden is my sandbox.

Another positive development (not that I saw it that way) was the sudden and wholly unexpected experience of becoming the chieftain's moll. Not inclined toward the fascination with things sexual (the domain of the girl clique), I was genuinely surprised when one day, in the hallway, the school's head guy—age fourteen, tall, the master of the students but not too smart—cornered me. He pushed me into the line of coats hanging along the wall and kissed me, telling me that I was now his girl.

Was this some papal blessing, or an ancient rite bestowed upon me? Since I was a new kid, anything was possible. I wiped my face, walked away stunned; I could not remember talking to him or even looking at him in any interested way. Now, however, I could not help noticing the societal sea-change, for rumor ran wild: suddenly I occupied a place of power and respect. No more catty remarks from the doll-girls; the young gang respectfully cleared the way for me and appeared grateful to carry out whatever tasks I may give them.

The only disinterested ones were my fellow "reading rats," and I liked them all the more for it. I do not remember the boy's name, but he reappeared again later, at Lunda, when his alcoholic father, a pot-bellied, foul-mouthed Bavarian, was briefly employed by the farm as a supervisor and lost his job within weeks. There seemed to have been no mother.

Nothing helped banish my general misery at school; it began to close in on me. Was it never having any mail, never a visitor, missing Vati, missing Mutti, missing Lunda? I notice in writing that this story has become all about my own experience, not that of my life with father or mother. For the first time, I think, I was truly alone, and one evening in the dining hall, without external provocation, my inner structure collapsed, and I broke into choking sobs.

Everyone fell quiet. The director's wife, who acted as mother figure for all of us, came over and, arms around me, took me for a long walk. For the first time someone seemed to notice, even showed interest in my situation. She wondered why nobody had visited me and was genuinely surprised when she learned my mother was in Germany, somewhere, my father too ill to travel–had nobody remembered to tell the school? Had the administration not informed the staff of the lives of their charges? Was it un-Germanic to worry about the children's burdens? At that moment, however, there was real sympathy, but also cheerful indomitability. The message was that we have to carry on, somehow–but it came too late for me.

The first quarter ended, and I packed everything, determined not to return. Once back at Lunda, I declared that if they made me return, I would run away at night, for I much preferred to be eaten by the leopards than spend another day at that place. My words must have carried some weight. Another victory over structured education. Now real learning could start, and it did.

At Lunda time was nebulous, fluid; it was counted by the day, not the hour; by the seasons, not the month. The sequence of events floated in this general mist, and memory dishes up single moments: the sound of the dogs howling at hyenas at night, the hours when we all sat together in the veranda, the rainy season dumping water onto the farm, turning it into a river. At other times, memory is seared into the brain by its numbing emotional power.

Time at Lunda had in fact taken on absurd shape for all who lived there. For old Mr. Gärtner it must have shrunk to the scale of the endless minutes it took him to lift a trembling spoon from his plate to his mouth, a minute that stopped all conversation while everyone around stared in fascination, wondering just how much of the food on this spoon, or coffee in that cup, would reach its destination. Time for him was just the span up to the point when all this would end–secretly observed and mourned, but never discussed.

For his wife, time had ceased to matter entirely, punctuated only slightly by her realization that on Sundays she would retreat to her garden to "do church" as she called it, either alone, or with me as her congregation. Seated on a small stone wall under a grove of coffee trees within the flower garden, she read a passage from the Bible determined by the *Losung* calendar. Only recently, during a conference in Ephrata Cloister, where Lutherans and

148

Moravians gathered, did I learn what that is: a calendar that guides the Pietist through the year with readings, thoughts, prayers, and songs, inviting contemplation and devotion. In Lunda we did not have an annual supply of new *Losungen*. Mrs. Gärtner had simply used the same calendar year in and year out. Did she realize that? It surely did not matter, for we happily searched the Bible and the Catechism for good passages and rolled them around in our mouths. When we came to the suggested choral for the day, she led us two in song with a breathy but crackling voice that was a pure reflection of her gentle personality. Afterward, we took a stroll through the garden admiring whatever flowers had just opened for the day–Pantheism of the finest, most natural kind–my only true religion.

For Vati, time must have become a burden that would have rendered weaker men insane or driven them to suicide. He could no longer walk, no longer even stand upright; pain wracked his whole body, and there were no medications, no doctor, no exit.

He occupied one Spartan bedroom in a little cottage, more a brick hut, a hundred steps from the main building. There was no electricity anywhere in Lunda, only storm lamps and candles. Servants were assigned to tend him, and rare visitors made it up the hill to see him. On my daily morning rounds, I stopped by his room; I admit with shame I did not always go there voluntarily but was called by a servant.

Did I not realize I was Vati's only lifeline, perhaps the fragile thread by which he held on to his sanity? I would find him sitting on the edge of his bed, looking out the window so he could see me coming up the path. When I entered, his crystal blue eyes lit up, and a smile would pass over his face, no matter how terrible the

Vati's cottage

pain of his swollen joints that had frozen his arms and legs into bizarre contortions.

His time must have been endless, punctured by pain, by the recognition of grave miscalculation, and the realization time was running out. Was it 1948 (later or earlier?) when he realized we had to leave Africa? When did he first ask himself whether he should wait and hope to get better or make a break–but

149

to where? To Germany in ruins? To America where he could no longer work? What resources he once had were either lost, confiscated, or destroyed. If he were to get them back, he would have to fight for them. Gradually, talk about bringing Mutti to Africa stopped.

In this desperate situation, there arose a certain estrangement from the Gärtners who, themselves struggling for sheer survival, did not want to pay Vati's salary nor did they feel responsible for paying for our travel out of Africa. Brief references on Vati's part gave a hint.

Yet, all this did not affect my own daily life, for somehow both Vati and Christel managed to keep the weight off my shoulders. Only today can I begin to guess the heroic effort it must have cost my father not to lash out against his condition, his friends, or perhaps against me. Rather, I would walk into his room, and he invited me to sit on his bed beside him.

Most of the time we talked, or he would show me pictures in *Life* magazine that some friend kept sending from America. One day he showed me a photo of Ingrid Bergman, saying, "Look, Ingrid Bergman. Isn't she beautiful? You have the same eyes, the same nose, the same face; some day you will be as beautiful as she is." Any image of Bergman—and that scene in Vati's room rushes forth.

If a rare letter from Mutti made it through the post-war mail system, Vati read it to me. She, too, at another end of the earth, suffering illness, rejection, and abject poverty—she too refused to be defeated. These letters contained no bad news that I can remember. Did they reflect any plans being made to reunite us, no matter how impossible the thought?

Vati sometimes asked me to read to him, probably as some kind of educational effort aimed at me, and a banishment of desperation for himself. Mostly, however, he talked about the past. Sometimes we sang. "Solveig's Song" from Edvard Grieg's Peer Gynt Suite was a favorite: *Ich hab es versprochen, ich harre treulich Dein...*[I gave you my word, I would faithfully wait for you...] Also big was *Dein ist mein ganzes Herz, wo Du nicht bist mag ich nicht sein...*[yours is all my heart; where you are not, I will not be, by Franz Lehar...]. Or he sang soldier songs from World War I. and told about the trenches in France and about coming home and finding his talents and training were unwanted.

Among his many lectures (for that is what they were, the most intense learning) was a lesson in tolerance. Vati told me about the Dreyfus Affair—his beliefs, his outrage, and his admonishment never to fall prey to such propaganda. Today I wonder: how could a man so ill, so isolated, so at the end of the road, still muster the intellectual energy to raise this subject to his unwilling child, whose thoughts at that point were directed at the next adventure on the farm?

On Sundays, two servant helpers would get him dressed and carry him to the main house on a chair outfitted with two long carrying poles. He joined all of us for breakfast or for the occasional visit by neighbors or travelers. The brief respite from utter isolation seemed to cheer him up, and he enjoyed talking. Only once did I see him lose his composure, and the memory is seared in my brain in the form of rage at the person who innocently caused it.

It was Vati's birthday. Tradition had it that all gathered on the porch, had coffee and cake, and brought a gift or two. The ceremony required that all sing what Mrs. Gärtner called the "Birthday Song," the Lutheran hymn, *Lobe den Herren, den mächtigen König der Erden...* [Praise the Lord, the mighty King of Earth...] which contains the verse that God blesses us with such gifts as He sees befitting.

At these words, Vati burst into uncontrollable sobs, trying to shield his eyes with hands so stiff they could no longer reach his head. One by one, the voices of the assembled trailed off into stunned silence. I ran to Vati and buried his head in my arms, glaring at Mrs. Gärtner, and stroking his hair until he calmed down.

We never did that again, and Vati came to the main house even more rarely. Instead, he was a virtual prisoner in that one room—a bed, a washstand, a dresser, a table and chair by the two windows overlooking the farm buildings—left to die in central Africa.

Here I must inject the present and tell you I can write this only at night, in the dark. It is as though daylight may pale the images, as though day might add cheer to thoughts too dark to be exposed and thus becoming absurd, or fake, or worse, self-pitying. I rise, driven by dreams or by the gradually increasing pain of arthritis—a tangible legacy, my haunting inheritance. Like a blind person, I have learned to walk the house in the dark, feeling each corner as I approach it, counting the steps to the kitchen, there to make a cup of coffee, hoping never to wake my husband. I cannot talk to him about what I write; he already knows too much, has had to carry too much of my burden, forever throwing his love of life against my Nordic melancholia.

The furtive moments of night, here in my office, in the room that has become the home of my brain, are safe to confront the contents of memory. To report all that happened, would be to sink into a litany of terrible decline and sadness. There was a futile trip to a regional Portuguese hospital, where Vati and I stayed for some time. There was having to watch how his range of motion grew narrower day by day, the pain greater at the same rate. All this within the context of a child's glory of life in utter freedom and beauty. Today the contrast is almost unbearable to contemplate, at the time it seemed just normal. For me there were still the cows, the cats, the gardens, the books in the library, and the wonderful hours of hanging around Christel and her chores.

Namibia

Best of all, there was a fabulous trip by truck to the South, into what we still called German South-West Africa, now Namibia, and a region resplendent in wildlife and moonscape desert. Christel needed a horse, hers having died from some disease that reaped all horses eventually. A neighbor, young Ewald by name, was to go along, and I was sent as a chaperone. The idea had been that these two people were to try out whether they could get to like each other and perhaps eventually marry and combine their farms. I remember Ewald as tall, dark-haired and quite handsome, although I can't remember him addressing a single word to me directly. Who had decided that I come along as "cover?" Whom were they trying to appease?

On the appointed day, Ewald showed up with his truck; we loaded stuff in the back, sat me on top, and off we went, heading south. If I was to police the pair for the sake of decency, it did not work. I remember traveling mostly at night to avoid the heat of day and finding a friendly farm where we could rest during the day.

On the flatbed truck, I stretched out in a sleeping bag and studied the riotous display of stars. The truck under me bounced around, but the stars were solid, so tightly packed together and silent, one could think they were a protective blanket over our earth (no starry night since has ever come close to those in Africa). Come morning, I could watch the herds of zebras rumble by, see giraffes nibbling in tall trees, antelopes heading for the water spot.

Whether we were gone a day or a week, whether we ever stopped at hotels, I can't tell, just that fantastic rumble through the bush, through stretches of desert, fording empty rivers, heaving the truck out of mud and getting splattered all over. Eventually we found a horse. Danger? What danger?

Leaving Paradise

Sometime late in 1949, Vati began to prepare me for the trip back to Germany. I was not kept informed of details, or who had set wheels in motion back in Germany, just that we would take a ship to Portugal and continue from there. Vati made local arrangements with Christel's help.

When the day came, a taxi arrived on the farm–three days earlier than expected since the ship's schedule had changed. In a great hurry, we loaded Vati and our few possessions into the car, hugged everyone, and left.

I was dazed with despair, and tears came in rivers, never stopping on the long car ride to the coast. Once in Lobito, the harbor town, we somehow got Vati into a hotel, there to await the arrival of the *Patria*, Portugal's proudest ship.

During those days, in this sun-splattered, sleepy city, Vati asked me to run some errands to banks and to the ship's offices. I remember being terrified, but I also realized that mine were the legs that had to do the running. I was 12 years old, walking the streets in a strange town, in a society that never allowed young girls to do so, certainly not a white girl. At one point, two nice elderly ladies stopped me and clucked at me, saying in Portuguese they were sorry to see me *toda sozinha* (all alone), but no one ever harmed me.

Erika's passport photo for the return trip, fall, 1949

The day we embarked, we arrived at the dock to find the usual confusion. There, before us, was the huge hull of the ship, rising and gently heaving in the sea. We saw no real gangplank by which to enter, only a long swaying stair that hung along the ship's side. No way for two men to carry Vati up that narrow ladder. So we stood at the dock: Vati on his stretcher, me crying, next to our luggage. People were gathering around, and many suggestions floated. Nothing worked. Finally, a tall Norwegian sailor from a nearby ship, stepped forth, took my six-foot-six father in his arms like a baby and walked up the many steps. Folks cheered and clapped, I remember trembling at the sight.

Somehow, we got into our cabin, somehow our luggage arrived there, too. Somehow, we said our goodbyes to Africa–Vati trying to get a last glimpse through the porthole of our cabin, I hanging on the railing upstairs and seeing the harbor slowly recede until it was only a narrow stripe between sky and water, numbed by a sadness that hung on for years and only gradually converted itself into memories that became more precious with passing time.

But we were on the road again, on a ship no less. During this trip north, we stopped at only a few harbors since this was a passenger ship. I recall only the brief glimpse of the Canary Islands through our porthole, Vati and I craning our necks to see the Pic a Tenerife gliding by. Later, I even got to see the lovely island of Madeira, taken along by some friendly passengers. And when we finally arrived in Lisbon, it was Christmas time.

Lisbon in the winter of 1949 was not the charming, somnambulant and poetic town tourists love to visit today. I do not recall seeing candy-colored stucco buildings and palm trees, parks where old men sit sunning their bones, stroking the cat and reading poetry; it was melancholy and yet glamorous in that way of ancient Mediterranean cities.

That wet and cold December, Lisbon was gray, dank, impoverished, and sullen. It had not been bombed, but lingering, corrupt dictatorship and war had left a general sense of decay and neglect. Most of all, perhaps, the city had recently ceased to be the port of last resort out of which uncounted refugees from Nazis and the war could gather in search of a boat to anywhere. Remember the last plane to Lisbon in "Casablanca"?

Vati and I, returning from years of news hibernation in Africa, knew little about that. We stayed in an old hotel in the lower city, the rooms and halls dark and gloomy, the windows looking out at buildings that were the same. Vati had his meals brought to the room; I sat alone in the dining room at a small table, feeling very grown up.

Again, Vati had to ask me to do errands for him, verify with the airline office that indeed we had a flight to the north in a few days; go to the bank to get money with which to pay the hotel. As he had done in Angola, he clad these outings in the guise that it would be fun for me to see the city.

That was fine with me. I had never gotten lost before, so he knew I would find my way back to the hotel. The lessons in Portuguese I received from Senhora Irene at the German school in Angola came in handy indeed.

Yet, in a desperate effort to protect me, Vati took a small lapel pin of an American flag from his jacket and attached it to my coat, saying, "This is the American flag; it will show people in the street that you are an American. It will protect you because nobody wants to hurt an American." I thought that was funny. But he insisted, instructing me to point to it and let people know I was an American, should anything arise that caused me to be afraid.

Again, he assured me: "This will keep anyone from trying to harm you, but first, please go to the black market and change some money, the banks do not give us true value."

From the proceeds, he promised, I could buy myself something pretty (I chose an embroidered Portuguese blouse, with little dancing couples on the front and an embroidered handkerchief that I still have.)

On that walk around town, I suddenly realized Christmas was coming. Christmas, which had been so marvelous at Lunda, with a huge tree I had chosen from among those in the garden, which I had helped decorate to the tunes emanating from the old Victrola. There had been singing, party games and wonderful food. Never mind, that the same ten records had been played for at least forty years, that the party games were played not at a party, but with the same five people, the white people who made up the household. There even were presents.

Now, here in Lisbon, I had barely registered the fact it would be Christmas. There were the shabby stores, their windows draped with dusty golden garlands that had seen many a holiday. There were few things in the shop windows. I was contemplating a few items that may be nice to have in our hotel room, things I might be able to buy with my reward for this errand. There was nothing enticing to be seen.

As I studied the displays, I noticed a man who also studied the window. In the reflection of the glass I could see he was tall, his sunken face gray and hidden by a large hat and turned-up collar. His frame was covered by a long coat, too large for his body. I turned away and went on to another shop window.

At long last it occurred to me that indeed we had been studying windows together for some time and that he did not look at the merchandise but at me.

Fear suddenly struck me; I turned a few corners, crossed a street, only to realize he was still behind me. Finally, I entered a shop to buy a trinket in order to see whether this man was indeed following me. I came out, and there he was.

So, I did as Vati instructed me: I pointed to my lapel flag and said "American." He looked at me, looked at the pin, turned around and hurried away. It took many years before I understood the global reach of America's power at the time, but I benefited from it that day. I have wondered many times since then whether he was a spy, a government informer, a robber or, most probably, a child molester.

After that, I no longer wished to explore the city. Vati and I sat in the hotel room.

Only once more did I venture out, and that was to buy a candle. It was Christmas Eve, and it seemed to me a candle was necessary to celebrate; I set it on the dresser at the foot of Vati's bed (I can still see the grey-veined marble top, the dingy wall behind it, the cramped room). In the evening we two lit the candle; we knew better than to sing Christmas songs, but we sat silently together, looking at the light for a very long time and feeling great harmony and love. Searching in a child's memory, I detect no sadness. I kissed Vati and said *"Frohe Weihnachten,"* and he did the same. There was no fancy dinner, no presents, no visitors, and yet this is the Christmas I remember above all others.

Where did this man draw the strength not to collapse in rage and despair? His body broken into aching parts and deformed joints so swollen they had a shine on the skin when I rubbed them with powder. His arms could no longer lift sideways, his knees no longer unfold completely, his ankles and feet now misshapen and gnarled, pointing in different directions. Yet his eyes had the same glint when we spoke, and there was unspoken acceptance, nay, an almost animal, instinctive stoicism. Or was it pride–which he had in abundance–that would not allow questions?

My father was not a religious man in the accepted, churchly manner. But yes, he had an inner life of connectedness to the spirit in all things, just as our ancients in the North had venerated all that existed, from stones and trees to man. Long before Christians ever appeared in our regions our people had a gnostic spiritualism that resurfaced again and again in German history, be it the medieval mysticism of Johannes Tauler and Meister Eckhart, or in the intensely personal, "inner light" of the Pietists that shunned outward displays of faith. And the farther north you search, the more intense is the presence. I believe these attitudes survived efforts of organized religion to suppress them or place them in their own service. I believe there lay the source of Vati's strength to endure. Never directly, but in conversations about the land, about animals, about his youth, even about his hopes for me, would this veneration and connectedness to a life of the spirit shine through.

And now, thinking back, the question arises: Why were we going back to the North? Was it mere necessity? Had Germany become the last secure place where, due to his German birth, he could benefit from the new democracy's health program, where he might be able to regain a fraction of his financial losses, perhaps even find healing? I am sure logistics were being discussed in letters between Vati and Mutti and other relatives, but I suspect it was also a spiritual homecoming. There was, after all, a house in Flensburg, high on a hill overlooking the city, the only one of his possessions that had not been confiscated, not bombed, and that had occupied his young dreams of success.

As we were gradually approaching this goal, flying from Lisbon to Zurich and from there on to Hamburg, a connectedness of thought between my parents must have risen with the increasing proximity; like the two lives in that moving tale, *Cold Mountain* by Charles Frazier. Two people's travels have a common goal that is measured in miles, but more importantly, in emotion and inner monologue. The progress of the journey has steeled and changed them into new beings so that they may enrich the joining and each other. In their case it was not the meeting again of young lovers, but a couple who knew fate had meant them to live out their years together.

In its outward manifestation, this growing together took the form of logistics; gradually, without my being aware of it, support systems were coming into play, and I no longer had to be an active participant. We arrived in Hamburg where things had been arranged for us; we arrived in Kiel, and a famous clinic was ready to accept Vati for treatment. Mutti—where had she been all this time? Why did she not greet us in Hamburg? Was she ill? Most likely, she was trying to gather whatever financial resources could be found in this desperate time just six months after the establishment of the new currency, when everyone, rich and poor, young and old, was handed a few bills with which to start a new life. Mutti was most likely trying to find a home, or anything that would pass as a home, for her arriving husband, now an invalid, and a twelve-year-old child, now a stranger.

Postscript

In September 2014, I was once again trolling Google Earth in my search for Lunda when it occurred to me to expand my reach by going to German Google and simply type in the words Christel Gärtner.

And there, inside a travel report of a Swiss family camping in a park in Namibia, was a reference to a 90-year-old lady, Christel, a refugee from Angola now living on a guest farm owned by a German family.

Words fail.

A telephone call brought joy and connection, and now letters can flow. When I called Christel, I heard about her need to leave all she owned on that Angola farm, and join the caravan of white refugees heading for Namibia, the country just to the south where numerous Germans still lived. She settled on an outpost of that safari farm, cared for by the family and was doing well.

In fact, on the phone she pointed out that tomorrow she would be on her way out to drive her herd of six cows to summer pasture (their summer) but why did I not come to visit? We could do these things together, as we had always done: hike in the steppe, watch the animals, sit and talk in the cool of the evening. Indeed, a small photo showed her outdoor kitchen, actually no more than a shed with roof and open sides.

Sadly, her invitation to visit comes too late. I no longer have a safari in my bones. It does not matter, the fact that she is alive and was able to escape is all that counts. I am so very happy about that.

Chapter 7

Flensburg

The Return

It was a reunion of the defeated. Both family and nation were groping for steady footing, a bag of bones, quite literally in Vati's case, metaphorically when it came to all of Germany. Our return in the last days of 1949 brought together a family on the brink of death and despair. Vati was now a paraplegic due to lack of medical care in Africa, a man who had lost every single resource that had once defined him: stature, pride, wealth. We encountered Mutti, an ailing woman who had suffered years of homeless existence; myself, I was no more than a confused teen who lacked basic education.

As to Germany, how could a people so deeply rooted in the land's history, so gifted and energetic, have fallen to such depth of cruelty, allowed themselves to be led by mad men, partially forced by terror, partially happy to cooperate? Now traumatized in body and soul, the survivors were left to face questions, grave questions, that would reside in the depths of their soul and strangle their voices throughout their lives.

Toward war's end, a massive stream of refugees had arrived in Schleswig-Holstein, the northernmost state of Germany. Displaced eastern Germans arrived from hundreds of miles away, doubling the local population by over one million. They had walked, ridden in trains half filled with corpses, climbed on boats in icy waters, only to have the vessels sunk in the Baltic. One ship, the *Wilhelm Gustloff*, attacked by Russian torpedoes in January of 1945, took with it 9,000 souls, mostly refugees: It is recorded as history's single largest loss of life at sea.

Perhaps it was the shared nightmare that allowed survivors to move forward. People rarely talked about their plight, their experiences; stoic acceptance was the only possibility. Since the end of the war, women had stood in line for hours. They returned home with their shopping nets not filled and plump, but drooping with only a potato or two, the day's meal. Few small children played in the streets, for had the men not been away for years, had they not died? There were so few fathers.

Gradually, signs of recovery now appeared, sparse goods became available for purchase through the Marshall Plan–the single wisest and most magnanimous act ever voted on by Congress.

Our family fit right in: Hurt, damaged, impoverished.

Healing

Once our plane from Lisbon had landed in Hamburg, Vati was transferred to a hospital in the city of Kiel, most likely through the good work of an aunt and uncle who had lived there for decades. Miraculously, the Lubinus Clinic was up and running; people were being healed. Famous for its work with

orthopedic ailments, the hospital managed to obtain modern treatments, all of which were applied to Vati's painful condition: gold injections, physical therapy in hot tubs, the first modern efforts at stopping inflammation of the joints.

However, it was Dr. Lubinus, too, who confirmed the diagnosis, a gift from Vati's New York past: Caisson Disease, or "the Bends," a decomposition of the spinal cord that came with an engineer's frequent descents in caissons to inspect underwater construction in times when pressurized cabins did not yet exist. This diagnosis, worsened by rheumatoid arthritis, made it clear there truly was no cure for my father, only relief.

Vati learning to stand unassisted, early 1950s

But stand he would, it just took a few years, and did not last for long. First, he limped tentatively on crutches, later on canes, at times even on his own. It was the gift of a new life, however brief.

Amidst all this, we had to learn to be a family. For me it would become a first awareness of both cohesion and separateness, defining features of family life. We were an island of three, tightly bound by our new circumstances, and yet strangers after so many years of separation; strangers as well in the country of our origin.

Today I realize this account of my childhood has little dialogue. And indeed, still now, it is an inner conversation with the past, images that must be reviewed, questions demanding answers, so that I may understand who I am.

Stillness may also be the condition of an only child: Adults talk among themselves, give you instruction, punish you when they see the need, but they do not communicate to you how they feel. Therefore, this child, often left to herself, to struggle with yet another language, withdrew into silence, to an inner theater more populated than the streets she walked.

And then there is the northern soul–already thriving in silence. Just think of those two aged ladies spending an afternoon coffee hour in the film "Babette's Feast:" A quiet room, velvet and lace, muted colors, dimmed light. Raging wind hurls snow against the windows.

With the clinking of old spoons against old cups as background music, their conversation is a word or a glance here and there. And yet their silent warmth gives healing and love to a French woman who fled the revolution but had once been the center of Paris society with all its glory and sound. However, when given a choice, this foreigner does not return to Paris but stays in the Danish darkness with her silent friends. It is a happy scene, although my Italian husband would shudder; he could stand family visits to the far North only for a very short time, drowning in that stillness.

For us, this northern quiet became the road to healing. My parents must have discovered that the years of struggle had formed a bond stronger than individual desires. For had these two people–husband and wife–not survived, had they not grown? My parents' marriage, shaky as it had always been, must have found its core, that place in the heart where character resides, where lasting attachments give the strength to be there, one for the other.

And surely, forgiveness had to happen, for how can a man put aside the fact that, out of love, he had followed his wife to Germany, into the pit of disaster and war, giving up all he had built? How could a wife live with the realization it was her impetuous flight from the comforts and safety of New York into the jaws of war, that had rained misery over them both, and later their child? Only love, way deep down, profound love, could offer enough balm to take the path ahead in unison, for their own sake and that of their child. Surely, this love was hammered into shape on an anvil, spiced by some hard pragmatism: What else was there to do?

Still, the years ahead would restore their union. They had found a love described by Gabriel Garcia Marquez: *"... they had lived together long enough to know that love was always love, anytime and anyplace, but it was more solid the closer it came to death." (Love in the Time of Cholera, 1985)*

Meeting my Mother

There had to have been that moment of encounter, one early January day in 1950, when mother and child greeted each other after a separation of almost four years.

Was it at a train station? On a street? In somebody's house, in Hamburg, in Kiel?

Surely there were tears, at least on the mother's side, perhaps an awkward hug. A kiss on the forehead? Impossible. The child was now almost a head taller than her mother.

When Mutti and I first stood face-to-face, she was fifty-five years old, aged—a stranger to me. I knew her from letters read to me, the words forming images of the face, the person, without change. Weightless fragments buried deep in the psyche arose again: Mutti's asthma, her imperious ways, her stories, her music, her fortitude in the shelters, her own body covering mine when bombs were falling nearby: all demanded caution. Greeting my mother on that nebulous day was the beginning of an arduous path.

Mother and daughter, early 1950s

Loving my mother would take time.

Over these troubled years, Mutti had become a vague remembrance of her former self. Never slim since her days in New York, her body now carried folds of fat tightly packed into a corset. Never having exercised, nor caring much about nutrition, she had used food for comfort: "I eat out of sorrow; I eat when I am angry; I eat when I am lonely," and given her situation, that had been most of the time.

After Vati's and my departure in 1946, Mutti had remained alone in our Graz apartment, hoping for an exit visa to arrive from the States. Instead, as a newly hated German, she soon suffered expulsion from Austria.

One has to wrap one's mind around the fact that Mutti had not been allowed to leave with husband and child because she had not been "denazified," that is, cleared of possible Nazi infections. Earlier, she had faced uncertainty because of her "tainted" ancestry; she was now a displaced person, given one day to leave the country (the good Austrians having forgotten that Hitler was a native son, and that once they had rejoiced at "unification"). Our friend, Anni Torsić, who had once saved us from Russian soldiers, had promised to send our possessions whenever we would call for them.

How to compare misery or hardships? Had Mutti's fate been worse than ours out in the world? After all, she never had the benefit of adventure. How did she endure the fact she was unable to see her only child grow into teenage? All I can tell you is she did it with great sensitivity and with that same stoic acceptance surrounding all of us.

I am not so sure I was able to do the same; I became a grouchy brat at the doorstep of teenage. Adults took control of the tasks at hand, asked no questions; no information was conveyed together with the kindness shown. I felt like a shadow, invisible. After all, I had gone from spoiled child to refugee, to displaced person, to adventurer in Africa, and now a child again.

Rebuilding a Life

Let me recall the modicum of normalcy that would be the gift of this decade. It required detours; nothing was simple in a society of vanquished people counting their dead.

Gradually it became clear that Vati's savings and investments had all been confiscated, ground up by the war, and in some cases frozen in the now inaccessible eastern bloc. Only the monthly rents from the large house on the hill in Flensburg remained. It was this grand building, on a prominent street that once fed the ambitions of a fourteen-year-old carpenter's apprentice, had driven him to get an education, to emigrate to America and make enough money to buy it. Now the rental income was hugely reduced since numerous refugee families still occupied every inch of space–and they could not pay any rent at all. Worst of all, there was not an apartment available, even for the owners.

Klein Wolstrup

On this road to healing, we were supported by relatives and friends who entered and exited our fractured existence. They were like markers of belonging, guiding three people who seemed to belong nowhere, thrown about like so many snippets of paper blowing down a wet street.

Instead, these connections carried us like melody and refrain like a color that reappears in a composition, fitting and needed; they held the soul in place. And, oh, how many times these same, few, individuals were there when most needed!

One such anchor was Dina, the daughter of Vati's eldest brother who, long ago, had been called to Langenhagen to care for me right after my birth. She was competent and gifted with much strength, a daughter more than a helper.

The Jessen family: Hans, Dina, Hans, Jr., Peter, early 1950s

In the years of our absence, Dina had married Hans, a farmer living in Klein Wolstrup just outside of Flensburg. This gentle man's kindness and grace in the face of trouble was enormous. I will never forget the smile coming from his eyes when he spoke, which was rarely.

During the war, with all male members conscripted, Dina had held together farm and family with almost super-human energy–plowing the fields with horses, bringing in the hay, doing laundry without running water, cooking meager meals for all, raising two small children by herself. Under these circumstances, the farm had remained in antiquated condition, but whole, until her husband returned from the war, an injured veteran.

Now, five years after war's end, this beautiful old farmhouse and outbuildings were filled to the rafters with people. There was the farmer couple, their two little boys and grandfather. There was also an East Prussian refugee family of eight that lived in the large dining parlor, cooked in what had been the laundry room, slept in tiny servants-quarters and grew by one more person when the son-in-law suddenly returned from Russian captivity. He had walked to the village from heaven knows where and how long, without any means of notifying wife and child. Who had told him where to find them?

Yet, when we discovered that there was no room in our own Flensburg house, Dina and Hans moved together just a little more, clearing a bedroom for us. There we

The Jessen farm house, built 1895

lived for a year and grew to love each other, establishing a close family relationship with their children, now grandparents in their own right.

This house full of people had enough kids to form a rowdy gang, climbing trees to reach the best ripe plums, sitting on the low roof to eat them, playing chase games, running 'til dark. How did the adults stand it? Came winter, we raced our sleds on the frozen road until darkness took over, around the garden hedge, to the farm yard, barely avoiding the dung heap. What a release for the silent teen! We also worked in the fields and attended the village's one-room school.

Living in Flensburg

It remains a footnote of World War II history that Flensburg was one of the last unoccupied cities. For less than a month in May 1945, it became the seat of all remaining Nazi military leadership. With Hitler dead in his bunker since April 30, Admiral Karl Dönitz was appointed president, and he chose the Naval Academy outside of Flensburg as the Reich's headquarters.

When the Instrument of Surrender had finally been approved by the Allies, the decision was broadcast on May 8, 1945, from that little radio tower across the fjord from us, by then the only official radio station still on the air. In subsequent years, the city had come to life again, the struggle to house the refugees being the primary concern.

The city had remained somewhat intact, bombed less than others, due perhaps to constant obstruction of weather or some political concerns, this being a town directly on the border with Denmark. The city's relative wholeness gave it a comforting aura.

Old Flensburg main street

Finally, after almost a year, there was an apartment, actually half of a large one, in our once fashionable building above the Flensburg fjord, and one day, in early 1951, our furniture arrived from Graz.

Remember our apartment in Graz? Our friend, Anni Torsić reappeared in our lives when most needed. She packed up our belongings, commandeered a railroad car, had it filled with our stuff and managed to bribe officials into rolling it downhill, at night, from Austria into Germany. The price was one carton of American cigarettes. Later we learned this mode of transport–and payment–was a well-oiled machine serving international exchange long before the border-free European Union came into existence.

Said shipment arrived in Flensburg–all the delicate antique glasses, the china, the American bedroom furniture, and most astonishing when considering the calamity of the times, even that black portfolio full of letters and pictures that now offers me insight into the past. All was heaved into the *belle étage* on Am Burgfried 12. And of course, as had happened

Marine Academy, Muerwik, built 1907-10

many times before, the grand piano was lifted by pulleys through the living room window. The communists had not broken a single black or white key.

This furniture now had its own history of war. Had the communists played the grand? Did they sleep in my bed? With whom? Did they sing as beautifully as the Russian soldiers gathered in the garden across from us? Were these Communists drunk on Moscow vodka every night, or were they just bureaucrats like all other party folks the world over?

166

Many years later, during my last year of school, I visited Graz and Mrs. Torsić, still living in that dilapidated building. I was tall and strong by then, she small and tired, worn by years of struggle, her blonde hair streaked with white. Her mother had died, her daughter moved on to Vienna. But in Anni Torsić's eyes shone the ferocious strength that once protected all of us. She had long ago abandoned the idea of saving the world through communism, had seen first-hand the murderous actions of its leaders, the total impossibility of any social good coming from their hands.

And, besides, she told me:

"I was invited to Moscow, got to meet Stalin, looked into his cold eyes. Then he thrust into my hands the largest bottle of stinking perfume you would ever want to smell. That was the final straw: perfume for a fighter in the cause?"

I never saw her again. I do at times visit Graz and lay thoughts of gratitude, like a wreath on the stoop of that old building, the same stoop where, as an eight-year-old, I sat watching the stream of refugees, where I sat on the day the war ended. More harmony through repetition, more melody for the soul, but now with new tonalities.

~*~

To live in Flensburg, you had to ignore the eternally gray skies, the wind, the rain. One did not talk about it; one silently endured.

Within that setting, our family slowly built a pattern determined by Vati's treatment. Errands were done on foot, descending on winding steps down to the ancient city. Later you lugged your bags up that hill, just like robber barons of long ago may have dragged their looted goods from the harbor.

Daily needs, however, were met six houses down, in a small mom-and-pop store. There you became a known entity, greeted each day by name, all gossip invited and passed along to the next customer. Once trust had developed, you learned that in back, through the arched drive, the shopkeeper also ran a semi-legal rum factory, selling that precious liquid in bottles you handed him. Strong rum, rich and golden brown. When added to hot water—not too much water—and some sugar, you could drink it hot, hot, hot; it was essential to making bearable the storms and gray existence.

Soon we learned the town had about one hundred such rum factories, some corporate, large and legit. The reason was historic. In the days of the sailing ships, rich Flensburg entrepreneurs owned plantations in Jamaica whence large fleets imported sugar cane syrup. This cargo was then distilled with the pure artesian water that rose out of the deep, from far-away Sweden. It had made for very good rum, for a very long time.

167

One can only imagine how impressive, and chaotic, our harbor must have been on days when the fleet came in, how drunk the sailors after months at sea, how busy the whore houses along Oluf Samson Gang, the town's red-light district down by the harbor—two blocks of ancient row houses with roofs hanging low. Once, long ago, the original owners sat on rickety chairs by their front door; later, these chairs had been taken over by scrawny, aging women who passed their lives confined by circumstance. Today, this small

street is gentrified, the houses are placed on the historic register. Boutiques sell you old photos and tourist trinkets.

We were never, under any circumstances, to walk down that street, but we ogled it with great interest. So long, Oluf Samson Gang!

Oluf Samsung Gang, one of the city's oldest streets

~*~

Memories of the early days are rich in normalcy and hence fleeting. At times there were spats and scoldings. After all, I had seen many things but had no idea how to be a fourteen-year old in a withdrawn Scandinavian society.

Into this vacuum falls one of those gifts only fate can bestow on you. A friend and piano student of Mutti's in the dark years of our absence, had been her intellectual refuge. This person, now in her nineties, recently sent me an antique glass, a gift from my mother, together with a 1951 letter in which Mutti describes our growing together and my own early reaction:

"We all have to accept constraints... but a warm room, a good book, those are wonderful things to have and we are daily thankful... Every day anew I celebrate the happiness of our being together in our own home and with husband and daughter. We are so happy that we really do not wish to go out; even Erika says that it is most beautiful right here."

Walking

For my parents, life in its outside appearances may have arrived at that place where the end alone is left to contemplate. The arc of action and rewards had closed; a writer may be tempted to lay down the pen.

What today fills me with almost jealous emotion, is their absolute refusal to do so. Moreover, if their tales at coffee time in Flensburg could hold a teenager's attention, so that I can now recall their smallest detail—that alone is proof of their power, the true drama, the victory of the spirit.

I do not remember how, and when, Vati was able to walk again. In a painful and laborious process, he had learned to stand, move haltingly from room to room. One day, he turned to Mutti and said: "I think I should try to go down the stairs, go for a walk."

"Carsten, are you sure?" was Mutti's worried response.

We looked at him in disbelief, exchanged glances of fear, but helped him into street clothes; we did not dare discourage him. And walk he did—on those long legs, now very stiff, with ankles so swollen we could hardly fit socks and shoes on them.

I cannot tell you what force of will it took, how much pain, for Vati never mentioned it. All I saw was lips tightly clenched, eyes sternly focused on the task of making frozen limbs move.

Carefully, he stepped to the stairs, trying to adjust to the new crutch. Leaning against the wall, he hesitantly placed the crutch on the terrazzo step, grasping the iron rail, slowly lowering a heavy foot onto the next step, placing the other, posting the crutch, finding his balance—over and over until we were out on the street. Ten minutes of will and pain for him, ten minutes of worry for us.

My parents, setting out on their daily walk to the fjord overlook

Yet, all three of us celebrated the achievement, the happiness of being able to walk ever so slowly around the corner. We walked the two blocks of the promenade, past the School of Economics, past the Danish high school, all the way to the *Schöne Aussicht*, the beautiful vista, that spread the entire town at our feet, from the fjord to the distant hills of Denmark.

On days when Vati and I walked alone, I learned to adjust my steps to his halting gait, never sensing the need to run or change. Tomorrow, Mutti would walk with him, resting on a bench, slowly returning home. Surely, during that outing, they exchanged ideas and remembrances, tried to find a way forward.

Watching our progress, stopping for a kind word or curious question, were the tenants of the building who paid the rent in person and stayed for a brief chat—genteel folk who complained about the political situation and the refinement lacking in "those refugees."

Others, the ones living in the garrets, had no fancy airs and subsisted on poverty provisions. They froze in winter, sat with blankets around their legs and told us it was actually tasty to cook dinner with lumps of flour in broth made from bouillon cubes. Oh, and they had a little garden plot for potatoes and greens. It was a world of damaged people, wearing polite smiles, rarely laughter.

None of this obstructed the view of a future that may be possible for the country, for its people, for us. No, living in Flensburg, finding healing and family—these experiences lie at the core of all things remembered. Coffee hour shed light on the past while giving sustenance for the future. This is the reason for my frequent returns to the city. It is the source for this book's title.

Mutti in Flensburg

Mutti must have felt excluded from the bond between father and daughter. I do not remember her showing resentment or sorrow; perhaps I just could not tell. How should I know to be a daughter, show love and closeness to a woman whose views on what was allowed had not been tested?

Over the following years, dedicating herself to Vati's care and to my education, Mutti fought her own declining health, heart ailments, and asthma. Yet, she took up the burden. Her inborn resourcefulness came to the rescue.

Now that food began to be plentiful, Mutti celebrated survival with a smile. She took great pleasure in setting a bountiful table for the much-loved visits that brought our relatives, Hans and Dina, to town. She would search the stores for special meats, cheeses, a glass of port, and arrange it all in the dining room, hoping this would be the day Vati was well enough to join us.

Visits brought light back into her eyes, a spring in her step. Her stories took precedence over tasks at hand. While regaling Hans with some tale about New York (did I mention earlier that my mother loved men?) she placed the pewter milk pot into the heating niche of our tile oven, came back to it when the story was finished, only to find that its little metal legs had melted away, the milk now a greyish, curdled lump.

"Oh, well," she smiled, "it *was* a good story. More coffee?"

When a day lacked all relief, however, nothing happened that called for her spirit to shine, on those days her face turned limp, her eyes dull. Vati, knowing from early years how her moods could rise and sink, smiled and said, "See? When Margarethe Müller is bored, her nose gets long, it hangs into her coffee cup."

Mutti failed to see the humor in this.

What words could Mutti find to rebuild trust in a husband? Perhaps it was the power of her gift that could make this man sink into a state of calm enchantment? Did he see it as a treasure placed into his hands, to protect the music and the woman who could fill the room with sound? Did fate present it to him like a sacrifice to be burned on some altar of forgiveness? How was it possible I had to discover the truth in faded letters?

Deeply immersed in creating sound, Mutti looked out the window, her green eyes reflecting absence. These escapes became more and more rare as time went on. Adding hurt to sorrow, it turned out the piano desperately needed tuning. Vati and I could not hear it, but her perfect pitch conveyed painful dissonances. Sadly, in the beginning there simply was no money to bring in a piano tuner.

Remarkably, her lovely hands, tiny and sinuous, with fingers coming to narrow tips–those hands had remained agile. It was as though all former energies and capacities of the body had come to rest there. Hands fell into elegant repose like those of a Baroque *putto*; when playing, however, they stretched beyond an octave, became forceful tools with a life of their own.

Sometimes, in later years, Mutti would lie in bed, and I joined her for a talk. She then stretched those hands high up into the air, working her fingers as though playing a particularly fast Beethoven. With obvious pleasure she said, "Oh, just tell the men to look at my hands; forget about the rest," and some story about early conquests would follow–always ladylike and a bit melancholy in the telling, but with glinting eye. I cannot say for certain whether these men were real or imagined, but I have an idea.

Normal Life

In those early years in Flensburg, we moved forward like blind people, sliding a hesitant hand along a wall, hoping to be guided in unsure progression, not knowing where obstacles–or the wall's end–may be. It was a triumph of the will!

Gradually, our excursions grew to include a bus ride down to the harbor, a rare meal at Piet Henningsen, a fine 17th-century pub. Its low ceiling had massive dark beams between which hung dusty ship models. You could still sense a hundred years of bar fights, of drunken sailors stumbling onto the street and staggering to their boats just feet away.

Now the few tables were once again laid out with white cloths on dark wood, tiny windows with hand-blown glass panes gave a view of boats from a low angle. The kitchen served herring and potatoes—luxuries at the time—with a jug of Flensburg beer. In later years, you could attend an evening of poetry reading at Piet's—entrance fee, one glass of *Grog*, hot mulled rum. Today you fall into the establishment knowing it is a place with a fancy menu; still, the flavor remains.

There were happy days in those years of the mid-50s, when we three got on one of the pre-war excursion boats, paint peeling, motor coughing. They lumbered out to Glücksburg, a fancy little resort with a castle-moat, built in 1582, whence came the last empress of Germany, Auguste Viktoria. Walks on the beach promenade, a cup of coffee at *Café Rosenterrasse* [terrace of roses] were highlights.

Vati and Mutti on a Christmas walk along the harbor, 1954

This excursion we two displaced Americans, Dad and I, could make. We were, however, unable to take the "butter boat" that visited the nearest village on the Danish side. There the German locals traveled to buy cheap Danish butter and cheese. During the half-hour trip through international waters—all one hundred yards of it—they also got royally drunk on custom-free rum and beer, but no official cared or measured the length of that bit of internationalism.

Vati and I could not go because our passports had expired, and the State Department blocked all travel except to the States. We tried, but failed, to convince the bureaucrats that here was a man too poor, too ill for the journey. However, we did not worry about the Department of State, or how cheap the butter was in Denmark.

How Much School Have You Had?

Was I aware I led the life of an aged person? I do not remember it as a burden, just normal day-to-day. Love for my father was the rock to which I could cling.

It is not surprising, however, that in those dark days of Westchester County, New York, I had developed a stomach ailment that kept me in bed many times. Doctors treated me with Belladonna. Later, in Angola, I was sent to the Swiss nursing station not far away, in hopes the missionaries there could help calm my stomach.

Gradually, this too, was healed, but the young person who had returned from these journeys was numb, turned inward for protection. People ask me how it felt to live through these troubles. I have to answer that I cannot remember feeling anything.

What remained, and has been with me for life, is fear—an inner scream that rises in nightly dreams: being on the run from forces unknown, trying to climb fragments of stairways that hang off collapsing buildings, having tasks impossible to carry out. These scenes have become my companions. I am always on the move in unknown territory, always tasked with some responsibility that can never be carried out because new obstacles rise turn after turn. These dreams, and the historic events that brought them on, have had lasting impact.

~*~

How is it these dreams arise when my reminiscences turn to school? Well, I am always in some classroom. The teacher towers over my desk: "You have not had algebra before? You do not know that here, in this country, we write divisions with a caret, the solution to the right, the dividing lines on a slanted descent below the number, decimals a period, not a comma?"

"No."

"How many years of school have you had?"

"Three."

"Oh. We will soon have a test, try to learn it." I am scared.

Over and over, in several languages, and with differing degrees of kindness, this message had been clearly stated to me: "You are about to fail."

Hence, schooling, and my attitude toward it, had become abysmal: Excused from nursery school for ceaseless screaming; kicked out of nunnery school for unholy speech; refusing to return to African boarding school because of loneliness. Formal education in three different languages. Although fluent in spoken German, I could not correctly spell many words, never did learn where to place a comma–in my entire life. Yes, I was well trained in history; it had happened outside our own front door or had been brought to life in the stories at coffee hour.

Not long after our arrival, I faced the requirement of public education at one of the city's three Gymnasiums. These were highly competitive public prep schools, one each for boys and girls, the other co-ed. During the Founder Years of the early twentieth century (the German equivalent of the Industrial Revolution), with money and ambition plentiful, the Flensburg city fathers had chosen three prominent hills on either side of the fjord to build these schools, their importance within the city's social structure clearly stated by their towering location and architecture, a signal that knowledge was a summit to reach for.

Admission to this school began at age thirteen and led to the *Abitur* exam after seven more years. Upon graduation, you were automatically admitted to any German university for graduate studies.

It was spring of 1951, the beginning of the school year. Who were the twenty students sitting in a classroom, all terrified at the prospect of tests that would last two weeks?

I was not alone when it came to gaps in schooling, it was the norm. Many children lived in cramped housing or Quonset huts hurriedly built for the wave of refugees. In the face of these conditions, special admission exams had to be developed that would test for the ability to comprehend and react. At the end of the exams, we were tested on this material alone, thus giving everyone a chance. Much time was spent in conversation between teachers and students.

Once accepted and organized into classes, we remained together year after year with minor re-groupings. This continuum developed a deep sense of belonging and friendship among the classmates. Still today, more than half a century after graduation, we travel from far and wide to attend a reunion once every five years.

Who were our teachers? Most were elderly women, some brilliant, some unqualified. The few male teachers who had been too old or ill to fight, were now called back to work. Our first director was a soft-spoken Jewish scholar of philosophy, a survivor, who led the school of some 700 girls with a gentle hand. The second was a Moravian. She was stern and intellectually demanding as is the tradition in this variant of Protestantism which, like our Quakers, takes pride in education. When we encountered these individuals in the corridors, we were expected to curtsy and utter a polite greeting; both of them inspired us with awe; they deserved that courtesy.

Our teachers were aware it would be our generation's task to make life in Germany possible, perhaps even meaningful and productive. It would be up to us to help create the so-called "German Miracle." Prompted by the benefits of the Marshall Plan, Ludwig Erhard, an economic genius, became Minister of Economics, an appointment he carried from 1949 to 1963. His vision developed the Social Market Economy, to this day the effective balance of capitalism and social responsibility.

This promise of a shared burden moved wounded war veterans to once more go deep into the earth as miners to bring up almost inaccessible coal and iron ore. Their labor grew into the new steel industry, the engine of rebuilding. At the time, we too, sensed the mission. As did they, we already knew there was a cloud over our youth and future.

We would have to show the world how to live every waking hour under the shadow of crimes committed in our names, often with the willing participation of elders around us. We, our teachers, in fact all Germans, had to confront this calamity, ask questions, find answers. It meant accepting a stigma, generation after generation. Perhaps, some day one could stand for a new beginning, vowing never to forget, never again to wage war.

However, our teachers remained silent.

Just as we young people never spoke of personal experiences, hurts and losses, our educators avoided all mention of recent events. There was a huge elephant in the room. When it came to avoiding this obstacle without getting trampled by history, we were on our own.

Imagine the burden heaped upon a young person who discovers that her family participated in the deportation of a large number of Jews and intellectuals, lent the underpinnings to the policies enacted. Or, having had a much-loved uncle with a major role in the financing of Hitler's atrocities.

This is to this day what it means to be a German.

Still today, it can happen that a person, upon learning your national origin, will abruptly turn away as though seeing a leper, slashing your heart with the realization that your accent has raised horror in a heart, brought terrible memories. It can mean that, in a job interview, you are told in harsh terms: "I hate you; I hate your stinking Mercedes cars!"

This is what it sometimes means to be German.

And again, speaking of Mercedes cars—the symbol of haughty perfection and enhancement of manhood—Saul Bellow, my favorite author in the American language, the writer whose sensibilities are so closely tied to the old world and to my own, wrote about Mercedes cars in *Humboldt's Gift*: "Murder Jews and make machines, that's what those Germans really know how to do." It haunts you, and it is true.

Or, even more terrifying, a person may smile, head bent near your ear, telling you in a conspiratorial voice that America went to war with the wrong country, should have sided with Hitler and beat those damned Russians, ignored the Jews, and thus together we could have dominated the world. You turn away. You carry guilt, your genes carry guilt. It is your heritage.

This is what it sometimes means to be German.

In the early years, we students may well have been truly innocent of the elephant in the room, our parents too preoccupied with survival. But later, I am afraid we, too, drank from the fountain of feigned ignorance.

Somehow, in spite of it all, a new generation had to be prepared for the future with minimal resources, with an absence of modern books. Mainly, I would now say, learning happened by word of mouth and later conversation. And yes, German rigor was applied, demanded.

What became of those early students, all girls, trained in the sciences, several languages, social studies? Most of them took on the work of rebuilding a country. The issue of women's liberation, of women's access to positions of responsibility, had taken care of itself; war and the decisions of men, had done it for us.

A class outing to the North Sea, 1953

For me, school was the place of refuge, a stage upon which to act out youth, be one of the many. Still today, a luminous image rises in many a dream. It must be a metaphor for numerous experiences: There is a child in that school; she is given a trivial task, such as delivering a paper to the teachers' lounge. I am that child, quite young, and I walk along the silent hallways, sensing learning behind every door, admiring the lovely tiled walls with terracotta decorations. I

176

skip over stripes of sun reflected on dusty floor, then turn the columned corner to the open stair hall, tall and wide, with a painting of Saints Peter and Paul on the wall below. Light from a two-story window washes the painting and the bottom of the stairs. A deep well of wide wooden steps, scuffed and eroded from thousands of feet, spreads out before me. I start with a jump, skipping steps as I fly. Still today do I feel the air swishing past my ears, my braids flopping, my weightless state landing one foot on a step, bouncing off again into flight. A wave of joy carries me on, free of all limits.

Hiking in the dunes, 1953

Class trip to the beach , 1955

At the office, I curtsy before the teacher, hand in my paper and return in the glowing satisfaction of having carried out a trust, perhaps being accepted? I was home now.

School offered diversions: Class trips, hikes, school plays. My old photo album is filled with boat rides, camping trips, group scenes of happy girls, arms around shoulders like a warm blanket, or the sun's rays on a balmy day.

Julika

And yet, I often felt alien, left out of my classmates' conversations. Then came the day that changed it all.

We were now fourteen or fifteen years old; our class had traveled to Amrum, the most windswept of the North Sea islands, to spend a week in a camp and observe excavations of Stone Age grave sites. Sitting on the benches of the small boat that took us from the mainland, were two teachers and twenty wind-blown girls, knapsacks at their feet. After a long hike through fields and dunes, we arrived at the dorm by the sea–just a sun-and-wind-battered shack that had survived both the elements and World War II. A shed, really: one door, a few salt-encrusted windows, outhouses in the dunes.

Julika and Erika on a Danish border marker, ca. 1954

Teachers and students stood in confusion, "Where is the hostel keeper? We hiked all the way from the harbor. We had an appointment!" These angry teacher words were directed at the sea or the dunes, for there was no official to answer this question.

Suddenly, a girl, "The New One," who had just moved to our town, said, "Give me a boost; I can open that window. It's just a bit too high."

Soon she stood on my hands and shook loose the rickety window, bracing it with her shoulders when it began to flap in the wind. The effort made glasses slip from her nose, dark curls forming a wild-wet cap around her head. Undaunted, she climbed in and, moments later, opened the front door from the inside.

All poured in. Expected action took up its rhythm, no one expressing thanks or surprise, least of all, the teachers. They were in a quandary. After all, it was a deed that rained success upon us, but also a deed that broke rules, and German education of the time lived by rules. Better not praise that new kid, her spirit of enterprise may come to haunt you as a teacher.

As for me, I cannot recall anything but the dizzying feeling of having been part of something overwhelming, something that ignored fears; I had smelled greatness.

This event was the birth moment of a deep, binding friendship with the girl called Julika. It still fills my heart with delight at every visit, every phone call, every letter. Never did the astonishment leave me that this bundle of self-confidence, this fearless girl, would be my friend for life, and I readily signed on for a wild ride.

This included a class trip to Denmark, right outside of town, the passage a plain border marker, but the path ahead unknown as far as identification might be required. Keenly aware of my inability to enter this country, I stayed behind. Julika declared that she, too, would stay behind, in protest. We considered it to be an act of defiance that I sat on the border marker eating my sandwich. My friend's loyalty once again confirmed our bond.

Over the years of our education at this pillar of higher learning, Julika and her parents fought on our behalf, demanding more freedom to let spirits develop and allow student initiative into the classrooms. Julika's father taught educational psychology at the local teacher college. Her mother had spent several years in America, there soaking up the self-confidence and the singing speech by which members of that country's upper classes assert themselves, endowed with that inner steel that says: "I am entitled. Here is why. Do please prove me wrong." This was the gift Julika and her parents laid at my feet, one never learned but worshiped. Fear had already won the battle inside.

As time went on and our friendship became known to our parents, this family helped in many ways: visiting, giving advice relating to education, adding another kid to the three already squeezed in the back seat of that VW bug and driving out for a picnic on a Sunday afternoon. In later years, there were house parties, dinner dances, events that allowed glimpses of another world. We felt privileged; these were dizzying heights.

Many times, I heard Julika's mother talking about the years of hunger. Her finishing sentence always: "What would we have done without our Americans?" She was referring to her classmates at Vassar who had launched a package stream, intent on keeping this family alive. This long reach even extended to my first months in the States, when a simple phone call from this lady resulted in an interview, and a job, at the Smithsonian Institution. This help formed an entire life.

Three friends, Julika, Gertrud and Erika camping on the island of Amrum, 1955

Julika became a social worker, moving to the encircled city of Berlin. She tended to those most needy and hurt in Kreuzberg, the city's poorest neighborhood at the time. There she convinced funding sources to build a women's bath, the only place Turkish

House party at Julika's, 1956

immigrant women were allowed to go without supervision from husband or family. Today, their daughters demonstrate against oppression in their country of origin, returning to tell Julika all about it.

This friend, who has been a violinist all her life today straps her instrument to her back, climbs on her bike and rides to the next rehearsal or chamber concert. She is a mother and grandmother, her daughter is our daughter's best friend.

The last time I visited Berlin, we tried to visit a former classmate who had fallen ill and did not answer the doorbell of her apartment building. For a few moments we stood on the sidewalk, then Julika said: "Hold it: I'll ring all the doorbells; someone will buy my story. I can get into any building!"

I knew that.

The Life of Teenagers

As we grew, and spread our sights beyond the school yard, the city was large enough to offer movie clubs, concerts and a fine municipal theater, all open to us without charge; and the city was small enough for us to know every medieval church, every side street, every hill; we could walk home safely at all hours.

And boys, yes, there were boys, shy love affairs in later years. We had two schools from which to draw recruits, especially the august boys' Gymnasium that differed from ours in only one subject: instruction in Ancient Greek. The first explanation said girls were capable of learning Latin, but Greek, no, that could not be expected. The second, and more understandable, yet no less sexist, was that this ancient language was useful only for the study of theology—and pastors were, of course, male.

Living in the North, you had to learn to live with the howling wind, the lead-colored waves on the fjord, rain pelting your face until it burned. Storms would move in after the early sun had promised a fine day. The town's cobblestones glistened in fresh moisture, walls had a deep glow. For the folks of this town, rushing from the bus terminal to their work, it was the challenge of daily life. Like always.

But, come summer, those precious few days of sky so clear your eye could ride along the undulating shoreline until it sank into the distant sea—on such days, white billowing clouds shared the drama with the sails of a regatta. Sunlight danced on the waves, fractured the scene into a million glistening dots as though nature herself was a canvas by God, the Impressionist painter.

The land was hilly, gently reflecting the glaciers of the last ice age that had rolled before them rocks, earth and sand, finally sinking into the ocean. Now these hills were covered by ancient villages and farm land.

On those rare days of summer, you could jump on your bike, meet a gang of friends, pedal up the steep incline from the harbor and make it to a beach in one of the many coves of the fjord. Or you could bike through the rape-seed fields—a sea of yellow singing to the sky, heightened by its complementary, the blue waters. You could even race through the villages in wild abandon, farmers and small kids shaking their heads as they watched you speeding to the open Baltic Sea, a day's outing.

If you happened to be riding with Hanna, the gifted class musician and leader of our very own small chorus, you could stop in a village, enter the ancient stone chapel, its Romanesque architecture unchanged since the twelfth century; there, you could sing in the hallowed space—just you, the sound and the altar.

Once at the beach, your gang swam in the icy waters; you licked the salt off your lips, rode the wake of passing sailboats. Then, spreading out in the sand like a reptile, you absorbed the sun, letting it enter body and soul,

Heading for the beach, 1957

while enjoying the closeness of friendship, or the timid love of a fine boy. Yes, early love affairs were chaste, another one of those antiquated words that give me pleasure to write. Remember Paul McCartney singing about *Norwegian Wood*, a night spent talking? Yes, this was the North, a repressed society. Later, that would change.

181

The sun of spring was a blessing of all things natural that every Scandinavian will recognize and recount like a rhapsody—heavenly days that released hedonism in a stoic world: hikes and picnics in wooded meadows, Maenadic dances, song and shy kisses. The subconscious whispered of ancient fertility rites, of ceremonies with rum-fueled mating rituals. And this—life, warmth, joy—had to be celebrated in nature, in the forests, in the protective coves of dunes—sand so warm and soft, framed by golden grasses that swayed in the wind, the distant sea sending soothing sound. It came naturally, it *was* nature. Today, even the city of Berlin, famous for spitting in the face of most bourgeois notions, has a day when parks are free for all things one may wish to celebrate, an urban orgy, topless and otherwise. Prudes had better find another place to take a walk, but this ritual, too, is as ancient as nature waking from a long winter.

Of course, only later, when classes focused on Greek Mythology, on Nordic ritual, did we understand we were simply following ancient rites. Our young had done it forever. Who knew that these festivals—spontaneous, loud, uncivilized—had legendary ancestors?

On these outings we were allowed to leave without an adult present, we were by then somewhere between age fifteen and eighteen and had absorbed many a lecture. We were expected to use care when swimming, to watch out for each other, to be home in time for supper. But whatever happened on these outings remained forever private, removed from the adult world. In those days, life took on new meaning.

Graduation at Mr. Schmidt's dance school, 1956

In later years there were loves, break-up tragedies and, seen from today's vantage, very sedate and protected affairs. Yes, my boyfriend and I did smuggle three bottles of wine into the art studio, the darkest room of a school dance party. We were planning to share them with our friends in anticipation of slow dances on the wings of wine. The cheap bottles exploded in the heated room just as a teacher-monitor walked in.

We were not punished or expelled, we were after all, 18 years old, and

182

according to this society, quite mature enough for drinking, although it *had* been announced that only soft drinks would be allowed on the school grounds.

However, the art teacher really did feel sorry for us. He grinned, said: "Oh, what a shame!" and left the room. Next Monday, in art class, you could still smell the acrid stench of cheap wine.

Triumph

While my teen life was unfolding, Vati's triumph of healing, of walking, even for a few years, had followed an arduous path, one obstructed by hazards so treacherous they almost crushed the wanderer. Yet, one day, triumph came by bus, or at least in the ability to take one, out to the country.

I do not remember how many years after our arrival this took place, but we three–father, mother and teenager–made it to the Flensburg bus depot, rode through farms and fields, until we stopped near the village of Klein Wolstrup, a name that to this day sings of love.

From the bus stop on the highway we entered the "Cow Path," an unpaved lane shielded on both sides by ancient rock walls. White-blooming thorn bushes grew out of these stones, sending waves of scent into the path. Through the dense growth, the eye caught meadows and fields, a quilt of fresh clover, golden oats and yellow blooms dancing in the sun. Carefully, tentatively, we three walked what may have been a half mile to the farm owned by cousins Dina and Hans.

Father and daughter, Klein Wolstrup, ca. 1954

This property, tended by generations of ancestors, is nestled in the rolling land of Anglia, the original region whence came the early settlers of England, there creating an almost mirror image of this rural world. Today that region of scarcely more than twenty square miles reaches from the city of Flensburg to Schleswig, the state capital. One cannot imagine a lovelier, gentler countryside.

Anglia was peopled by inhabitants who were most likely not Viking–those lanky, red-bearded giants of Norwegian origin, their noses hooked, their narrow-set eyes white-blue. Anglians, by contrast, are fine-boned, often brown-eyed and,

183

according to some legends, of Celtic origin. Even the cows are different from the Holsteins; they are small, brown, rich in buttery milk. The Anglian dialect is close to Danish, traditions leaning more toward the good life–weddings and births celebrated in week-long festivities. Anglians take pleasure in sitting in the warmth of their parlor, drinking a fine glass of *Glühwein,* hot mulled red wine.

On that fine day, we three had succeeded in returning to the farm where we had spent a year waiting for our city apartment. Dina and Hans had become our anchor and refuge.

Our arrival was a triumph worth celebrating! It is captured in a photo of father and daughter dressed in celebratory garments: Vati in suit and tie, myself wearing a flowered spring dress. It may have been my birthday, fifteen or sixteen, or just a family feast of the mid-1950s, a victory of the will.

There we pose, in a barren corner of the back entrance, shielded from the never-ending wind. Vati's hand rests on my lower arm, holding my other hand. He is standing, unsupported by crutches. The radiant smiles exchanged between a very tall father and his daughter looking up to him, are a triumph as well–of survival, of the fact that nothing, nothing on earth, could dampen the joy of the moment.

Invisible in this photo is the surrounding family, the garden filled with flowers and anchored by a centuries-old chestnut tree. No matter, the psychological space of this image is taken over entirely by the exchange of glances. This connectedness is heightened by hands and arms that form a knot in front of us, as though this, too, were a symbol. What cannot be seen, but the writer knows, is the history behind this day, the vast difference between this picture, and a photo taken in 1946, during our last days in the States when pain and defeat had carved its signature onto both of our faces. Hidden from view are the years since then, the migrant existence, the search for a place where we could be a family.

Vati's smile could tell another story: Over the years, he may have found a way to conquer remorse or anger when he realized that following his wife to Germany in 1932 had robbed him of all he had achieved as a young man in America: success, financial security, professional standing; all that was lost. Did advancing age help in this coming to terms, or had it been hard won through bitter inner battles? No matter, this smiling face reflected a man at peace. Sadly, there is no photo showing the day's triumph reflected on Mutti's face.

Hidden from view is the future, the days ahead. I am sure my father, then around sixty-five years old, saw his fate, knew how fleeting was this moment, how near the day when his doctor's prognosis would become reality, when his daughter would grow up, go her own way, even if the girl in the photo could not imagine such a time. Like all young people, she lived for the moment.

Triumphs, by their very nature are pinnacles, the culmination of long struggles, a precarious balance, like a dancer's, on a single toe. They cannot last. In fact, the day soon came when suffering could no longer be ignored, even by a teenager. This photo foreshadows that there, in this house, Vati would later spend long summer weeks, confined to his bed, but carried into the garden by Dina and Hans, so that he could see the sky, could talk to the family. Mutti would pull a chair next to him after having been chased around the flower bed by the gander, the family's watch goose.

Both knew their daughter, having finished her school day, would soon arrive by bike having ridden the few miles from town. We three would be included in celebrations of farm life, the eating of roasts and mountains of cake, demanding a new kind of fortitude.

Dina now became my parents' other child for reasons of love alone. Her family was truly our own, her sons my siblings, especially young Hans, with whom I have maintained a close friendship, enriched by numerous visits on both sides of the Atlantic, and with whom I would later explore the family's ancient roots.

A few years in the future, it would be this farm where Mutti, too, found care after I had returned to the States so as not to lose my citizenship. Someday, it would become her resting place, next to her husband, in a graveyard surrounding the ancient church.

Mutti

Mutti was not included in this image of triumph, but she was now the solid rock that held all together. Consulting with Vati, she took over all business matters, the care of our aging building, our sparse income, our way to cope with losses, my education. Her fortitude now shone from her grey eyes, her ready smile. Remarkably her asthma, the terror that had dominated her earlier life, seemed to have subsided except for rare attacks. Heart ailments now plagued her, but she carried out her daily life with few complaints and came to luminous life during the stories at coffee hour.

On her old typewriter, she carried on a vast correspondence with relatives and friends, and her best escape was reading books, especially American women writers, whose praises she sang to anyone willing to listen. She was well known at the local library.

Mutti's warmth, gradually growing, now encompassed me, her teenage

185

daughter. I longingly remember how she would sit at my bedside when I was ill, gently telling stories, bringing things to eat and drink, resting to give me comfort, sharing a tale or two of her youth.

On outings or rare travels, she was able to make friends with people in the street, on a park bench, in a train. Her smile was open, sincere, not a trace of judgment. Over the years of supreme hardship, she had developed an ability to send out signals to people, that they mattered, that she would respect confidences and keep them to herself.

"I don't know why, but people talk to me about the most personal things in their lives, uninvited, as though seeking reassurance. I know how to listen, maybe that is it."

Exiting the Triumphal Arch

When you visit that great city of Rome, there to be confronted with the ancient monuments, you stand in awe before the Arch of Constantine. It was built in AD 312-15, celebrating the emperor's triumphant achievements, specifically the Battle of the Milvian Bridge that brought him to power and Christianity to the Romans. The emperor's victory parade approached the arch decorated with reliefs celebrating the great man, the great empire. It was at once the goal and highlight of the parade, and its formal conclusion. Light flooded through the openings, suggesting a shining future. The narrow passage was brief, like a flash of hope and glory. Those who enter, know the brevity of triumph. Scholars who study the rise and fall of empires have referred to these arches as monstrous toys that by their very existence advertise the end of something.

Likewise, using "triumph" when describing that shining day when we traveled to the country, I now realize that it carried both glory and foreboding.

Gradually, almost unnoticeably in the course of the later 1950s, Vati's steps grew slower, his crutches became a painful challenge. I do not recall the day, the year, when his shoes no longer closed over swollen ankles, arms no longer stretched enough to reach for his hat. Fewer and fewer were the days when Vati managed to stand on his feet.

When did the day come, weeks or months later, that Vati found it impossible to descend the stairs from our apartment, when he told us that today was not so good; he would rather spend a few hours in bed–and could he please have some pain killers?

Now, a male nurse, a veteran, arrived every day for a few hours. He was an East Prussian from a region usurped by Russia, all his possessions and family lost. Half the height of his new patient, balding, but with a cheerful smile, this good man brought news from the streets and stories from his life in war. For brief moments he stopped working, sat down on the side of the bed and memory flowed: "Well, we had marched until we couldn't march any longer; no more ammunition, no more food; during the day we hid in the forests, but eventually we made it to the American side. Man, they offered us cigarettes even before putting us into prisoner camp; the black guards were the best. We were damned lucky.

"Next morning, at roll call, we grinned—and the 'Amis' looked surprised—when the count showed more inmates than they had the night before. Well, we knew that these guys, who had climbed the fence or maybe even found a guard who opened the gate, were hungry, sick and tired. They had managed to avoid the Russians and a trip to Siberia."

These stories brought a smile to Vati's face, and he remembered life in the States during the 1920s. "My partner and I were building a part of Pulaski Skyway in New Jersey. It was Friday evening, payroll time. I was prepared to hand out the payroll in cash, but first I had given the proper share to the Mafia boss in charge of that project; then I drove home to pick up my German Shepherd in case there may be another visit from the bosses. Only then did we make payroll and close shop."

The nurse's eyes widened in wonder. "Where the hell was the police?"

Vati's answer: "They were too scared."

Or, he told about Christmas in the trenches of World War I, reminiscences identical to those of many a soldier along the French lines. Both men nodded. Only those who had been there could talk about it, and it became a bond only they could share at this moment.

After that, more exercises, more encouraging words.

Our doctor, himself an amputee, climbed the stairs to our apartment to note the changes, prescribe stronger and stronger pain killers; possible treatments were few. These insights were not shared with me and must have been private conversations between my parents.

In view of Vati's quiet acceptance we did not feel free to let sorrow rule our day. It would have been unseemly in the presence of this quiet suffering. And anyway, the light in his eyes still shone, there still were moments during coffee hour, when one of Mutti's stories would make him smile, days when his face lit up at the news that I had brought home a respectable report card.

Gradually, my day in Flensburg was bifurcated by a double life: classmates, laughter, silliness, sometimes even learning: a place to be young.

Then, rushing home to help with Vati's care, tell him some stories, jokes, or reports on some small success in the outside world.

In spite of friendships and the help of many, our daily life became hard. I felt the pressures of the final two years of school, the multiple exams to be faced, the difficulty of maintaining the strength to lead this double existence. Only once did I rush from a classroom in tears when a teacher, ignorant of my situation, criticized my lack of homework. Classmates rose to my defense, became my fortress and strength. Gradually everyone knew of the struggle.

We three, and friends around us, faced it together. I was reminded again and again that I could soar on the wings of their hopes, their gift of love. Never did I hear the words "suffer" or "hard times." We were in this together, and dignity forbade complaints.

~*~

At one time, our decade in Germany, from 1950 to 1960, had almost approached normal life, had offered some patterns I could draw on for my own adulthood.

Still, how do I explain the realization—it came late in life—that my own youth hardly prepared me for the mechanics, let alone the resilience needed to become a mother, to start a new life in the United States, to navigate the pitfalls and decisions demanded by this new country?

So often I was too foreign, building patterns and rituals that, to me, appeared unassailable, pitting them against habits that would have made us just like all the others. This otherness appeared in the ways one celebrated Christmas or St. Nikolaus, or in our son's question: "all American families keep their cereal boxes on top of the refrigerator, why can't we?"

More significantly, how do you learn parenting by negotiation, by reasoning, as taught by the school we eventually chose for our children. We made that choice partly for its excellence, but to a great extent for its insistence on the dignity and rights of the young person in an environment that was multi-ethnic and multi-cultural. As parents, we wished to give our children a fine beginning, but there was also our very own desire for healing. It is a monument to Richard's patience and love that these needs were always understood and supported. Our children were students in those schools, but so were we; their traditions and methods were new for all of us. For me, the golden moments, their lightness, would always play out before a dark screen, a condition that demanded to be hidden from the children. Still, of all lessons, love and endurance were the gift bestowed.

Chapter 8

Death in Schleswig

Das Erwachen	The Awakening

Ramón Jiménez (tr. Karl Krolow)

Meine offenen Augen!	My open eyes!
Tragt mich ans Meer,	Carry me to the sea,
Um zu sehen ob ich einschlafe!	For to see if I can fall asleep!
Solange sie fern sind,	As long as they are distant,
Werden sich meine offenen Augen	My open eyes
Nicht schliessen.	Will not close.
Es weinen die Erinnerungen,	Memories cry,
Bis sie ein Meer	Until they form a sea
An Tränen und Sehnsucht schaffen…	Of tears and longing…

(Part of a poem found amid old notes taken at a poetry conference.)

It was a late winter day in 1959, exactly ten years after our return from Africa. The taxi raced along the highway from the city of Kiel to the town of Schleswig; I could not again ask the driver to please speed it up.

In my hand I held all the cash I owned and the cable I had found in my dorm room when I returned from class: "Vati near death."

189

It seemed like an eternity, that forty-mile drive from the university to the State Hospital. Once arrived, I raced through the garden door toward Vati's room. There, in the deserted hallway, stood a stretcher, low on the ground, white sheets covering a long body. I had arrived too late. I do not remember feeling shock or screaming recognition of death's finality, only silence, mute awe, and a strange sense that the universe had opened a realm, one that could now be felt as a true presence. Something beyond our world had called a soul, just as our ancients knew when they had a tiny window in their house, near the roof, that was left open at the coming of death, so the soul could make its way to eternity.

Quietly I knelt beside the stretcher and whispered to the white sheet (I dared not remove it, and I am glad I did not):

"Vati, Vati, I came as fast as I could! You will always, always be with me. I will carry you in my soul, that is where you will live. I will try to make you proud of me. All I do will be my gift to you."

I rose and never cried, nor did I cry thereafter; stony silence was the only possibility. The promise made that day to the figure under the white sheet has held. Others may have eternity, a godhead, or moral teachings as their signposts. All I had to do was search my heart and mind, where henceforth Vati lived, and the answers were clear: He had given me an almost Calvinist imperative of that which is right, and the absolute of what is wrong; clear as day and night, as beauty and the order of nature. Try to live up to it, you had the example. Only much later would I learn to value the shades of gray, the ones we cannot live without.

The weekend before, Mutti and I had visited Vati, now hospitalized in the city of Schleswig for over a year. She regularly traveled down from Flensburg, while I headed north from the University of Kiel. In quiet understanding of an impending end, I had transferred to the closest university and now spent most weekends on the train, knowing how much a visit meant to my father.

The Staatskrankenhaus (state hospital) in the small, ancient town of Schleswig, was a nice enough place for the mentally and physically ill who had nowhere else to go. It was the stop at the end of the road, when insurances and private funds had been exhausted, the last corner of a socialized state that never lets you down but does have its final stations.

This hospital was situated in a fine park, its high walls, hedges and trees offering the silence of places that society would rather hide and forget. Yet, a modicum of kind care had been provided at no cost to patient and family. I learned much later that this institution gradually deteriorated under poor

190

management and very questionable medical practices.

Earlier in his stay at the hospital, Vati's eyes still showed traces of warm recognition and pleasure, but gradually stronger and stronger doses of morphine had dulled the body's ability to function, and the smile, faint as it was, faded away. No longer did he sit up in his bed. Deformed, racked by pain, rotting from bedsores, his body had stayed alive for the simple reason that his heart was too strong to die. It would not give up its right to beat even in the face of the obvious. Does a heart sometimes punish its own body? Does it have a life of its own? Is there an outside force that determines when death comes? Does this force have no mercy? Death would long ago have been a blessing.

Now Vati was dead. Numbed, we mourned. Actually, it was more like a crawling, gradual death of its own kind, a pain that ripped apart body and soul. There was only the desperate feeling of waking from exhausted sleep and having reality take over section after section of the waking mind—rolling like a huge, crushing boulder. Being awake meant loneliness, loss of an anchor, better yet, a limb.

The Last Steps

I can hardly remember the funeral. A path led to the village church in Klein Wolstrup, an ancient stone building with a wooden tower, surrounded by old graves. A late storm blew snow into our faces, covered every grave. Plants gently bent under the white.

With Mutti at my side, I carried the urn from the ceremony inside the church to the small grave site. In numb determination, step by step through the snow, we led the silent family—Dina, Hans and their two sons. Someone placed the urn into the grave, now snowy white as though a fine linen had been spread to receive it. We threw a bit of earth onto the urn; the group stood in silent prayer. Then, nothing; memory leaves me again.

But one thing I do know: On this short procession, cradling the urn from the snow, I grew to be the protector of my father's legacy, just as I had protected him when I brought him home from Africa, cradled his crying face in my arms when misery overcame him, and gave him the smallest sense of Christmas in Lisbon because we were alone.

This moment now, on that snowy path, surrounded by high walls and swaying trees, that walk also brought the strength to know my own feet. They, and this memory, have carried me.

At the same time the inner focus became an emotional moat. In the end, what has remained is love. It does not fade, it has been my guide over all those years.

~*~

Today, in the nights of my waking and writing, images arise that are in stark contrast to our technicolor present–travel, holidays with the young families, visits from abroad, the grandchildren. My beautiful house and garden often ring with music and laughter.

Yet, come evening, deep melancholia rises. Visions, like flashes of lightening, create unconnected impulses that have no time, no anchor in reality. A sight, a sound, a smell–dark, all of them–appear uninvited. And yet, in their contrast, they give added meaning to the moment, like a musical chord that lies at the base of a melody, giving it substance, making it richer. Then it all fades again, mercifully, for the mind slowly hides in its depth that which it cannot tolerate.

What remains are ways of seeing the world.

Yes, Mutti and I now had a chance to rest, but mostly there was a void where purpose had lived before. For years, our thoughts had centered on Vati's care, on his needs, on the desperate effort to move an arm or a leg to ease his pains, to lift him to a chair, to help him sit up in bed so he could eat, to bandage swollen joints.

Do you know the intimacy of giving your father a shave?

Now, what were we to do; how to return from there toward a plan for the rest of our lives? It is not easy to confront the freedom of choices when there has been no practice, no chance to envision rosy futures. Even departing to study at the university, first in Hamburg, then in Kiel, had seemed like an interlude; the real purpose was soothing my father's pain.

And here is the stark truth: While the future was bright and wide open for me, Mutti now stood before a void. Where should she find the strength to formulate one?

Back in Flensburg, Mutti and I went down to the city, walked along *Grosse Strasse*, main street, looked at a few shop windows, discussed a fine dress or a set of shoes, and ducked into a café. In the past, these outings had been our own small vacation, now the erstwhile pleasure of relief was gone. Slowly, haltingly, we went through life's daily motions and exhaled. I would fall asleep at night, unable to bear the thoughts of my loss, sleep deeply, and, waking in the morning, would believe for just a moment that nothing had happened.

Alone now, 1959

Yet, some sort of reasoning had to help us gain perspective, find words that, years later, would explain our lives and give clarity to history as we had experienced it. So, the question rose: How did Vati, the builder of highways, docks and a fancy hotel in Palm Beach–how did he come to end his days in that Schleswig hospital, a mere twenty miles from his ancestral village? How did Mutti, the piano prodigy and later the indulged matron, end up on a rickety train from Flensburg to Schleswig for a weekly visit with her dying husband?

To understand, let us retrace the course of Vati's last months at home and his eventual move to a hospital in Schleswig where he would spend his final year of life. Then it will become clear that this move, the one that brought death in Schleswig, was a step taken by choice.

In his marriage vow, my father had once given unquestioned love to his wife, had followed that with a second gift of love when he gave up life in America to follow her into the disaster of war-time Germany. His third gift, a gift to his child, was perhaps the most noble one of all.

It would become Vati's final gift of love.

Living with Pain

The art of medicine, the strength of love, the power of steely determination–all had brought this family a new beginning in Flensburg, one that lasted some years, even if dominated by pain and limitations. One could almost say that father, mother and child prevailed and managed somehow to absorb the normalcy of their new surroundings, make it their own. Only when seen from the barren heights of disaster, of loss, only then can you rejoice in the magnificence of simple daily life.

It should be praised in song.

Eventually, the day came when we found ourselves unable to care for Vati. Mutti must have convinced the health services that help was needed. We knew hospitalization would soon be a necessity, but all of us wished, and Vati longed for, care at home as long as possible.

Off and on, the social health system had sent Vati to spas where he could get relief in hot-spring baths, receive new medications and therapies. All offered brief respite from pain and, for Mutti and me, some relaxation. Healing, however, could no longer be expected.

When did a doctor at one of Vati's hospitals tell him there was more decay in the spinal cord, that his legs no longer received impulses, that arthritis made his ankles swell and ache, and that this was just the beginning?

Facts remained facts.

Quietly, and in his accepting way, Vati went from handicapped person back to the invalid he had been upon returning from Africa in 1950. All Mutti and I could do was follow along. Care changed from efforts to bring improvement to the never-ending tasks of reducing pain.

Resting in that large American bed in the Flensburg apartment, he looked out the windows, enjoyed a rare beam of sunlight, checked the hour on the clock tower of the boys' Gymnasium. It told him of the school-day's end, the time when we three could sit down together over some coffee and talk.

In dreams, oh, many dreams and thoughts, I see Vati sitting on the edge of his bed in Flensburg. He is very thin, his immobile shoulders protruding from his shirt. His swollen knees are exposed, large and shiny; hip and knee connected to thighs thin as sticks; between knee and contorted ankles, the same. With his cramped hands, he tries to massage his knees, slowly circling over them, but his fingers refuse to bend. He does not speak, does not complain. In his seeming acceptance of fate there is something ancient, almost mythic, a gentleness that forbids rage against the fate that has befallen him.

In later months, I needed to bike home from school at lunch time to give him the shot of morphine Mutti could not bring herself to administer. To stare at that needle, stare at the skin to be violated, but knowing the relief it would bring! Then, back to school to practice for the class play; on the way passing the boys' Gymnasium, glancing and wishing that one of the guys I knew, or hoped to know, would be out in the school yard.

The Family

This confined life, Vati's inability to descend the steep stairs to the street, brought new degrees of isolation. Friends would come occasionally, Onkel Karl and Tante Käthe, then still living in Brandenburg, would come for a week's visit; conversations were lively, laughter could be heard now and then. Their son, Eberhard, having recovered from Russian internment, was now established in his own practice in the city of Hamburg. He would arrive for brief visits, review medical treatment plans, suggest new therapies, gently warn Mutti and myself of what was to come.

It is hard to explain, harder to understand, but Vati's relatives, with the notable exception of Dina and Hans, rarely visited. Most of them had remained in the north, and is seems that the years of absence, the entirely different choices made in life, had made my father, and in fact all three of us, strangers. Perhaps the sight of their disabled relative was uncomfortable?

At times they would come with their cars to take Vati to a hospital or a spa for relief. Others, seeing the need, would invite me to their homes on the islands when it was discovered that I had a touch of tuberculosis, since who knows when. Whatever help came our way was appreciated.

On one occasion did the tragedy of our situation become clear to me, the comparison to what could have been, the almost Greek tragedy of soaring heights followed by a fall and broken hopes.

One of the relatives who made the journey to Flensburg, wrote to her family that the conditions and the suffering she had found was a "*Jammertal*," a vale of lament. She left the letter on the table of her room, intending to return later. I happened to see it and suddenly understood our life in the abstract. There it was; it had been given a name: vale of lament. I never forgot those words but accepted life as I knew it. We had found a way to live, we were doing what needed to be done. A combination of duty or pity, but chiefly love.

Tante Adele

True and dedicated, concerned for Vati's and our well-being, were Mutti's sisters, foremost Tante Adele, who had returned to Germany sometime in the mid-1950s after having lived in the Sates for many decades.

She had taken up residence in what remained of the Berlin apartment building that had once been her childhood home. From there poured forth a constant stream of letters and *Manchester Guardian* newspaper clippings meant to enlighten the family and report on possible treatments or new political outrages. Clearly, her views had mellowed little since her anarchist days in 1920s New York.

At times she had visited us in Flensburg, sitting by Vati's bedside, the two of them reminiscing about New York days. My own memories of days spent in her company during our stay in New York, 1946 to 1947, had remained vivid for me. One did not easily forget Adele, and I felt a special kinship with her, which grew as the years went on.

The two sisters, Adele and Margaret, visiting Germany, August 1927

Shortly after graduation from gymnasium, perhaps in 1958, I visited her in Berlin. I recall walking through dilapidated, bombed-out streets, rubble removed. Gaps in the street line, however, reminded me of a mouth with missing teeth. The Berlin Wall would soon be built, making the division between East and West absolute, in fact deadly. *Prinzenstrasse* was mere blocks from the future Checkpoint Charlie.

There I found No. 19, where once had stood a Victorian apartment building. A rubble-strewn lot now revealed a rear building, its faded stucco blistering, chunks falling to the ground ever so often. Ancient cement, now powdered, rained off the exposed brick, creating little piles along the facade, which in turn killed anemic dandelions. Outhouses on the right were leaning against huge, bare walls that seemed to be reaching for the sky. They were the sides of neighboring buildings that formerly sidled up against other walls, now gone.

Looking up, I saw an open window on the second floor, rickety and scarred, the sill sporting a pot with a young orange tree–such a fragile symbol in that gray scene.

And behind that, nose turned to the faint ray of sun, Tante Adele: Her white hair pulled into the tightest of buns, gave the impression she had planted a dumpling on top of her head. Below that, a strong, curved nose, high forehead, and a mouth with missing teeth. Age had bent her spine to the point she could barely peer over the window sill. One arm resting there held a glass of scotch, the other hand flicked her cigarette ashes into the courtyard. No neighbors could be detected. Was she the only resident in this ruin?

In the days that followed, we both sat at the window, and she educated me about the tragedy of the Russian Revolution, its betrayal of the people. She described the beauty of the ideas generated by its thinkers, their fates and losses.

Then she turned to me and said: "But we can't give up. Look at Mao, he is trying. It is an experiment; his ideas will forever be the promise of a more just world."

Poor Tante Adele, had she overlooked the fact that anarchy in its idealized form is a concept too demanding for the real world? Did she, in her darker moments, realize that both anarchy and her very own anarchist were not worth the noble gift she had made, the gift of a life?

Sad to say, eventually Tante Adele had to leave her burrow in Berlin, victim of that city's politics and urban renewal. The property was simply confiscated for new housing construction. She returned to the United States and roamed the country, retreating into that realm between memory and oblivion where she could feel whole.

One day, around 1967, she ran out of options and money. She was found at the Chicago train station and taken in by Catholic Charities. We brought her to Washington, I became her guardian, hoping to keep her comfortable in a home nearby where we could visit.

Then, one morning, the home called, reporting that she had disappeared during the night. Again, no trace of Tante Adele. A national search went out that finally located her in New York. She refused to return to Washington, so arrangements were made to place her in a home that accepted her Social Security income. Cut off from all contacts, refusing to communicate, she died in her early 90s in the city she had loved.

If there is solace to be found in the locus of one's resting place, then I was able to make a small, final gift: Her ashes were placed at Green-Wood Cemetery in Brooklyn, in the company of many a creative soul, Henry Ward Beecher, Leonard Bernstein, and Jean-Michel Basquiat among them. As the *New York Times* reported in 1866: "It is the ambition of the New Yorker to live upon Fifth Avenue, to take his airings in the [Central] Park, and to sleep with his fathers in Green-Wood."

Growth of the Spirit

In 1957, as the last year of school neared its end, I had turned twenty, very late for graduation; we all had lost years to war. Families and classmates started to ask questions about plans for the future–leave town for a university?

Attend the local teachers' college? Spend a year in another country to learn a language and new ways of life?

Looming over every decision, large and small, was Vati's care. The effort demanded most of our energies, so the tendency was to push things off, wait for some solution, the reality of which we all doubted but clung to anyway.

Gradually, carefully, we three approached the question as to what I would do once I graduated from Gymnasium. For some time, in the course of our talks at coffee hour, my parents had asked me about my hopes for the future, what I wanted to do. Having somehow passed the first of my school's two-year state exams, sciences and math, I soon learned I was exempt from the grueling oral finals before state education representatives in 1958, our year of graduation. It gave time to think while my classmates were studying.

Graduation Day, 1958

Gradually, tentatively, one thought entered my deliberations: I would study to become a physician, specialize in rheumatoid arthritis, and find a cure for the disease that had claimed my father's late years. Yet, at the same time, I knew I really needed to break out of that cycle of suffering; the visions of my father would forever dominate my daily work, and painful memories might even come between me and my ability to care for others. I knew, without wanting to admit it to myself, that I needed to escape–to a place, and to tasks, that might nourish the soul and strengthen my future life.

And there was that other dream: Over the past few years, I had developed a great longing for deeper understanding of art, heightened by my love of reading and seeing. For some years I had spent hours staring at works of art in any book I could find, making small comparisons, learning about distinctions of style and age, developing an interest in whatever art was to be seen nearby. Our ancient region was rich in treasures and museum collections. I loved the interior of our medieval churches, their fresco ornamentation, carved altar pieces, and splendid baptismal fountains. A class trip to Germany's south had given us the chance to see the splendor of Baroque architecture–deep and lasting impressions that became my own modest contribution during coffee hour. My parents listened with interest, and today I must believe with a bit of pride.

Was this need to spread my wings engendered by their stories at coffee hour–by the glimpse at a wider world of human action, human ambition? Was I drawn to the promise out *there*–not here in this small city with small ambitions, small choices, beautiful as it may be?

And so, one afternoon, I asked to be allowed to study at the University of Hamburg, which of course was free to all who could show a valid degree, the Abitur, from a high school. The only cost would be food and board. This university had the remnants of a once fabled art history department, led originally by three scholar/teachers who had fled to the United States, there to become the leaders at major universities and research institutions.

In early 1958, the Abitur degree in my pocket, my desire to study in Hamburg brought forth the stark question concerning Vati's move to a hospital. Seeing that staying at home was no longer an option, that funds no longer remained to allow both private care and the basic costs of a university education, Vati decided to be moved to the State Hospital in Schleswig. It was the healing, and dying place of last resort, mostly peopled by the mentally incapacitated and dying veterans. He had earlier spent some time there when doctors decided some tests and new medicines could be tried out. Cortisone had just come into use against autoimmune inflammation, and it promised some help.

A lovely, ancient town only 30 km south of Flensburg, Schleswig was nearby enough to allow Mutti to visit on weekends, myself riding the train from Hamburg, the three of us gathering for whatever remnant of family life we could muster.

Vati made this choice in the absolute clarity that was his own: He knew it had become impossible for Mutti and myself to care for him, even with the help of the male nurse who came daily–it was clear, inevitable, never discussed, simply obvious. With my being absent from the family for months at a time, Schleswig would be the only answer, and Vati accepted it without expressing a hint of doubt. There were plans to bring him home for "vacations," when I could be home between semesters. But it was clear; of course I would go to Hamburg, of course all family resources would be channeled my way. I knew, and my parents knew but never mentioned it, that my eventual leave-taking would be a blow.

I do not recall the day when the ambulance drove away, when the large bed in the corner room stood empty; there no longer were tasks that demanded every moment of the day, no reason to enter that room. Mutti and I sat in the living room, looking around as though strangers in our own home. The sudden finality of this change left us mute. I do not recall the early trips to Schleswig before the semester would start in Hamburg.

I do remember working at Dina and Hans's farm that summer, helping with the harvest, loving the freedom to test my physical strength and, in a way, reliving settings that recalled the years in Angola. I was there for the monumental event, when the horse-drawn wagons and ploughs were replaced by a newly purchased tractor, now making the horses obsolete, their future unthinkable. Young Hans drove the empty wooden wagon, standing on the backs of the two fine brown horses pulling it, and careened around and around the farm courtyard, tears streaming down his face.

I was there when the old hand-pump in the washroom was replaced by a total-electric system with heating in every room, the lovely white tile oven that had heated the room with coal and wood fires, now a decoration. Yes, modernization, industrialization had come to Anglia, and one by one, new experiences, new ways of living, turned the old ways into traditions, venerated but dead. Today, a few farmers tend all the village's fields, their layouts strictly controlled by laws that guard the ancient configuration of the land, hills and valleys, the stone walls many centuries old. The farmers have become wealthy from the leases and from changing the historic farmhouses into apartment buildings, the stables into parking garages. Yes, it was the tractor, on that day, and the crying teenager, that clearly spelled out the end of something.

Gradually, as I rode my bike on those country roads on my way to the hospital in Schleswig, I noticed these changes throughout. Suddenly, the churches protected by ancient walls, the graves tended weekly, the flower gardens in the village blooming in those short summer months, all these images settled in my heart, and I learned to love things that are ancient, that tell of earlier generations and their patterns of life.

The Shining Example

I have reported how Vati ended up in the State Hospital in Schleswig. This sacrifice, quietly decided upon without self-pity or complaint, was my father's gift that gave me a chance to enter a life of study and independence.

The life we three had spent for close to a decade, a life centered on father, mother, daughter, in the embrace of the known, all this changed with that first train ride to Hamburg, a large city by the sea, a harbor town wealthy for centuries, now almost rebuilt after the war's bombings. Our art history institute at the university was reduced to a few rooms in the basement of the museum, books were still packed in boxes retrieved from the bomb shelters, and credit was given for those students willing to help unpack and shelve them. The lectures were fascinating, opening a world of thought about art, the mystery of that which hides behind the visual image.

However, very quickly, old hierarchies emerged from the rubble. Professors were all male, all known to have made inner adjustments when the question of leaving or staying under the Hitler dictatorship had confronted them. Students, too, were mostly male. The fact that training in art history, as in all other fields, was on a graduate level, meant that the few doctoral candidates were a daily, intimidating presence for us freshmen. Spread on their chairs, uttering their wisdom and critique with nasal voices and arched eyebrows, professor and doctoral students made it clear they noticed this first semester student's limitations. I certainly would not be able to grasp the morsels of wisdom exiting their mouths. In fact, they barely acknowledged me. After my first, trembling presentation, the professor turned to his followers and asked: "Well....should we let her continue, or do we suggest she go to secretarial school?" The wise young men were silent, their feet on crossed-over legs languidly tipping up and down.

Then there was that old, totally blind teacher of Latin whose class one had to take if not enough credits in Latin had been earned in Gymnasium. This poor man had internalized Cicero word for word, knew every page, every sentence from his days with sight. He could correct from memory our trembling efforts at translation. Errors were met with booming ridicule. Had this man lost his sight in the war? Did he follow us in Braille? No personal words were ever exchanged, I was terrified.

Bitter determination dried my nightly tears, and besides, I loved the lectures. Often, I attended evening events, presentations, all free, by specialists in philosophy, sociology, archaeology. My brain was struggling to hold the mass of information.

My new home, a lucky draw in a lottery of available sublets, was one small bedroom in an unheated apartment one floor above a rowdy bar. The owners had moved to the country; I was the only resident. On my way upstairs, I greeted the bar's waiters, the visiting prostitutes and their clients. To this day I can sing for you the songs howled by drunken sailors deep into the night.

I loved my new life, although I had never been so alone in the past. Decisions were mine; the way I spent the day was mine. There were so many things to participate in without being in a group, but rather an anonymous observer, a role that suited me beautifully.

Besides, I had two cousins, much older than myself, who lived and worked in Hamburg, Eberhard with his wife Christel and new-born Martina, and Elfriede, Dina's sister and her husband Reinhardt, an international business man. Both men had spent years in the war, had been prisoners; one had spent years in Russian captivity but survived because the Russians needed surgeons. The other, 19 years of age at war's end, had been the second oldest sailor on one of those last-minute U-Boots that sailed up the Mississippi, never detected. When the crew learned the war was over, they returned their ship to Norway, there to hand themselves over to the Allies, who looked at these young men, kids really, and told them to go home. These relatives' doors were always open for me, their parties were my parties, their birthdays my birthdays. By spending time in these two households, I saw the life of people in mid-career, the rewards, the pressures, the fun that could be had.

But come Sunday, the thought of Vati in that hospital became a huge draw. I would wake up, contemplate my options for the day–walks in town along the lovely lakes, visits to museums, the cousins, more reading in the library–and the decision was clear: I would hop the next train north and drop in on Vati, relishing the surprise in his face as I entered the room. I remembered that light in his eyes. Eventually, Mutti would arrive from Flensburg, there would be a reunion, a cup of coffee together, a faint remembrance of coffee hour.

On these visits I could not help noticing that Mutti struggled to make these trips from Flensburg, that her asthma had returned, her steps slowed. My mother appeared to have shrunk, folded into herself. She lived for visits from her family, rare, but much loved. She had made so few friends, and life must have been empty after all these years of daily struggle. Henceforth I tried to visit her in Flensburg in addition to our meeting at Vati's bedside. Dear friends, Julika and family, and of course Dina, reached out to her.

~*~

Beginning in early 1958, Vati and I started a weekly correspondence between visits. In an effort to recapture its spirit, I searched the black portfolio–the one that has opened the past for me–and there are the postcards, notes and pictures Vati called his "Sunday greetings," meant mostly for those weekends when I would remain in Hamburg. The ones that remain, date between April 1958 to February 1959, the time between my first semester at the university and his death the following spring.

Vati's notes, always dated and on proper cards, addressed me as *"Häsekin"* (little bunny) or *"Muschilein"* (little kitty) and sent me wishes for the coming week. Still written in his smooth, regular hand, they are his final expressions of love without self-pity or complaint, the marker of his sacrifice, my passport to a life of study and hope. They were his last means of giving me strength, of showing he was well aware of the mountain I had decided to climb. One of Vati's first cards addresses this gift:

[January 27, 1958, postmark]:

> *My dear Ekalein* [little Erika]*: Thank you for your mail. The*

calendar is hanging over my easy chair, and even if I cannot fully appreciate modern art, so I know that my smart daughter will soon enlighten me. Also, the transparency you made was much appreciated by my doctor, the surgeon....You write about your favorite restaurant. It must come right below the NY Stork Club...this way you meet many interesting people.... For your presentation, lots of good luck. Just wait, once you are on the podium, the words will come by themselves...Vati.*

Schleswig, 4/30/58 – Dear Ekalein: I am happy that you are content. Surely you will master all that is new. However, Mutti is very lonely; good that Tante Adele will soon visit.... Mutti and I are glad that we can make your studies possible. Your success and happiness will be all the thanks needed. Just remain our cheerful Eka. Soon we will see each other and you will have much to tell. That I am looking forward to, your Vati.

Vati's postcard, April 30, 1958

My own notes, never dated, reflect my fear of the new, the intimidating comments from professors and my grim determination to face them down. Every note asked about the pain he lived every day. I sent Vati postcards of works of art or reports on literary conferences, since in the early semesters I also studied literature. I continued to complain about pressure and too much work.

5/29/58–My dear Muschilein! Your card just arrived and now you are to have a Sunday greeting so you can overcome loneliness.... Your and Mutti's visit were of course a holiday for me in the endless monotony. Yes, one has to become a bit more modest when laid low like this. But after all, one used to have action and excitement enough. It would of course be lovely to have the quiet time in one's own home.... Meanwhile, the preparations to bring me outdoors are going on. Slowly, as befits a state institution. Today my male nurse brought me a lovely bunch of yellow tulips from his garden. That is all the news. I kiss you, Vati.

One of my cards, sent from Florence, my first trip to Italy as a student at the University of Hamburg (an aged bus, one driver, 30 students from every corner of the earth). Overwhelmed, enchanted, I needed to send Vati a sign of gratitude for having made it possible:

> *July/58—My dear Vati: Today, we again experienced so much that I must share my joy with you. These magnificent art treasures, beautiful buildings, those romantic corners and the vino—everything, everything calls me to remain. Every morning, a delicious bakery in hand, we stroll through the market, in the evenings we meet at a trattoria.... Everywhere, men, many men, only men! Only good that we are always guarded by our group; we girls are looked at, and studied, like wonders of the earth! Next greeting from Rome, love, Eka*

There is only one card from the summer months which I spent in Flensburg on an internship at the municipal museum. This proximity allowed for frequent trips to Schleswig by bike.

On November 5, 1958, Vati wrote:

> *I send you my Sunday greeting.... Here fall has come and soon I will again be able to see through the hedge of the garden and see the path outside.... You describe to me a fall day along the Baltic Sea. Such a quiet day of fog near forest and water is a wonderful, calming experience. I remember such a day in Graz: Evening was coming, and it was All Soul's Day. The cemetery on the slope of the hill lay in fog and there were hundreds of lights on the graves.*

Vati expresses his frequent worries about Mutti's state of mind, her isolation and illness. Never wavering in his love, he longs for her visits:

> *12/4/58—...I do hope that she will be ok by next Sunday. For Sunday with that visit is the only ray of light in this vale of misery. Every second one doubly so because then my big daughter, the art history student, appears. The closer the clock comes to 10:00 a.m., the more often do I glance at it, and then out the window. I look forward to good talks....*

As subsequent letters (sometimes two and three a week) show, advancing illness had not diminished either Vati's spirit or his concerns for his wife's wellbeing. I find signs that the few times during semester breaks, when he had been able to "vacation" at home with us, had brought him joy. However, he knew that by now they had become impossible. In recognition of that fact, I had transferred to the University of Kiel after the second semester. From there it was little more than one hour's train ride to Schleswig.

Often, Vati tried to give me courage in the face of a seminar presentation. At the university in Kiel, a much more supportive, congenial spirit prevailed, centered on the task of educating a new generation of art historians. One of the leading professors, however, had spent time at American universities, returning with the determination that his department would be established on a seminar format, stress group-learning systems, thus fostering an open exchange of ideas. I remember at least one fellow female student.

1/9/59–Hold your head high, it can't cost more than that head! You will master it! I just read a book where it was said "he talked like a first semester," so it seems that this stage does not yet count for all that much, if only you keep talking, and my daughter will indeed present something. Remember, no master just falls from the sky.

Mutti, in her infinite ability to find solutions, and with the help of hospital officials, had made contact with a retired teacher, a kind lady who gave us shelter during these visits in return for company and conversation. She was skinny, hook-nosed, and given to preaching, but was a soul of kindness and generosity. I do not know whether money ever changed hands. Evenings, she would serve us a simple meal when we returned from visits; there was a room with two beds, and a warm greeting at the door, no questions asked until we were ready to speak. Fräulein Schmitt, you are remembered with deep gratitude. At one point, later in our friendship, she even offered us the use of her apartment while she visited her brother in America–her great adventure in the planning of which Mutti was a great help. Sadly, by the time summer, and her trip, came around, we no longer had reason to be in Schleswig.

Subsequent visits became ever more sad. Vati would briefly open his eyes, greet us with the faintest of smiles, drift again into sleep brought on by stronger and stronger doses of morphine. His life, his soul, were still there, but retreated into a realm we could not reach, and he could no longer leave. Would we be there to hold his hand, once more stroke his forehead?

It was not to happen. On my last visit to the hospital, I knelt beside a stretcher and spoke to a figure covered by a white sheet.

The Decision

With Vati gone from our lives, we had to find ways to carry on, decisions had to be made. It may have been weeks or months during which Mutti lived in Flensburg, I returned to Kiel as a commuter, adding to my schedule a one-semester teaching job at a local teachers' college. Most of my memories involve sitting in old-fashioned trains, bone tired.

I don't know when, but gradually the idea of America arose in my mind.

The external impetus was my citizenship established by birth to an American citizen. However, at the time it required to be confirmed by a five-year, continuous, presence in the States prior to one's 28th birthday (don't ask me whose brain at the Department of State thought up that rule). I was 22 years old, confronting the difficulty of applying for German citizenship on the one hand, and the realization that if I were ever able to reclaim Vati's financial losses–the confiscated houses, the blocked accounts, the large insurance policies, I would have to do so from America. This, too, was a legacy to be carried, a task to accomplish in my parents' memory, a redemption.

I remember the day the decision was made. It was afternoon, coffee time; we sat at the table at the foot of Vati's bed, now empty; Mutti had just put on her nice afternoon dress, and the light was streaming in through the many windows; her typewriter had been pushed aside–her letters would be written later. Gently, cautiously, she raised the question as to what might be my plans for the future. I told her I had decided to go to America.

Her face was gentle, she looked down and said nothing for just a short while. When she looked up again, her green eyes seemed turned inward, as though living in some distant past, and she said: "This is what I did, and it is time for you to be free."

That is how I came to America, how Mutti came to spend her last years under Dina's care, forced to observe from afar how her daughter built a life, and a family, in the United States. Difficult was

Mutti, 1960

the struggle to get established in a new environment, few the visits back to Germany. From far away, Mutti relished my rare early successes, a press photo of my first exhibition opening in New York as a staffer at the Smithsonian Institution, a catalogue that carried my name. Did these small events give her a sense of history repeating itself, believing that her own struggle for success in New York found an echo?

Mutti died unexpectedly, early in the year 1966 while in hospital for observation. Only days earlier, I had called her with the news that, in a few months, there would be a grandchild.

~*~

Here it becomes imperative to discuss the process of remembering and writing. Again, I have stalked the computer, knowing I had to continue, knowing this chapter speaks of the end and, yes, the tragedy of my parents' lives.

Today I can report to the figure under the white sheet in the hospital that life has been good. Dreams shared during uncounted hours at your bedside, Vati, when morphine shaded your eyes–they took work but did deliver. Dreams, yes; plans, no. The swimmer whose body is pounded against the rocks by wild surf does not make plans but dreams of survival.

Vati, I must tell you that your sacrifice, your choice of spending over a year in a mental hospital so I could attend the university, was not in vain. The hopes you held for your daughter–that she could do anything to which she put mind and heart: art history, scholarship, a life of the mind and the soul–all this did materialize. You gave her belief and daring; you gave the strength; you gave the capacity for love that could grow and be there for the future.

I can report to you, Vati and Mutti, that your two grandchildren are beautiful, gifted, and accomplished adults, some of your great-grandchildren are tall as Vati's Viking genes would tell them to be. They all have ravishing smiles; there is Mutti's gift of music and humor, of sharp intellect, rich soul and even a set of eyes as ice-blue as were yours, Vati. So, you see, there is long life for both of you.

My parents, in spite of all their unexplainable actions and decisions set an example of strength almost impossible to follow. I raise my arms to them; I try to live under their gaze. I must remember the good moments, the laughs, the resolve, the times when we were happy: I must relive the *Haferhocken* story or a Beethoven sonata by an open window–that should be their legacy and their future. In short, what must shine in memory are the stories of

COFFEE HOUR IN FLENSBURG.

The End

67153139R00120

Made in the USA
Columbia, SC
26 July 2019